The Final Decade

CHRISTOPHER LEE

THE FINAL DECADE

Will We Survive the 1980s?

HAMISH HAMILTON
LONDON

First published in Great Britain 1981
by Hamish Hamilton Ltd
Garden House, 57–59 Long Acre, London, WC2E 9JZ

British Library Cataloguing in Publication Data
Lee, Christopher, 1941–
    The final decade.
    1. Atomic warfare
    I. Title
    358′.39   UF767
    ISBN 0–241–10424–6

Text set in 11/12pt Linotron 202 Baskerville, printed and bound
in Great Britain at The Pitman Press, Bath

For Alexandra who is $5\frac{1}{2}$
and Victoria who is just 9

Contents

	Preface	xi
1	Overview	1
2	The Soviet Soldier	14
3	The Soviet Military Machine	31
4	The Warsaw Pact and Nato	61
5	The Western Military Machine	76
6	Future Weapons	97
7	Nuclear Effects	119
8	Civil Defence	139
9	Conclusion	175
	Short Bibliography	182
	Index	183

Preface

During 1980, one of Europe's most respected military experts, a former chief of the British Defence Staff remarked, 'There is a whiff of war in the air.' It was perhaps a sad omen that as the United Nations Disarmament Decade drew to its ineffectual close, the Soviet intervention in Afghanistan signalled the beginning of one of the most testing decades the world has known. For many people throughout the world in high office, in military commands, in their simple homes, the whiff of war was very real. In January of 1980 I was sitting in the Washington office of the former director of the United States Defense Intelligence Agency, Lieutenant General Daniel Graham. His was a more stark comment: 'The 1980s have gotten off to a lousy start.'

In Europe the sale of nuclear fall-out shelters has become part of a boom industry. Civil Defence policies on both sides of the Atlantic are being dusted off and re-examined. Defence spending is increasing and in the United States the White House has called for improvements in the plans to protect military and civilian leaders in the event of a nuclear conflict. The various campaigns for nuclear disarmament are once again on the march, but this time with renewed vigour and also indications that the traditional protesters are being joined by more conservative elements of the population. The sickening scent of world instability is spreading.

There is, consequently, a more determined debate on the future of Western nuclear weapon policy. A speech made in 1979 by the late Admiral of the Fleet Earl Mountbatten of Burma is becoming a cornerstone of that debate, although extracts are often misused either deliberately or unintentionally. It has become known as the Strasbourg speech. Because it is rarely quoted in full, few people have had the opportunity to make up their own minds about its contents. This is what Lord Mountbatten did say:

'Do the frightening facts about the arms race, which show that we are rushing headlong towards a precipice, make any of those responsible for this disastrous course pull themselves together and reach for the brakes?

'The answer is "no" and I only wish that I could be the bearer of the glad tidings that there has been a change of attitude and we are beginning to see a steady rate of disarmament. Alas, that is not the case.

'I am deeply saddened when I reflect on how little has been achieved in spite of all the talk there has been particularly about nuclear disarmament. There have been numerous international conferences and negotiations on the subject and we have all nursed dreams of a world at peace but to no avail. Since the end of the Second World War, thirty-four years ago, we have had war after war. There is still armed conflict going on in several parts of the world. We live in an age of extreme peril because every war today carries the danger that it could spread and involve the super powers.

'And here lies the greatest danger of all. A military confrontation between the nuclear powers could entail the horrifying risk of nuclear warfare. The Western powers and the USSR started by producing and stockpiling nuclear weapons as a deterrent to general war. The idea seemed simple enough. Because of the enormous amount of destruction that could be wreaked by a single nuclear explosion, the idea was that both sides in what we still see as an East-West conflict would be deterred from taking any aggressive action which might endanger the vital interests of the other.

'It was not long, however, before smaller nuclear weapons of various designs were produced and deployed for use in what was assumed to be a tactical or theatre war. The belief was that were hostilities ever to break out in Western Europe, such weapons could be used in field warfare without triggering an all-out nuclear exchange leading to the final holocaust.

'I have never found this idea credible. I have never been able to accept the reasons for the belief that any class of nuclear weapons can be categorised in terms of their tactical or strategic purposes.

'Next month I enter my eightieth year. I am one of the few survivors of the First World War who rose to high command in the Second and I know how impossible it is to pursue military operations in accordance with fixed plans and agreements. In warfare the unexpected is the rule and no one can anticipate what an opponent's reaction will be to the unexpected.

'As a sailor I saw enough death and destruction at sea but I also had the opportunity of seeing the absolute destruction of the war zone of the western front in the First World War, where those who fought in the trenches had an average expectation of life of only a few weeks.

'Then in 1943 I became Supreme Allied Commander in South East Asia and saw death and destruction on an even greater scale. But that was all conventional warfare and, horrible as it was, we all felt we had a "fighting" chance of survival. In the event of a nuclear war there will be no chances, there will be no survivors – all will be obliterated.

'I am not asserting this without having deeply thought about the matter. When I was Chief of the British Defence Staff I made my views known. I have heard the arguments against this view but I have never found them convincing. So I repeat in all sincerity as a military man I can see no use for any nuclear weapons which would not end in escalation, with consequences that no one can conceive.

'And nuclear devastation is not science fiction – it is a matter of fact. Thirty-four years ago there was the terrifying experience of the two atomic bombs that effaced the cities of Hiroshima and Nagasaki off the map. In describing the nightmare a Japanese journalist wrote as follows:

'"Suddenly a glaring whitish, pinkish light appeared in the sky accompanied by an unnatural tremor which was followed almost immediately by a wave of suffocating heat and a wind which swept away everything in its path. Within a few seconds the thousands of people in the streets in the centre of the town were scorched by a wave of searing heat. Many were killed instantly, others lay writhing on the ground screaming in agony from the intolerable pain of their burns. Everything standing upright in the way of the blast – walls, houses, factories and other buildings, was annihilated . . . Hiroshima had ceased to exist."

'But that it not the end of the story. We remember the tens and tens of thousands who were killed instantly or worse still those who suffered a slow painful death from the effect of the burns – we forget that many are still dying horribly from the delayed effects of radiation. To this knowledge must be added the fact that we now have missiles a thousand times as dreadful; I repeat, a thousand times as terrible.

'One or two nuclear strikes on this great city of Strasbourg with what today would be regarded as relatively low yield weapons would utterly destroy all that we see around us and immediately kill probably half its population. Imagine what the picture would be if larger nuclear strikes were to be levelled against not just Strasbourg but ten other cities in, say, a 200-mile radius. Or even worse, imagine what the picture would be if there was an unrestrained exchange of nuclear weapons – and this is the most appalling risk of all since, as I have already said, I cannot imagine a situation in which nuclear weapons would be used as battlefield weapons without the conflagration spreading.

'Could we not take steps to make sure that these things never come about? A new world war can hardly fail to involve the all-out use of nuclear weapons. Such a war would not drag on for years. It could all be over in a matter of days.

'And when it is all over what will the world be like? Our fine great buildings, our homes will exist no more. The thousands of years it took to develop our civilisation will have been in vain. Our works of art will be lost. Radio, television, newspapers will disappear. There will be no means of transport. There will be no hospitals. No help can be expected for the few mutilated survivors in any town to be sent from a neighbouring town – there will be no neighbouring towns left, no neighbours, there will be no help, there will be no hope.

'How can we stand by and do nothing to prevent the destruction of our world? Einstein, whose centenary we celebrate this year, was asked to prophesy what weapons would be used in the Third World War. I am told he replied to the following effect:

'"On the assumption that a Third World War must escalate to nuclear destruction, I can tell you what the Fourth World War will be fought with – bows and arrows."

'The facts about the global nuclear arms race are well known and as I have already said SIPRI (Stockholm International Peace Research Institute) has played its part in disseminating authoritative material on world armaments and the need for international efforts to reduce them. But how do we set about achieving practical measures of nuclear arms control and disarmament?

'To begin with we are most likely to preserve the peace if there is a military balance of strength between East and West. The real need is for both sides to replace the attempts to maintain a balance through ever-increasing and ever more costly nuclear armaments by a balance based on mutual restraint. Better still, by reduction of nuclear armaments I believe it should be possible to achieve greater security at a lower level of military confrontation.

'I regret enormously the delays which the Americans and Russians have experienced in reaching a SALT II (Strategic Arms Limitation Treaty) agreement for the limitation of even one major class of nuclear weapons with which it deals. I regret even more the fact that opposition to reaching any agreement which will bring about a restraint in the production and deployment of nuclear weapons is becoming so powerful in the United States. What can their motives be?

'As a military man who has given half a century of active service I say in all sincerity that the nuclear arms race has no military purpose. Wars cannot be fought with nuclear weapons. Their existence only adds to our perils because of the illusions which they have generated.

'There are powerful voices around the world who still give credence to the old Roman precept – if you desire peace, prepare for war. This is absolute nuclear nonsense and I repeat – it is a disastrous misconception to believe that by increasing the total uncertainty one increases one's own certainty.

'This year we have already seen the beginnings of a miracle. Through the courageous determination of Presidents Carter and

Sadat and Prime Minister Begin we have seen the first real move towards what we all hope will be a lasting peace between Egypt and Israel. Their journey has only just begun and the path they have chosen will be long and fraught with disappointments and obstacles. But these bold leaders have realised the alternative and have faced up to their duty in a way which those of us who hunger for the peace of the world applaud.

'Is it possible that this initiative will lead to the start of yet another even more vital miracle and someone somewhere will take that first step along the long stony road which will lead us to an effective form of nuclear arms limitation, including the banning of Tactical Nuclear Weapons?

'After all it is true that science offers us almost unlimited opportunities but it is up to us, the people, to make the moral and philosophical choices and since the threat to humanity is the work of human beings, it is up to man to save himself from himself.

'The world now stands on the brink of the final Abyss. Let us all resolve to take all possible practical steps to ensure that we do not, through our own folly, go over the edge.'

I make no comment on what was said at Strasbourg. Instead, I have produced what I hope is a worthwhile contribution for those who wish to decide for themselves whether or not their particular governments, their particular power blocs, are going the right way to preserve the peace of the 1980s. This is no part of the international peace campaign, nor is it a plea on behalf of what are commonly called 'hawks'. What I have written is not a learned thesis for some centre for strategic studies; it is, instead, for those who do not know what is really meant by the Military Balance – but want to find out.

ONE

Overview

The ease with which Third World countries are able to buy modern weapon systems from the two Superpowers, together with the spread of nuclear technology, makes it almost impossible to reject the notion that nuclear war is inevitable. There are those who believe that it is now too late to stop it happening. There are those who believe that it will happen during this decade.

Military spending throughout the world is running at a rate of something like one million dollars a minute. Although it is very difficult to pin down an accurate picture of world military expenditure, it is generally accepted that about six per cent of global output goes on so-called defence spending; and there is absolutely no reason to suspect that the spending rate will slow. In fact there is every reason to suppose that it will increase, that it will do so rapidly and that, in spite of a general world recession, many of the existing budgets will rise by at least four or five per cent for any foreseeable future.

The alliance of Western nations in NATO (the North Atlantic Treaty Organisation) has publicly promised to increase its various defence budgets by a minimum of three per cent in real terms every year (that means three per cent after inflation, which in many countries is running well into double figures). Furthermore, the dire economic problems of many member nations of the Alliance have not blunted the resolve to increase defence spending. There is almost a sense of panic buying in the military air.

Perhaps one of the more interesting aspects of military spending is the way in which it proceeds without any real public debate and at a time when it might be imagined that more social needs would appear higher on any government's list of priorities. For example, during 1980 the United Kingdom economy was bad enough for the Thatcher Administration to impose strict and often controversial limits on public spending. This meant that most government departments had their budgets either cut or severely restricted. At the very best, few departments showed real growth in their budgets. As a result, medical, social and educational services were drastically curtailed. Yet in one forty-eight hour period alone, three major multi-billion dollar military programmes were announced. The total cost to the taxpayer was estimated as being somewhere in the region of 14,000 million dollars, and that was a baseline figure. At the same time, employment figures released by Whitehall showed that the number of people out of work in the United Kingdom was approaching the two million mark and was to rise even further. One local authority had just announced that it was having to shut down school meals services because there was not enough money to run them. There was little or no public condemnation of the Defence Ministry's capital expenditure projects. The indignation demonstrated in the House of Commons by the Labour Opposition was short-lived.

In the United States, with her bizarre system of military accounting, the mood is far removed from those seemingly far-off days when the then Presidential Candidate, Jimmy Carter, promised to cut defence spending. Again, in 1980, the events in Afghanistan and Iran and the pressures of an election year (and some critical analysis by other NATO members following the 1978 Alliance Summit in Washington) forced military expenditure as high up the political flagpole as it could go. More or less everybody saluted.

By the fiscal year 1985, the defence budget of the United States is expected to be about 225,000 million dollars. (Those are 1980 dollars and unless there are some radical policy changes in the White House and changes of heart in Congress, that figure may be safely assumed to be somewhat on the low side.) On paper it is well ordered, but in reality the US military budgetary system needs total reorganisation. It is, for example, doubtful whether the United States could pay for all the equipment that she has ordered. The system is uneconomic and inefficient and an indication of the massive problems in arriving at, and assessing, the various defence budgets throughout the world.

Spending in the Soviet Union presents for the Western analyst further problems. There are few open documents and such information that does exist tends to be unnecessarily complicated by such agencies as the CIA. To get a general picture of spending in the USSR, it is normal to go to Western sources. Some of those sources have somewhat obscure qualifications to the figures they supply, they often have dubious reasoning behind their own assessments, and there is always the tendency to believe, rightly or wrongly, that some Western analyses of Soviet defence spending border on the suspect science of guestiganda: a credible guestimate plus plausibility equals acceptable propaganda.

But, just as the defence budgets of the Superpowers and their satellites are absorbing more and more of the assets which are increasingly difficult to find, the Third World appears determined to place itself in the same, or at least a similar, position. In the Third

World, military spending is outpacing Gross National Products by about 50 per cent.

In the relatively rich Organisation of the Petroleum Exporting Countries, OPEC, member states are increasing their annual defence budgets by approximately 14 per cent. And, just as the Boers trekked with their bibles in one hand and their rifles in the other, the Third World is backing its various and varying philosophies with the best weapons it can possibly carry.

During the 1970s, something like three-quarters of all major weapon exports went to the Third World.[1] There is little to show that this trend is not continuing in the present decade. By 1981, business in arms exports is expected to be worth about 25,000 million dollars a year. The arms business is a boom industry, one of the very few which is reckoned to be an overall good investment (although various conglomerates may well wilt). Furthermore, the industry is not restricted to the so-called industrialised nations. The export market to the Third World is dominated by four countries: the United States, the Soviet Union, France and the United Kingdom, and in that order. However, nearly sixty countries now produce major weapon systems. More than 40 per cent of those countries are classified as being in the Third World.

The passing of conventional weapon systems to a third country has long been considered to be one of the simplest ways of currying favour; it is also one of the more lucrative. If one country can dominate another's military imports, there is more to the deal than gaining good will. Firstly there is the financial gain. Many modern interceptor jets cost in the order of 20 million dollars each. But there is very little use buying a jet without the weapons that go with it, or the spares, or the back-up services. A major buy from one country may well attract orders from another. All this means business at home, continued production and therefore job security; hence it is difficult to see how objectors to a sale would get much support for their objections from a fully employed and economically sounder home base.

Secondly, there is the political and diplomatic strength to be gained. Quite often political concessions form part of any major military deal. This is especially so when Western countries deal with the Third World. If the negotiations are handled properly and do not, as happened with the Soviet Union and Egypt, collapse at a later date, then that political understanding can benefit the arms-selling country, and over a considerable period of time.

The main problem arises when that weapon system is used in anger. It is perfectly acceptable if it does little more than fly, sail or rumble along border patrols. It is something for a military attaché to smile

1. Stockholm International Peace Research Institute.

upon during National or Armed Forces Day Parades. But when it is put into operation, that is another matter. Or it should be. When, for example, the F-15 jet was sold to the Israelis, it was on the understanding that it should only be for self-defence. Shortly after it went into service, it was used during a border incident with the Syrian air force. There are many, and not just Syrian, observers who are unable to accept Israeli claims that the F-15 operation can, in any way, be interpreted as a self-defence exercise. Washington had doubts and has expressed them. But that has all been swept aside. The F-15 builders now have a telling slogan on their advertisements for the jet. It says simply 'Combat Proven'.

If the border incident should turn into a full-scale war, then what is the position of the original weapon supplier? Does he replace aircraft, tanks, ships and missiles as they are lost in battle? If he does, is he not prolonging that war? Presumably he does so, because what he wants politically is for his 'client state' to win. But what might happen, for instance, if the United States is supplying one side and, let us say, the Soviet Union is the arms supplier for the other aggressor? Is it not possible that there are circumstances where the two Superpowers could find themselves facing each other, all because of somebody else's war? It was a dilemma so clearly illustrated during 1980 when Iraq and Iran went to war.

Just as the scenarios being put forward for the 1980s are changing, so are the perceptions of weapon systems. It takes perhaps twenty years for an idea for a modern warship or aircraft to graduate from the buzz-brain of the conceptual strategist to the funded drawing-board, and then to appear as something that can be flown, sailed or fired in combat. Therefore it is easy to see that conflicts tend to be engaged with recognisable if not traditional weapon platforms and systems. What does change – and often this change is a radical one – is the public awareness of some weapon or weapon support system. It may be that the army, or the air force, has had a weapon for some years, but it is not until there is a use for it that the public latches on to its existence. One example of this was the surface to air missile (SAM). It was not until it had been used in the Middle East between the Arabs and Israelis that the general public came to accept it as just another weapon. When precision bombing arrived in South-East Asia, it was the newspaper reader's first introduction to this guidance method. Defence is a complicated business for the average man in the street. To begin with, it is not easy for him to understand its technology. In some cases it is so complex that only a few specialists in the Services may ever quite grasp the ins and outs of some new system. Another problem is that information is hard to come by. It is either classified, or appears too insignificant to worry about when it does appear in the lengthy but invaluable Congressional Reports. Consequently, new systems have to catch the imagination. When they do, then the authorities must treat this phenomenon with respect. If they do not then they are in trouble.

Such a state of affairs occurred with the popularly termed Neutron Bomb – the Enhanced Radiation Weapon. Washington's attempt to get this weapon accepted into Europe, into the NATO Alliance, was so badly handled that the whole project had to be cancelled. (It prompted one European official to observe: 'After this, I don't believe Washington could sell a lifeboat to the skipper of the *Titanic*.' This is an illustration of the kind of mistrust that still exists in many European elements of NATO.)

Yet there is every sign that the 1980s are already so unsettled that the more controversial weapon systems will be introduced into the Western armouries. It can only be a matter of time for enhanced radiation and reduced blasts munitions – neutron warheads. France has already declared that she is in a position to go ahead with final development plans.

There is little to stop the United States from expanding its Chemical Warfare research, and, if the public relations are handled properly, there should not be too much opposition to chemical weapons being introduced into regular service. The then British Defence Secretary, Francis Pym, said during the spring of 1980, in an interview with the author, that he believed the West including the United Kingdom should examine the possibilities of building these weapons in answer to what Margaret Thatcher's government sees as an ever-increasing threat from Warsaw Pact forces. The engineering that has brought about the development of binary nerve gas weapons[1] has made deployment that much easier and, according to some experts, safer.

Again we are seeing a changing philosophy, or at least a changing attitude to weapons which hitherto were taboo. There is a trend, albeit a small one, to believe that chemical weapons are acceptable. The reason stated is simple: some now think that chemical warfare is an alternative or preferable to nuclear confrontation. Others remain convinced it is nothing more than a step in the escalation to full-scale nuclear conflict. 'It's part of the lateral thinking in modern strategy,' one NATO official told the author. When, however, he was pressed for some definition of his phraseology, no further explanation was forthcoming.

At the moment, the only two Western nations with large chemical weapon potential are France and the United States. It remains

1. See page 114.

difficult to estimate the full capacity of the French stockpile or even the extent of the research carried out at the Centre d'Etudes du Bouchet, not far from Paris. Like most Western countries, France surrounds her chemical testing programme with the same secrecy as she does her nuclear capability.

It is very likely that more information on the American capability will come to the public's attention if a decision is taken to go ahead with construction on a reasonable scale. A decision to do so will arouse at least some public and Congressional debate and investigation. Furthermore, if the United States goes into the business of binary nerve gases, then it does seem likely that new facilities will have to be built to cope with the different production processes. Some of the existing American stocks are probably obsolescent. It will be interesting to see if they can be 'saved'. But during recent years there has been a large programme for building chemical weapons, perhaps much larger than people think. We are no doubt talking in the region of millions when considering the numbers of artillery shells to carry, say, sarin. Some may be surprised that, all these years after the First World War, agents such as mustard gas are still stored in great quantities with facilities in such places as Colorado, Utah, Indiana, and in West Germany. The revulsion, at one time widespread, seems to have died down except on the part of the traditional pressure groups, most of which have made little impact.

Apart from budget notes by the United States Department of Defense and some public statements, there are other signs that the Western Allies are preparing the public for a full-scale production programme for chemical weapons. At the time of writing, it would seem that this subject will begin to dominate many sessions of NATO Council meetings and the more general Defence Planning Committee meetings of the Alliance. The public relations exercise started in the middle of 1980, with carefully leaked reports from Washington, that the Soviet forces in Afghanistan were using nerve gases. By the time these leaks made their different ways about Washington, New Delhi and the European capitals and then back to Washington, the State Department especially was ready with hazy but eagerly snapped-up answers. Consequently, the 'word' from Washington was that the Soviets were definitely using chemical agents in Afghanistan, although the evidence for these assumptions was, at the very best, vague and certainly circumstantial.

It seems that the Chemical Warfare lobby has learned a great deal from the blunders of the Neutron Campaign, which was successful in foiling American attempts to base the so-called Neutron Bomb in Europe. If the West does turn to chemical weapon construction during the 1980s it will be largely on the grounds that the Soviet

Union is already ahead in the military game and has actually deployed such weapons on a large scale. This would be in line with much of the public comment on the size and complexity of the Warsaw Pact forces. It is very difficult for anybody outside the Intelligence Services to judge the strength of some of the Western claims about chemical weapons, but, as there tends to be a readiness to accept the general claims that the Soviet Union is getting bigger and better at most things military, the actual evidence may not be too closely questioned. At the same time it would be difficult to turn away from the argument that, if the Soviet Union has managed to produce improvements both in quality and quantity in most areas of warfare, and if one accepts that the Soviet system champions the theory that an army must be efficient in all its forms, then why should anybody doubt the existence of large chemical warfare units.

One area which will go unchallenged, and perhaps rightly so, is that which might be described as exotic weaponry. If the strategic pessimists are wrong, and we do get a chance to look back on the 1980s, then what will undoubtedly impress the public mind are the areas of warfare which until now have been best left to the science-fiction writers. The idea of space war is no longer incredible. Indeed it is credible to such a degree that both East and West might believe it to be unavoidable. As a general figure, it is accepted that about 70 per cent of all satellites have some military value. It was always accepted that the idea of using a satellite as some high-flying spy was not only common sense, but it was also comforting for some. To get some early warning of an attack, especially a missile attack, held obvious military value if little comfort for those in the target areas. But military science has gone many steps from there. It has reached a stage where, in many cases, it is almost reliant, perhaps too reliant, on satellite technology.

Looking at this area in its simplest form, satellites are now expected to identify enemy formations, evaluate them and track them, as well as providing the more traditional intelligence of early warning units. They must also provide a constant communication relay for ground, sea and air forces – and the mundane jobs of checking out weather patterns should not be ignored. The modern commander needs to know what elements may influence his tactical and theatre operations and, while long-range forecasting is rightly seen as one of the more mistrusted sciences (it is more of an art form), the short-range weather forecast could easily decide the form of an engagement and therefore influence the course and the outcome.

If satellite observation and communication were to play such an important part in any future East-West conflict, then it should hardly be surprising that both sides have given a great deal of thought to anti-satellite warfare. As any cat burglar will testify, there is nothing like neutralising the alarm for making a life of his particular crime that much easier. Military men go along with this concept and it now seems reasonably certain that the Soviet Union, at least, has carried out experiments in space to determine the best ways to neutralise Western satellites.

Perhaps romantically, perhaps realistically, then, any future war would begin in space. And not a stone's throw away from this concept is a subject that really has been the province of nobody else but the sci-fi buff: the death ray. It can be called that if only to attract attention to its simplest property, which is the transmission of a beam of energy in order to destroy a target. Work on charged and neutral particle or high-energy beams has been going on for some time. Once again it does appear that scientists working in the USSR have taken a lead over their American counterparts. The day may not be far away (and everything is being seen in the context of the current decade) when a beam of some sort will be capable of destroying or crippling a satellite. There are obvious technical problems and much of the praise for bringing these to more general attention must go to the staff[1] of the American publication *Aviation Week & Space Technology*. (This journal is often called, in Washington, 'Aviation Leak' – and with good cause.) One of the problems highlighted is the availability of a power source for any beam weapon. A high-energy beam needs a huge source of power. At present, therefore, the generator has to be physically big as well as powerful. To achieve the best results it would seem desirable to project that generator into space, but this presents problems because of the sheer size of the machinery. Immediately, then, it is reasonable to suspect that the Space Shuttle system has a value other than the peaceful experiments envisaged for this troubled craft. Space Shuttle and the present concepts of space building could well become the ideal, indeed the only, means of getting a big enough power supply into space for any beam weapon. And so the 1980s will see a greater emphasis on the military aspect of space exploration. There are indications that many scientists and scientific bodies have chosen to ignore the implications of some of the work they are doing. Possibly one reason for this is that it naturally brings into question the method by which much of their experiments are funded.

Anti-satellite development, or ASAT, is fast becoming one of the most important areas in modern military thinking. So important is space exploration, that the US Department of Defense has established a Space Defense Center inside one of the fifteen buildings constructed in Cheyenne Mountain, Colorado, the home of the all-important North American Defense Command – NORAD.

1. That of Clarence A. Robinson, Jr. and Philip J. Klauss has led the field.

Apart from these more exotic forms of weaponry, the conventional systems are going through a modernisation programme, almost unprecedented in peacetime. The tensions of the first months of this decade have only enforced the conviction of all military planners, that the chances of being caught flatfooted, as were the British in 1939, are all too great. Consequently the weapons development lobby has never been so powerful, nor so successful.

In the Soviet Union, work on new types of tanks has included what might well be an extremely effective form of armour-plating. It is said by some to be so good that many of the anti-tank warheads owned by the West may be less than effective. The development of the Backfire bomber is well known in the West. What is not generally reported is the deployment many years ago of the Soviet Fencer jet, which is best described as a long-range attack aircraft. Although smaller than the American Fl-11, the Fencer shows a keen resemblance to that particular swing wing aircraft.

Well known to the Western public are the Soviet SS-20 missiles. The very existence of these weapons has played a major part in the NATO publicity campaign to make more acceptable the deployment in Europe of a new generation of American cruise missiles. But this area of medium-range missile production is just beginning and there are more missiles to come during the next couple of years. These will include the Soviet SS-21 which is already in production.

Probably the biggest change in the Soviet military system has come within the navy. There are five types of nuclear ballistic missile-firing submarines, and a new one, described by some intelligence officers as 'a giant', is being built. For the first time, the Soviet Navy is constructing a large, nuclear-powered aircraft carrier and nuclear-powered cruisers. Equally important, although not such headline material, is the development of long-range supply ships and a means of deploying marines at sea over equally long ranges. The *Ivan Rogov* may not bristle with missiles, yet for the West its capability is extremely relevant when the overall threat is assessed.

In the West, Britain's decision, announced in July 1980, to buy the Trident ballistic nuclear missile from the United States is seen by many analysts as more of a political than a military triumph. There is a justifiable concern that Britain's conventional force structure will suffer as a result. The development of the tri-national Tornado jet will do much to reinforce a doubtful air capability within Europe but, at 20 million dollars a copy, the Tornado remains an expensive option.

Western armour is gradually being modernised, although whether it is being done along the right lines is open to question. An equally intriguing development is the decision to allow West Germany to build larger warships than previously. Some believe this is the beginning of a much greater freedom in weapon development, one which will strike fearful chords in the Soviet Union and, to some extent, among the West German people themselves.

Across the Atlantic, the United States is in something of a difficulty over her future weapon programme. There are new-found reasons to spend money on defence projects, yet there does not seem to be any sensible way of controlling the overall costs of many projects. As a result, far too many projects are over-subscribed, too many companies are bidding for the same programme, wastage is unnecessarily high, claims which seal government contracts often cannot be honoured, and energies are often directed in an unreasoning manner. Although substantial on paper, many of the air force formations are outdated. Too many worthy programmes are destined to be doubtful starters because the concepts are wrong.

Perhaps most crippling of all, is the level of manpower in the United States forces. Sometimes, brilliant military commanders are being compelled to pull together their forces with too few men, some of whom suffer many of the dreadful social hangovers of Vietnam while others are, to put it kindly, ill-educated. Considering the importance of the United States in the Western Alliance, there are those in NATO who have to resort to the old story that the strength of NATO is best illustrated by the fact that there has been relative peace between the two major power blocs during the past thirty-five years or so.

And now there is a further element in the military equation. Civil Defence is being examined on a larger scale than ever before in peacetime. At least one authority believes that 160 million Americans could, and perhaps would, die during a surprise attack on the United States. The British government expects that three quarters of the population would perish under the same conditions. The Soviet Union has long recognised the importance of Civil Defence and has a large, although not necessarily a good, Civil Defence programme. The whole subject has advanced from the simple idea of protecting the civilian population during a nuclear attack. Awkward questions are being asked. Is Civil Defence part of the overall deterrent? Might it be seen as an aggressive action? Although few would doubt the expertise and enthusiasm of Civil Defence experts on both sides of the Atlantic, it is obvious that, until somebody discovers there are votes in the subject, little worthwhile will be done to put matters right. It is undoubtedly one of the major miscalculations in national and All-iance defence thinking during the past thirty years.

However, there are those who see military procurement and technology as the least of their worries when it comes to assessing the chances of avoiding a major war. It is clear that this is a concern felt not only in the Western camp with all its political and social divisions, but also in the Eastern bloc. There are two main segments in this concern.

Taking the Eastern bloc first, there can be little self-assurance in Moscow that the structure of the Warsaw Pact Treaty membership is sound. While the events of the past few years in both Rumania and Czechoslovakia should not necessarily be seen as a widespread and Sakharovian disaffection with the Soviet system, there remains an element of instability which cannot be, and is not, ignored by the Kremlin. Some would point to social misgivings in Poland and claim that, taken with Czechoslovakia and Rumania, this represents a clear uncertainty for the Soviet Union. Add to this the tensions along the south-west Asian and Sino-Soviet borders, and it can be seen that Moscow should be far from smug.

In the West, there is a major leadership crisis. Rightly or wrongly, the European members of the Alliance were unable to give unanimous support to the United States over Afghanistan and the Moscow Olympics. The United States was deserted, and not simply in the political sense, and some commentators spoke of the possibility of her going into isolation as a result of this lack of support. A more accurate assessment might have been that Europe in general was quite prepared to isolate the United States. There remains a feeling that this was not a matter of public opinion in Europe being anti-American. It was more a case of indifference. True, there was some support for President Carter, but most of it appeared in the correspondence columns of newspapers. However, what happened in Afghanistan did not produce the gut reaction that some Western leaders supposed that it might.

It became apparent, during the early part of 1980, that political mistrust of the Carter Administration was verging on the absolute. Even American diplomats in Europe were saying that the Administration was suffering because of repeated ineptitudes. More interestingly, those same diplomats put the blame not on their President but on his advisers.

The NATO alliance itself is going through yet another wallpapering exercise. However, the basic cracks are defying most efforts to disguise some very old walls that are not only creaking (they have done that for a long time) but give every sign of crumbling.

On the southern flank, Turkey and Greece continue to worry the Brussels Secretariat. Italy's ability to stumble from one crisis to another never ceases to amaze the Alliance command system. The action replays of non-government in Belgium are almost accepted as a continuing flaw in the NATO cross, which was made no lighter to carry by the Dutch decision in December 1979 to reject the plans for basing cruise missiles in the Netherlands.

Mrs Thatcher's public support for the White House has, admittedly, been seen as unbending, although it is questionable whether this open support could suffer close inspection among the British electorate. The sentiments often expressed in Britain during the run-up to the Presidential election, certainly during the summer period, tended to revolve about the simple question: how was it that the United States had thrown up two such dubious candidates for the leadership not only of the United States, but also of the Western world? It was, perhaps, an uncharitable attitude, but it was one that was hardened by what was generally seen as an equally uncharitable American attitude towards the former Shah of Iran. Remembering that most people do not understand, nor can they be expected to understand, the ins and outs of the Iranian question, there were those who wondered, if the United States could dump such a former ally, then would it not be possible that they too would be dumped if it so suited the Oval Office? Perhaps it was an unsophisticated fear, nevertheless it was a real one.

But more crucial than anything else is the sense that the Western leadership has no real grasp of what is generally described as the 'world situation'. There are numerous examples of this lapse to be found during the past few years and those who would readily say that the United States is the prime example of the diplomatic and geo-political illiterate should beware. After all, it was Britain, the most agile colonial analyst, who remained convinced, right up until the time the results were declared, that Joshua Nkomo would win the election in Zimbabwe. (If it were any comfort, an East European diplomat told the author shortly after the elections that it was the view of the Soviet bloc that Robert Mugabe stood little or no chance of gaining the leadership.) Nor was it the exclusive privilege of the Carter Administration, or to be more exact its officials, to mismanage foreign policy. Angola, Cuba, Vietnam, it does not matter where the chronicler sits, there is a time and an example to redden most diplomatic faces.

Furthermore, there is some evidence to suggest that, eleven months before Christmas Eve 1979, there was every opportunity for the United States to provide further diplomatic, economic and cultural aid for Afghanistan. This would have been with the blessing of the Soviet Union; in fact it was almost at Soviet bidding. (The terrible death of Ambassador Dubs in Kabul in February 1979 made this a non-starter, assuming of course the opportunity was ever recognised in the first place.) It would have been interesting to see how a State Department under General Haig would have reacted in similar circumstances.

What Afghanistan did, was to make the world nervous. Some countries – and not only the smaller ones – saw it as a simple contest between the United States and the Soviet Union. In their eyes, the Soviet Union won. More significantly, they believed that, in spite of her remarkable technology, her almost overwhelming array of weapons, her economic power, her leadership of the Western world, her trumpeted vows to protect the weak from the bullies, in spite of all these things, they believed the United States was powerless to act. Equally demoralising was the fact that the so-called Allies of the United States were unable, or unwilling, or both, to act in support of Washington. France sneered (as was to be expected), West Germany called for caution (understandably) and Britain, trying to maintain the myth of that 'special relationship', produced little more than fine, although sincere, vocal support.

What does not appear to have happened in Western Strategic thinking is any serious examination of the possibility that the Soviet intervention was a Soviet *defeat* – not a victory. Considering the intervention represented a distinct failure on the part of the Soviet Union to control events from Moscow, this factor should have been more seriously considered.

As a result of that international nervousness, together with the need for the President of the United States to counter the impression that the arm of Western military might was muscle-bound, furious diplomatic and military promises were made, remade and introduced. To some extent, they did little more than give the impression that the Alliance is as weak as many believed it to be: this, in spite of the public proclamations on occasions such as the Venice summit. Instead of a calming of the nerves, there must remain a strong suspicion that the Western world has started the 1980s displaying little diplomatic and strategic learning. For this reason alone, there were many who nodded in agreement when Chancellor Helmut Schmidt offered the warning that it was still possible that the world had not learned the lesson of August 1914. And, writing in *Foreign Affairs* in the spring of 1980, Aleksandr Solzhenitsyn began with these words, 'Anyone not hopelessly blinded by his own illusions must recognise that the West today finds itself in a crisis, perhaps even in mortal danger.'

TWO

The Soviet Soldier

There have been something in the region of 270 armed conflicts this century – so far. It is almost impossible to account for the total number of people who have died during these various wars, revolutions, uprisings and punitive campaigns. But, as a starting point, it might be remembered that at least 20 million Soviets died during what we in the West call the Second World War. Since that war, at least one analysis indicates that a further 25 million people have perished. At the time of writing, that comes to an average of 714,000 people being killed every year, although this figure is of course not standard for each twelve-month period. It should be noted, however, that this total would necessarily include a huge number of civilian casualties.

Observing the way in which most countries have managed publicly to distance themselves from modern wars in, say, Chad, Kampouchea, Vietnam – and incidentally the way in which some countries have managed to distance themselves from their allies taking part in some of these wars – then some might begin to believe that Solzhenitsyn's warning of crisis and mortal danger is largely irrelevant. Yet there was a period during 1980 when many people throughout the world held their breath. Others were too busy fighting to do so, and other had seen it all before, said so, and might have been forgiven for muttering, 'What crisis? What mortal danger?' Of course Solzhenitsyn must not be taken at face value, whatever his popular credentials. He would not have us believe that he should be regarded as some guru of grand strategy. In fact his main concern would often appear to be that the West does not begin to understand the Soviet Union, its people, its systems, and therefore cannot begin to read the signs that litter the détente circuit.

To that mesmeric marketing myth, Average Man, the art of strategic analysis (can it *really* be classified as a science?) is best left to those who claim some authority in that particular direction. Instead he (Average Man) is content to cope with the steady flow of information, much of it contradictory and contra-distinct, that comes from the seemingly endless official, quasi-official and decidedly unofficial sources.

And, of course, that flow of information is going out to an ever-changing generation. In the West, many of us live with the pettifoggery of tit-bit information. We know a little, we think we should know more, yet life is really too much of a struggle, or too easy, for the gathering and analysis to be anything but a physical and intellectual hassle. In Western Europe it is possible to live in complete communities where all-out war is becoming little more than a memory. In some cases it is even less, it is somebody else's memory. In the United Kingdom for example, the majority of men under the age of forty have never been in military uniform. And so, although the hundreds of British soldiers killed in Northern Ireland (and Northern Ireland is part of the United Kingdom) are very much part of those 25 million deaths since the Second World War, they have little if any effect on the everyday lives of the majority of British people. This attitude, which is marked in other European countries, presents a problem to NATO planners. It has often been said at NATO headquarters in Brussels and further down the highway at the Supreme Headquarters Allied Powers Europe (SHAPE) that, while it is a fine thing to tell everybody that the peacetime strength of the Alliance has maintained that peace for more than thirty-five years, there is a very real danger that public complacency will undermine that strength. There is no great reason to believe that this fear of the military is confined to the West.

NATO spends *more* on defence than does the Warsaw Pact. In terms of defence spending as a percentage of any one nation's Gross National Product, then the Warsaw Pact probably spends more than NATO. But however the figures are juggled – and they are juggled – the accepted need of both sides to fund increasingly large military budgets is not only an economic headache, it is becoming more of a social problem. More governments on both sides are beginning to say so. The Danes, even the West Germans, are presenting problems in the NATO camp. In the Warsaw Pact communities, Rumania has publicly disagreed with the Soviet Union's demands that all Treaty nations increase military spending. However sophisticated the arguments, both sides eventually reduce public reasoning to a simple gut emotion: fear. In the West we are told that, in spite of international treaties and 'understanding', the Soviet Union is building up its forces at an unprecedented rate, that this is provocative and that the West must be prepared. There is sufficient evidence to convince most people that such is the case. Most people have heard about the Soviet SS-20 missile which is capable of hitting every European city. The Backfire bomber, until recently a hazy snapshot on our news pages, is now detailed as the main manned air threat to us all and, with an air-to-air refuelling capability, is capable of delivering its deadly missiles to New York or Washington DC. There are three times as many Warsaw Pact tanks in Northern and Central Europe as there are NATO tanks. And so on.

Furthermore, we are told the Soviet Union is quite able and willing to use this arsenal. We are reminded of the events in Hungary during 1956, the tanks which rumbled into Prague in 1968. During the last couple of years we have witnessed, or have been told about, the truly remarkable air lift of troops and equipment to the Horn of Africa. We have seen the so-called proxy troops fighting in Africa and the considerable Eastern bloc presence in the Peoples Democratic Republic of Yemen (PDRY) and its formerly British base of Aden. The Soviet Navy is alive and apparently very well in every ocean, including the Indian. As a finale, we have had the events in Afghanistan.

And what of the Eastern bloc? More particularly, the Soviet Union? To Western ears, there may be a familiar ring to the warning bells tolled in Moscow. In the Eastern bloc they are told that, in spite of international treaties and 'understanding', the United States is building up its forces at an unprecedented rate, that this is provocative and that the Soviet Union must be prepared.

Of course this is an over-simplification. The way in which both sides put over the message tends to vary, especially in the West where the political ball games tend to be a little faster than in the Eastern bloc. Nevertheless, in the Warsaw Pact countries the story still runs along similar lines and the evidence to support the claims is handled equally deftly.

The decision to go ahead with Cruise and Pershing II missiles in Europe is roundly condemned. The Trident submarine-launched ballistic nuclear missile in the United States and now in the United Kingdom is denounced. The decision on what amounts to the gradual rearming of China by the West is labelled an aggressive move. The plans to introduce the MX to the United States's ballistic missile system is equally provocative. Ironically perhaps, the false alarms in the American early warning system, which occurred in 1979 and 1980, were seen as ideal propaganda chances. The Soviet claims that America was dancing on the brink of a world war might easily be dismissed, except that they were echoed by some elements in the British Parliament. And, again, the people of the Soviet Union and of other Warsaw Pact countries are not short of examples of the West's willingness to use its not inconsiderable military power.

British and American forces fought alongside each other in Korea. The skies are still searched for another U-2 flight. The Bay of Pigs still smells (especially as Cuba is a client state), American involvement in Vietnam (atrocities are well, if not accurately, documented), the Dominican Republic, and Angola can hardly be ignored. The British are remembered for Suez, Borneo and for Cyprus and Aden. They are still seen in Belize, Gibraltar, Hong Kong and the Falklands. British officers, both mercenary and seconded, are listed in Oman. The CIA's involvement with SAVAAK in Iran and elsewhere is recorded with as much pleasure and propaganda value as KGB operations are in the West. The Kremlin does not forget that, for every MiG delivered to a Third World country, an American Phantom will go to another. Finally, President Carter's announcement of the setting up of a Rapid Deployment Force was seen as the latest evidence that the West in general and the United States in particular was willing to use its military system.

Of course it is possible to argue the reasoning behind any military action. But few in the West will bother to justify the other side's actions – even if they were justifiable. The same might be said with a greater degree of certainty about the East.

And that is how the two sides live.

Many who do stop to think about the possibility of war find a quick refuge. It usually takes the form of a flat statement that goes something like this: 'There won't be a war. They know they'd destroy themselves as well as us.' But then the doubt follows. 'They wouldn't, would they?'

So, if Average Man *does* get frightened every so often, what is it that frightens him? Is it The Bomb, as it was called during the later 1950s and early 1960s? Is it because few can begin to believe there is a way of stopping a Third World War happening? Is it because Washington has said the United States will not permit another Afghanistan and that means war, and that in turn means nuclear war, and few believe it is possible to have a nuclear war without its becoming full-scale, and that would mean the end of much of society as we know it in the Northern hemisphere? Is it bits and pieces of all these things?

And could it be that the memory of the United States not being supported in Vietnam, not being obeyed over Afghanistan, failing tragically in the Iranian desert, finding herself with more than 50 per cent of her enlisted men using drugs, raises too many doubts about the Western political and military systems? A glance into the Soviet Union, beyond the tanks, missiles, ships and planes, to newsreel film of seemingly super-fit, rigidly uniform ranks of almost too-clean-living young men is enough for many people to believe that, come a war, there would be no chance for the West against the Soviet machine, made up not just of weapons but also of equally programmed men. However founded the fears, it is clear that an understanding of the Soviet military system must begin with a look at the people who drive the tanks, fly the jets, con the ships and press the buttons. So, instead of launching into what the defence business likes to call an examination of the military balance, it is first necessary to see what makes the Soviet soldier tick – to see whether or not he is 'ten feet tall' as some analysts would have us believe; for unless the system behind the weaponry is fully understood there is little chance of being able to make a fist of judging whether or not those divisons, squadrons and fleets are as good as Western analysts say they are. To understand the Soviet soldier some basic questions need to be asked. For example: is it possible that one day the Soviet Army would stage a coup d'état? Or is the loyalty of the armed forces beyond question? If so, loyalty to whom? Their generals? The Soviet President? The Party? Are soldiers members of the Communist Party? How does one join the Party? Who runs the forces? What are their names? What is the KGB's connection with the army? How much does a soldier get paid? And if he is not ten feet tall, how tall is he; how good is he?

About 300,000 Soviet troops speak hardly any Russian. That figure is a rough estimate but it illustrates two things. Representing, as it does, approximately 11 per cent of the conscripted force, it indicates the extent of the forces. Secondly, it indicates the size of the problem facing the Soviet system which has to draw its forces from 15 per cent of the globe's land. There are an estimated one hundred major ethnic groupings within the Soviet Union which is split into fifteen Republics. To the Westerner, a Soviet citizen is usually displayed as fair-haired, perhaps stocky, invariably blue-eyed. Surprisingly, the lightning sketch writers rarely see Soviets with dark hair and bushy eye-brows. Yet they vary from the pen-portraited Yuri Gagarins, to the flat faces and weathered skins that are quickly ticked off as Mongols. It is a country that knows and suffers extremes of weather, hardship, deprivation, religion, atheism, oppression, beauty, ugliness, culture and emptiness. It could be, then, any other vast country. Except that it also suffers isolation. Everybody and his brother has been to Moscow, where you take your own bath-plug, can sell your Levis for twenty pounds sterling, and wonder which building is Lubyanka. But Moscow and Leningrad are not of the Soviet Union, they are certainly not of what we once correctly called Russia and now incorrectly call Russia. And it is from this that comes the Soviet soldier.

As a youngster, not yet in his teens, he will be very aware of the military. He will probably have seen more military parades than his Western counterpart. There will be parades to celebrate famous victories, especially those in the Great Patriotic War, Armed Forces Day parades, Anniversary parades, May Day parades and just parades. Because the conscription system touches most families, he will feel the breath of the military on his own household, perhaps more than his Western counterpart, because the Soviet conscript rarely comes home. It has been said this tends to make the military and the very thought of military service that more awesome. And, right from his early school days, the young boy will become personally involved with military styles if not the military itself. The notion that, if you can grab a child when he is still at his primary stage of education, then you will have his loyalty for all time, is not merely the perspicacity of the more learned Roman Catholic orders. Lenin emphasised time and time again that no generation could expect to see the fulfilment of its promises. Youth was all-important.[1]

When he, or she, first goes to school, the Soviet youth will probably join the Pioneers. The Pioneers might be described as the kindergarten of the Communist Party. Just like the Cub Scouts, the Pioneers hold regular meetings and summer camps. At those camps they will be broken into groups along military lines and they will find themselves in battalions and sub-units. At play, they will be taught semaphore, tracking, map-reading, how to bivouac, first aid, just as any cub scout group might anywhere in the world. What cub scout groups do not normally do is exercise with mock rifles and practise grenade throwing and military identification. Pioneers do. Anybody with a couple of tiny sons knows how popular this might well be, and the children learn quickly. By the time the child is into his or her secondary education, he or she is ready for more sophisticated games. This is where the Komsomol comes in. The Komsomol is the Communist Youth League and, when a Pioneer reaches the age of thirteen or fourteen, he may well transfer to become a member of the Komsomol. He does not have to and might well choose not to.

They too have their summer camps and the more physically and mentally demanding war games. Because the Komsomol does not necessarily end when the boy's school days are over, many of its members find themselves involved in very grown-up activities. These include political discussions, Civil Defence training and even helping out with major projects in the region. Above all, they will surely follow the writings and directives of Lenin, especially his thoughts on the need to 'learn' Communism. For Lenin, this was not a matter of reading the slogans, pamphlets and books of Communist thinkers; it also included the idea of getting out and seeing Communism working and sometimes not working, of pinpointing specifics. Consequently the teenage member of the Komsomol may well be supercritical in the name of Communism and perhaps more so towards his elders than would the equivalent but apparently 'free' teenager in the West. He

1. In particular, see Lenin's speech to the Third All-Russia Congress of the Young Communist League on 2 October 1920.

will not necessarily question the system but he might well question the efficiency, or lack or it, in his particular part of Soviet society.

While he is in his secondary school or high school, whether or not he is a member of the Young Communist League, there will be a certain emphasis on military-type activities. These are not normally set out as a subject, but are accepted into the standard sporting programme for all schools. So, while it might be reasonable to expect a youth to complete the Tarzan Course of ropes, climbing and swinging exercises before he can get the required number of credits for high school graduation, the inclusion of such events and trials as throwing the stick-grenade may appear to Western eyes as somewhat incongruous.

However it should not be seen as such, when it is understood that every Soviet boy must, during his final three years of high school, complete a military acclimatization course. It is not a brief visit to the local recruiting office or drill hall. It is laid down that 140 hours will be devoted to this course. Naturally, there are not the facilities for everybody to complete this 140-hour indoctrination period. Some areas are so remote and sparsely populated that instructors are not to be found, although the law provides, in theory, for instructors to be laid on where there are groups of about a dozen students. Although it is not one hundred per cent successful, it is estimated that about three-quarters of the annual intake of conscripts have completed the pre-service training before they arrive at basic training camp. The instructors come from among retired and reserve officers and from the Komsomol. It is one of the first demonstrations to the young man that his military life will be more than influenced, almost dominated, by political motivation.

Another contact with the military might well have been with an organisation called DOSAAF. In very simple terms, DOSAAF is a group of volunteers – in their thousands and usually with a general officer at their head – who maintain liaison with the regular forces. They do two things very well. In the more populated areas they are able to provide some of the best sporting facilities in the Soviet Union, and these are not confined to running, jumping and throwing. If a young man wants to learn parachuting, as just one example, then the chances are DOSAAF will be able to fix it for him. Secondly, in recent years they have taken on some of the workload in the pre-military training programmes.

So, by his seventeenth birthday, it will be assumed that the young Soviet youth is no stranger to the military, its triumphs, its heroes and, at least by sight, its weaponry. It is on his seventeenth birthday that the first knock comes on his door. More accurately, it is a letter telling him that it is time for him to register for the draft, for conscription. And if he doesn't want to go? Just as in the West there are laid down penalties for outright refusal. The authorities do not actually throw away the keys, but labour camp sentences for this offence would tend to be rather lengthy. During August 1980, a Soviet draftee who refused to go was given a two-year hard labour sentence. However, there is no doubt that not everybody is looking forward to conscription and there are attempts to dodge the draft. Furthermore, there are quite legitimate ways of doing just that. Everybody in the Soviet Union lives in what is called a Military District,[1] just as people in the United Kingdom live in Military Districts.[2] The Soviet seventeen-year-old will get his registration call from the headquarters of this Military District and not from Moscow. If he, or his parents, believes that he can produce one of the various legal reasons for not being called up, then it is to that headquarters that his case must be made. He can be totally excused service or his service may be deferred for obvious reasons (again they are similar to those in the West). He may, for example, be the family bread-winner. Physical or mental health is another valid excuse. Possibly he may be starting a higher education course, although reading for a law degree, say, or a history course will not pass muster. It must be a course which the State agrees is beneficial to the system as a whole. Educational grounds vary then according to the importance of the course and sometimes to the influence his family may have.

If he does dodge the draft on educational grounds, it will only be for the life of his college course, but then he will only serve in the forces for about eighteen months. If he can keep his deferment going until he is twenty-seven, then he is exempted altogether. However at that point, and armed with a degree, he will probably be given a junior commission in the reserve forces and he will have to do regular reserve training.

Once it is decided that he is to go (and this would be in the vast majority of cases), he sits and waits for his eighteenth year and one of the two conscription periods that come round every year, The first is in May and runs for just over a month. The second is six months later. He is able to ask for drafting to any number of branches of the services, but the decision will be made by the drafting committee of the Military District. Every unit will have sent to the headquarters a shopping list of draftees needed by the regiment, squadron and fleet. There are other, and perhaps more standard, qualifications. Education, aptitude and fitness are the obvious ones although like the Services throughout the world there seem to be plenty of round holes waiting for square pegs.

1. See Chapter 3.

There are two other characteristics in the Soviet system that may not be so common in the West when it comes to drafting a new recruit: national origins and political stability. As has already been discussed, many recruits have only a smattering of Russian. Some speak none at all. Certainly then, these people are not going to be sent to a signals unit. Many of them will undergo a comprehensive language training course once they have been drafted, but others will simply be sent off to one of the 'back-of-beyond' units working, for example, on a construction gang.

Care will also be taken not inadvertently to put too many people of the same origins in the same unit. That should not be taken to mean that a company of infantry will have 120 men, each of some different cultural background. But there is an effort to make sure that the army does not suddenly find itself with a whole division of one of the more nationalistic groups. It is difficult to say to what degree this splitting of minority groups takes place, but it is certainly high on the list of recruiting procedures for the draft service. It may be imagined that the commander of a Military District, like any good general, will know his area, its people. Therefore just as he would not wish to have the added problem of wondering about 10,000 men, well-armed, trained and with perhaps suspect loyalties, he will also make sure that, when they are drafted out of his area, they do not end up together.

In fact it is a golden rule of Soviet conscription that, wherever possible, no draftee should serve in his home region.

An interesting sideline to this cultural and geographical splitting up is that the navy finds itself with recruits who have never before seen the sea, perhaps not even a boat. And the inclusion of one of these more obvious nationals in any parade, ceremony or promotional film is considered a must by the political directorate. There is a regular television propaganda programme (propaganda in this context is the Soviet usage, not the author's) which sets out to show how efficient, ready and willing are the armed forces. During each programme, the cameras will cut to the 'mandatory ethnic minority' to illustrate the oneness of the armed forces. It is similar to the style practised in the West, especially during the late 1960s and 1970s, when most films of this nature and even groups of plaster-cast models in department store windows had to contain the 'statutory black'. (An incidental characteristic of these naval films is that nearly every one ends artistically with a shot of a seagull. It appears to be almost obligatory. It seems that few Soviet sailors construe this endless repetition as being funny, while others actually find it peaceful.)

The other important consideration during the conscription process is political stability. An eighteen-year-old, ready for his army service, may be one of the minority nationals and feel quite strongly about the fact. Equally important, he may have taken this feeling a stage further; he might have become a political activist. You do not have to be a Ginsburg, an Orlov or a Sakharov, to be a so-called dissident. The unstable youth is weeded out and will end up in a non-job somewhere, perhaps again in one of the construction units.

At the other end of the scale, a good and active member of the Party is used wisely. He will quite possibly be conscripted into the KGB (Komitet Gosudarstvennoi Bezopasnosti – Committee for State Security). The popular view of the KGB is that of its more clandestine operations. But the KGB also runs about 190,000 border guards and, apart from the Officers and senior NCOs, these guards are conscripts. It is an indication that the national serviceman will easily find himself sent to a unit other than that of the traditional arms. Of those arms, the Soviet Union has its own pecking order. Very much at the top is what the West would call the missile forces. In the Soviet Union it is known as the Strategic Rocket Force. The best recruits tend to go to the SRF.

As we have seen, the politically reliable may be drafted to the KGB. The bright recruits not sent to the Rocket Forces will go to the various air forces (there is not a single air force as there is in, say, the United Kingdom), then the navy and National Air Defence Forces and finally the army. Apart from the five main groupings, there are postings to the Civil Defence Force which is far and away more important than its Western counterparts, construction troops and special engineering and signals units. So off he goes for two years in the services, unless of course he is drafted into the navy, when it is three years.

While there is a regular supply of conscripts, the supply of commissioned officer candidates is frequently below the demand of the services, even though it can often be a means of getting a more privileged life than many civilians enjoy. A potential officer may well start his future career when he is as young as thirteen years old. There are a number of navy and army boarding schools and, although Lenin might well turn in his Tomb at the thought of it, they do provide pupils with something of an élitist education. Competition for a place is extremely high and, as in many other countries, it will help a teenager if his family is well established in the armed forces or in the state system. But this is only one way in which to get a commission. There are a few cases where a conscript may be spotted as officer material and recommended for a commission. Even so, the rate of commissioning officers from the drafted ranks is certainly not as great as it might be in the West, and the potenial is not there as it was during Britain's period of national service.

The cadet officer will enrol when he is in his eighteenth year and it may be that he has achieved the educational standard necessary while still at school. Others will be taken from the universities. Depending upon the training selected for the cadet, he will go to college for three up to as many as six years at one of the 140 or so military academies. On the longer courses he will get some form of degree qualification. In spite of a certain uniformity in the training pro- grammes, some academies have higher reputations than others. Where a cadet was trained may well have an influence on his future career. This is considered by some to be especially so in the navy where there are about eleven colleges recognised to be in the top grade.

So we now have an officer and a conscript all ready to join his unit, squadron or ship. What happens to him? For our purposes it is probably best to concentrate on the young conscript.

The first thing that happens to him is that he has his hair cut. More accurately, his head is shaved. This not only has a traditional military ring to it, it has a further very practical value. For the majority of conscripts, conditions in the armed forces are extremely primitive. A minimum of privacy, stark living quarters, the crudest of sanitary systems are all, by some Western standards, designed to inflict the quickest and harshest of toughening-up processes on any young man. On one visit to a Soviet warship, the author found the same cramped living quarters, with almost no privacy whatsoever, that he would have expected to find in any destroyer. (It may surprise some readers to know, for example, that the captain's cabin in a Western ballistic missile-firing nuclear submarine has an open floor area of not much more than three feet by six or seven feet. In a cabin of this size the captain will have to sleep, entertain, and use it as his private office.) What was striking in the Soviet warship was the dirt. The crude washing areas for the ship's company appeared to be one stage from being rusted up and the general impression would have dismayed the average Western Chief Petty Officer. Naturally enough, the ship's accommodation was not cooled, since it was built for operations in Northern waters. It was interesting, however, to see in the officers' quarters air-conditioning units – they were Japanese.

Returning to the conscript, he is paid about four roubles a month which at 1980 exchange rates is little over two pounds sterling or just under seven US dollars. He is set on a comprehensive training course that will last him six months, by which time he is not only proficient in basic drill or square bashing, personal weapons, an elementary trade skill (perhaps armoured vehicle driving and basic repair work) but is considered to be ready to start training some of the new intake of conscripts. Training is generally done at unit level, with very few outside courses. The chances are that the conscript will never leave his unit or ship during the whole of his two- or three-year drafted service. Home leave is unlikely.

This idea of staying with the one unit throughout a man's service is not confined to conscripts. It is a general rule that sea-going naval officers will remain in one ship for many years. It is common to find that the captain of a ship has started his career as the most junior officer on board and has steadily been promoted to a command without serving in another vessel or even on a shore posting. (In the West, a naval officer would expect to stay for about two years in his first ship before going to a shore job, a course or even another ship. But it is extremely unlikely that an officer would be promoted within the ship, and few would serve in the same vessel twice during their whole careers.) The brief portrait, then, of the Soviet serviceman shows that about 80 per cent of the nation's approximately 3,700,000 fighting troops are conscripts. That would indicate that about 3,000,000 Soviet front-line troops are between the ages of eighteen and twenty-one. Conscripts make up about a third of the total armed forces and, for continuity and the need for a higher training standard, headquarters staff tend to be regular troops. The front-line soldier is badly paid, usually far from his home base, is reluctant to sign on as a career soldier, is used to rigorous training and living conditions, is physically fit and for most of his active life has been under supervision of the CPSU, the Communist Party of the Soviet Union, through DOSAAF, the Komsomol or at an earlier period the Pioneers.

This last point, the political domination, is probably one of the most important aspects of the Soviet military system that must be grasped and studied in some depth if anybody is going to begin to understand the military threat that Western politicians and generals say that we face.

The way in which the CPSU controls the forces of the USSR must not be confused with the loyalty which Western forces feel for the state, the crown or the government of the day. It goes much deeper than that.

One of the 'prayer books' of their armed forces is *Marxist–Leninism on War and Army*. It says, 'The armed forces of the socialist states are the main weapon for the defence of the new system's achievements. As regards their sociopolitical essence and historical purpose they are an organ of the socialist state, and the Marxist–Leninist Parties are their leading and organising force.'

In a similar guide-line, simply entitled 'The Soviet Army', there is a more definitive pronouncement: 'The Party has always regarded the Armed Forces as an important organ of the socialist state with the functions of defending the people's revolutionary gains from the encroachments of imperialist aggressors.

'The Party's leadership of the Armed Forces *is not a temporary, transient factor* (author's italics, *et seq.*), it is an objective law that holds for all stages of army construction. The existence, development and strengthening of the Soviet Army is inconceivable without the leadership of the Party, without its organisational, theoretical and educational work . . .

'*Only under the leadership of the Party* are the Soviet Armed Forces capable of carrying out their historic mission of being a powerful factor in the preservation and consolidation of peace and *preventing a new world war.*

'The whole history of the Soviet Union is testimony that the Soviet Army and Navy owe their invincible might, great morale, high fighting qualities and victories over our country's numerous enemies *solely to the leadership of the Communist Party.'* The tendency in the Soviet Union is to believe that the army is controlled by the Party. And members of the armed forces are encouraged to join the Party. Up to the age of twenty-five or so, they will be recruited into the Komsomol. This recruitment of the political elements applies more to the officer cadre than to the enlisted men. According to Soviet sources, more than 22 per cent of the navy and the army are now Party members. Something approaching 70 per cent are members of the Komsomol. Because there is a fundamental belief that politically committed members of the armed forces are bound to be loyal to the system, membership is encouraged, but not necessarily open to all. The CPSU believes that '. . . cultivating socialist ideas . . . the Party awakens in them a love for their country, staunchness, resolve and fearlessness in struggle, the willingness to make sacrifices for the sake of victory over the enemy, mass heroism among the officers and men, an indomitable will to vanquish any aggressor'.

During the Second World War, this ideal was put to the test in a very practical way. CPSU members were mobilised, conscripted into the army. By 1942, nearly 55 per cent of the Party had been ordered into the army. Something like 400,000 Party workers were killed, which, again according to Soviet sources, must have meant that nearly one quarter of the Communist Party of the Soviet Union was killed in action. But, by the end of the war, and with servicemen being encouraged to join the Party, there were 3,500,000 Party workers under arms.

Today the routine for joining is straightforward. A young officer, say, over the age of twenty-five wishing to join the CPSU must fill in a lengthy form detailing his family, educational and professional background. He will also have to declare his former connections with the Pioneers or the Komsomol although this is a formality as his record will be well documented elsewhere. He then has to find three sponsors. The sponsors must have worked with the young officer for at least twelve months and know a fair amount about him. They will have to have been Party members themselves for at least the previous five years. The application will then go to a meeting of the Party where it needs a two-thirds majority vote for approval. In theory, any rank can become a Party member. The non-commissioned ranks are encouraged to take their political education quite seriously. There are night classes for almost anybody. It is possible for enlisted men up to the rank of sergeant to be sent to long-term political training courses. These usually last for one year. And, for the selected few, there are two-year sessions. Some prefer these to military training programmes. There is nothing new in this control by the Party. One of the most important colleges in the whole of the Soviet Union is the Frunze Academy. Mikhail Frunze was only forty when he died in 1925, but he was considered to be one of the great party thinkers and military philosophers. Shortly after the Civil War, Frunze went to great lengths to show that the Communist success could not be seen only in military terms. What he said then is important today, because it further underlines that the Party *working within*, not just directing without, is the all-important element of the Soviet Armed Forces in the 1980s, just as Frunze believed it to be during those violent years between 1917 and 1920, when he said:

'Who introduced elements of order and discipline into the ranks of the young Red regiments set up to boom the cannon? Who in the hours of failure and defeat kept up the soldiers' courage and spirit and infused new energy into their shaken ranks? Who organised the army's logistics and established Soviet order, thus making it possible for our troops to advance quickly and successfully? Who by their persevering and painstaking work demoralised the enemy's ranks, disorganised his rear and thus paved the ground to future success?

'It was the *political bodies* of the army and it must be said they did it brilliantly. The services they rendered were immeasurable.'

Frunze and his ideology should not be equated in the West with some commander saddled with the task of handing out eulogies after a battle. His words contain the outline for the political domination that exists in the army today. The Party-Political Department of the Lenin Military-Political Academy has produced a detailed handbook on the role of the political bodies in the armed forces. One section makes it clear that modern pressures are just as nerve-racking as those recognised by Frunze: 'Today, on account of the revolutionary changes in the armed forces, the growing scope and complexity of their tasks and the character of missile and nuclear warfare, *which requires man to strain his entire moral and physical strength*, the volume of the political bodies' activity has become much greater and their *responsibility for the military training* and political education of the personnel has increased.'

The need for what, in the West, military commanders would term interference, is recognised at the very top of the Soviet system.

Military policy is drawn up in an organisation called the Defence Council, which is effectively run by the Party General Secretary (Leonid Brezhnev), the President of the Soviet Union (Leonid Brezhnev), the Defence Minister (Marshal Dimitri Ustinov), the Chief of the General Staff (N. V. Ogarkov) and will include the head of the KGB (Y. Andropov). The Defence Council reports directly to the General Secretary of the CPSU and the Politburo. The Parliamentary body of the USSR, the Supreme Soviet, does not figure in the decision-making of the armed forces (there are some Members of Parliament in the United Kingdom who would say this is a style not unlike Britain's). Policy decisions are then implemented by a Main Military Council. In wartime this Council would have the operational command of the forces.

Consequently it may be said that the Soviet Government does not run the Armed Forces. Furthermore it is Brezhnev who holds all the major commands. He is, as we have seen, President of the Praesidium, General Secretary of the Party and Head of the Armed Forces. Perhaps we have some little irony here. Lenin would probably have disapproved of the way in which Brezhnev has systematically gathered so much power in his hands. It will be interesting to see whether his successor is allowed to have so much power.

Direction of the Party's wishes comes from the CPSU Central Committee and it is implemented through a very important body called GLAVPUR – the Main Political Administration of the Soviet Army and Navy. In the Lenin Academy's directive, edited by Lieutenant General Alexandr Khmel, the Main Political Administration's function is clearly defined. It (the MPA) 'organises ideological work in the army and the navy, directs the Marxist–Leninist studies of the officers, *including generals and admirals*, and the political education of privates, seamen and non-commissioned and petty officers, and supervises the Party educational system'.

This political education also involves military education. Take for example a division. As General Khmel points out, 'There is no aspect of *combat training*, military discipline and combat readiness of army and naval units with which the political department does not concern itself'.

It is emphasised that nothing is done to undermine the authority of the commander. However, one of the commander's deputies will be the Deputy Commander for Political Affairs. And he will be found in the highest and the lowest military formations. A division will have such an officer and so will a small ship or submarine. He is called the *Zampolit*, sometimes the *Zampol*. And there are also on-the-spot political investigations.

The political department will organise raids on a regiment or warship where they will check on the political and military efficiency of the unit, its personnel including the captain or commander, and also the political resident. Before the political team arrives, it will spend a great deal of time studying reports of the unit or ship and its personnel record. These political evaluation visits usually last between four and seven days.

To keep the units up to scratch, the political officers will be working with Party and Komsomol organisations within the unit itself. They are usually formed into committees and run by their own general secretaries. Every six months or so, a regimental Party secretary will go off to a seminar of similar Party officials in his region or military district. For about three or four days they will discuss joint problems and personalities. In smaller formations, one-day seminars are set up perhaps five or six times a year. Although the military is an important element in these meetings, it is usual for the Party and Komsomol cell leaders to dominate them. They tend to do most of the talking. However, it should not be baldly accepted that these sessions are merely to reinforce Party dogma. New ideas are occasionally presented, but like political gatherings anywhere in the world it is unusual for anybody to jump in without first making sure the water is warm.

The political organisation is considerably larger than might be expected. Again using a large group such as a division or fleet, overall control is taken by the Chief of the Political Department. He is very much the policy holder. It is his deputy who organises military planning and the inspection tours, and puts his pen to the political recommendations that follow. Those recommendations will, however, go only to the Chief of the Department. Probably one of the most important people on the staff is the Assistant Chief, responsible for Komsomol Affairs. Recognising the importance of youth and remembering that the vast majority of the forces are under the influence of the Young Communist league, it is up to the Assistant Chief to make sure the Komsomol workers are thinking along the right lines. It is too important a stage in the political education of a soldier to allow him to go off at a political tangent.

It is down at regimental level that one can see the importance of the political bodies. The regimental deputy commander for political affairs has control of all personnel. As General Khmel emphasises, the deputy commander in a regiment, 'is first and foremost a Party functionary'. Military training programmes, including tactical operations, cannot be put into force unless they have the approval of the Party system, and this means the Party and Komsomol workers who are working within the military at every level. Behind them, in other words not necessarily alongside them, there is the KGB. Most units have a KGB cell, working to make sure political direction is continuing along the right lines. The KGB is the private security force of the

Party and it is accepted that it exists everywhere. There are many who believe it has cells within the military intelligence service.

In spite of this vast machinery, the Soviet military system is by no means faceless. The tank commander is still an 'armoured man'. The sailor can still be heard to speak disparagingly about soldiers and aviators. As with so many other aspects of Soviet society where there is political domination, the primary function of the commander, or military line manager, is to get his forces working as efficiently as possible. The resources which the Party can provide in its name are utilised to the full.

It is also remembered, perhaps not openly, that without the army there might be no Party. And so those Komsomol workers, the watchdogs over the vast majority of Soviet troops, have one main task. It is to 'educate young servicemen in the spirit of utter devotion to the Communist Party and the Soviet country, to Marxist–Leninist ideas and heroic traditions of the Soviet people's revolutionary struggle and selfless labour, to train them to be stalwart, ideologically staunch fighters for the victory of communism, ready to spare no effort and, if necessary, to give their lives in the defence of their socialist country'.

That is the man. What of his machine?

THREE

The Soviet Military Machine

The Intercontinental Ballistic Missile (ICBM) is the biggest banger in the Soviet firework display. It is the thing that rightly scares us all, perhaps because most of us have been told what it could do to us.

Yet the ICBM is but a part of what has been variously described as the Most Powerful War Machine the World Has Ever Seen, the Biggest Army in the World, the Threat to the West. It is up to the individual, be he the man in the street, the expert, the politician or the soldier, to decide for himself whether or not he finds the military behaviour of the Soviet Union threatening. What can be shown with some degree of objectivity is the very size, the scale, of the awesome creature that is the Soviet military system. That it is no less awesome than its Western counterpart makes it no less impressive. Even on paper, the amount of fighting power is staggering: around 3,200 nuclear ballistic missiles, about 3,700,000 soldiers, sailors and airmen, a minimum of about 10,000 *operational* combat aircraft, 50,000 or so tanks, more than 10,000 fixed surface-to-air missile launchers, 195 *major* warships and something approaching 370 operational submarines.

And it is here that any attempt to portray who has what runs into trouble. No matter how 'objective' an assessment may attempt to be, it will be misleading to anybody who wants to know the true strength of the Soviet Union, or any other major military nation for that matter. As an example of the confusion to be found when it comes to military counting games, it is worth comparing the above figures with the following: Soviet Military personnel, 4,900,000; tanks, 42,000; warships, 2,000; aircraft, 14,600; ballistic missiles, 3,000. Those figures come from a book compiled by some first-class military analysts and edited by a former senior air force office.

In assessing the relative strengths of the Warsaw Pact armies and navies there is a tendency to over-simplify. Every time there is a 'crisis' or a military debate, the temptation to trot out a series of graphics for easy consumption becomes almost overwhelming. This is especially true of Western newspapers, journals and broadcasting systems. Silhouettes of tanks, ships, jets and soldiers with rifles are paraded before audiences as a guide to who has what. If it were possible to leave it at that, it would be a reasonable operation. But the average audience cannot be expected to absorb it as a rough guide and little more. To begin with, as we have seen, the figures can often vary so much as to be meaningless, or nearly so. In the West, they are rarely displayed unless to show how much *more* of everything the Warsaw Pact has; therefore there is a further temptation in some areas for the chart to be on the heavy side. But this is not the really important aspect of this particular numbers game. What is important is that anybody who wants to see more than the end column of figures in this military ledger should have access to the rest of the books. It is impossible to get much more than a harum-scarum view of the Soviet Armed Forces without going beyond the line of figures which will show that there are an awful lot of them. Unhappily, just as there are few successful do-it-yourself accountants, there are fewer unqualified military auditors who are able to read the increasingly complicated figures and systems of the Soviet forces. Those figures and systems tend to disguise the essential information that any analyst needs to know about a potential enemy: capability and, more importantly, what he is likely to do with that capability.

However it would be absurd to believe that the numbers in what is normally called the military balance[1] should be dismissed. After all, 3,700,000 trained and armed men, 3,000 ballistic missiles and 50,000 tanks is a massive army no matter how many qualifications are introduced into the discussion. The fairground fighter may not have much skill, but if he is big enough, it is going to take a very big punch to knock him down. Indeed the most obvious thing about the Soviet armed forces is their size. Having examined the background to the majority of the Soviet forces, the conscripts, it is worth beginning any examination of the machine itself with a look at the very top. Who are the big names at the top of this very big force? Are they, for example, as scarifying as they are made out to be?

The first thing to notice is that the highest command of the forces either coincides with, or is very close to, the real leadership of the Soviet Union itself. Now, the same might be argued for Western forces. In Britain the Monarch is the head of the Services, officers receive a commission from the Crown, soldiers, sailors and airmen declare their loyalty to the Queen or King. However, it is interesting to note that, during a fairly recent seminar for middle ranking officers, those officers were reminded that their loyalty is in fact to the government of the day. Why it was necessary to remind them was not made clear; apart from some foolish rumour-mongering, there has not been any suggestion of a 'colonels' revolt' in the United Kingdom.

1. This term should not be confused with the statistics presented every year by the London-based International Institute for Strategic Studies. The IISS analysis, arguably the finest unclassified presentation published by any non-governmental body, in Europe, is entitled 'The Military Balance'.

The British Prime Minister will have, in his or her Cabinet, the Secretary of State for Defence. The same Minister is likely to be in any Inner Cabinet that might exist during a government's term of office. Furthermore, the most important secret committee is the Cabinet Defence and Foreign Affairs Committee.

In the United States, the President's closest advisers include the Secretary of Defense and the National Security Adviser. But, neither in the United States, the United Kingdom, nor in most other forms of democracies, is it the case that the serving military man has a position of political power.

In Moscow, the three First Deputy Defence Ministers are all soldiers. The eleven Deputy Defence Ministers are soldiers, a sailor and an airman. This does not make them politicians in the Western sense, but it does emphasise the very important link between the Party and all aspects of Soviet life. Others might of course dismiss the First Deputies and Deputies as merely holders of meaningless titles. President Brezhnev has undoubtedly managed a very close relationship with the military, and the fact that he appointed himself Marshal of the Soviet Union might be taken as an indication that he now regards his control of the military as something approaching absolute and that it is a sign of the Party's undoubted control. Some have argued that the military is being demoted in the powerful corridors of the Kremlin. This author is not convinced, especially as many of the arguments seem to centre on the premise that the last defence minister was replaced with a non-military man. This is not strictly true.

Marshal Grechko was a soldier who earned his promotion. For seven years he commanded the combined Warsaw Pact forces and then in the summer of 1967 he was appointed Defence Minister. There are those who say he was the complete Soviet commander, the true soldier who not only became part of the Party élite, but who made it work for him and the armed forces. Six years later, he was co-opted on to the Politburo, the generating room of Soviet power policy. Three years later he was dead and Brezhnev turned to a personal friend to take over as Defence Minister. The man he chose is today's Defence Minister, Marshal Dmitri Ustinov. Ustinov is certainly far removed from the fighting soldier image. Yet as Professor John Erikson, of Edinburgh University, points out, Ustinov was for many years a colonel-general in the technical branch[1]; and so, rather than talk about 'civilian' leadership of the Defence Ministry, we should emphasise the Party element and the institution of direct Party control. Ustinov's appointment perhaps represented the need for

1. Adelphi Paper, 152, IISS, London, summer 1979.

Brezhnev to keep at bay some of the younger elements of the Services and maybe the truly non-military members of the Party. To some extent, Ustinov is from the same school as the Soviet President and it is possible to imagine that if the Defence Minister should survive Brezhnev, he might be replaced as minister. He is now in his early seventies and is thought to have a distressing although by no means critical illnesss. He may be incontinent.

As with the civilian leadership of the Soviet Union, it is common in the armed forces to find a somewhat geriatric atmosphere among the general officers. Many are in their seventies, one or two are in their eighties. However the real strength of the higher command is relatively young, in Soviet terms at least. The youngest of the top three First Deputy Defence Ministers is Victor Kulikov, a Marshal of the Soviet Union and a very hard man to please according to some who have worked with him. If it were necessary to apply that overworked military cliché, a soldier's soldier, to any of the top ranking Soviet generals and marshals, then Kulikov would certainly carry the title against most comers. At one stage he was the Chief of the General Staff and he apparently spent some time sorting out a number of problems and jealousies at that level. It is said that he banged a few heads together and so he may well also have trodden on a few toes. On paper, Kulikov is seen by some as the most important of the top three. He went from the Chief of Staff's job to command the Warsaw Pact armies. It is a difficult job at any time and more so at the present.

This supreme command over the Warsaw Pact forces was established in 1956 and in 1972 diplomatically moved its headquarters well away from Moscow to Lvov. 1956 is a sensitive date in the Warsaw Pact in general and in Hungary in particular. Ironically, a special committee of Warsaw Pact defence ministers was set up in 1968, the year that Albania predictably withdrew from the Pact, protesting against the Soviet intervention in Czechoslovakia during that year. It can be seen that the job of Supreme Commander Warsaw Pact forces is one which requires a strong personality as well as a good soldier. Nor has it been forgotten that the late Marshal Grechko moved from this job to become Defence Minister. True to form, there are those who see Kulikov repeating the promotion act.

However, the man who took over from Kulikov as Chief of the General Staff might be better considered to be the most powerful military man in the high command. Marshal Nikolai Ogarkov is in his early sixties. He is not only regarded very highly in Moscow, there are many in Western capitals who see him as the Soviet military mind with which they must reckon. He built something of a reputation during the SALT II negotiations. His visits to some of the more uncertain governments in the Western camp, such as Ankara, are watched with special interest. He is a hard-liner, a convincing talker, and his broad forehead beneath dark, brushed-back wavy hair can be seen at most important gatherings. At the signing of SALT II, there were those who felt that he overshadowed Ustinov himself. His first-hand knowledge of command in the Far East and other military regions make him more than a corridor soldier. But it is in the corridors where he now makes his feelings felt and obeyed. And, considering that the General Staff's position is in the ascendant, then Ogarkov must be one of the most powerful men in the Party.

To those who still say the military is on the decline, it should be pointed out that the armed forces are becoming more technical than ever before. The application of that technology to the detailed military planning falls upon the General Staff more than it did. The Politburo may be able to tell the State Planning Ministry – *Gosplan* – to build more of everything, but it is likely they will begin to rely on the General Staff for more and more practical advice. It will be interesting to see whether or not Marshal Ogarkov's team will be able to keep pace with this movement.

The third First Deputy Minister is Marshal Sokolov. He is also the eldest, about seventy years old. It is unlikely that he would survive any major reshuffle of the top military.

But perhaps the most intriguing man in the whole Soviet military leadership is not in the top three. Nor is he a soldier. Admiral of the Fleet of the Soviet Union Sergei Georgivich Gorshkov is the commander-in-chief of the Soviet Navy and has been since 1956. For a quarter of a century, Admiral Gorshkov has been building a navy that started out as a relatively small coastal force and is today a headline-catcher in every ocean, in every port it visits throughout the world – and there are few places that the Soviet Navy cannot go. Because of Admiral Gorshkov's navy, Western commanders no longer believe they could keep open the sea lanes to Europe in time of war. Considering that it is believed that the majority of the supplies needed not only to support forces in Europe, but also to ensure food and oil supplies for the civilian population, must come by sea, then this Soviet ability, or rather its alleged ability, to hi-jack the Atlantic during a war makes the navy of Admiral Gorshkov a very important factor in the military balance. But who is the admiral? How is it that he has managed to survive when others have slipped, sometimes painfully, by the Soviet wayside?

He was born in February 1910 at the start of the decade of revolution. In 1918, with a budget of some 20,000,000 roubles, the Peoples Council, the Commissars, decided to establish the Red Army and Navy. Five men (Yurenev, Trifonov, Podvoisky, Krylenko and

Mekhonoshin) sat down to work out the rough details. Within a week, the job was done and on 11 February (two weeks before Gorshkov's eighth birthday) Lenin's decree on the Worker's and Peasant's Red Navy was endorsed by the Council of People's Commissars. At the same time, the first Soviet military academy was set up. It was later to become the M. V. Frunze Military Academy, and Gorshkov one of its most famous sons. He joined the navy in 1927 when he was seventeen and graduated from the Frunze Academy four years later. He was immediately sent to the Black Sea Fleet for a year and then was given the command of a frigate in the Pacific Fleet, which is where he stayed for the next seven years. By the time he left he was commanding a destroyer squadron, and he returned to the Black Sea for a bigger command, the cruiser squadron. He had what used to be described as 'a good war'. And it was not confined to naval actions. He spent much time organising shore assaults and got his first insight into the value and problems of operating with marines (known in the Soviet Union as Naval Infantry). By 1942, Gorshkov was deputy commander of what was then the Novorossiysk defensive region and in November of that year took command of the 47th Army. Three months later he was back in a sea-going command and again spent much time supporting and planning troop landings. By the end of the war, he was ready to return to the Black Sea and in 1948 he became its Chief of Staff. He was now on the politico-military trail (he had joined the Party in 1942). He became C-in-C of the Navy as a prelude to his promotion as Commander in Chief, six months later. He was automatically made a Deputy Minister of Defence. Gorshkov was then forty-six all but one month.

Although the diminutive Gorshkov (he is not much above five feet) was by then the head of the whole navy, it was not until 1967 that he was given the highest rank, that of Admiral of the Fleet of the Soviet Union. It is an interesting comment on the standing of the navy. In fact the navy did not begin to assume the importance that it has today perhaps until 1961, and most certainly after 1962 and the Cuba episode.

There is another general to be considered, if for no other reason than that he might be thought to have far more power than any Admiral of the Fleet or even Marshal of the Soviet Union. Furthermore, he is a member of the ruling Politburo. He is General Yuri Andropov, Chairman of the Komitet Gosudarstvennoi Bezopasnosti, the KGB. He works from an office in Dzerzhinsky Square in Moscow, the infamous Lubianka. The KGB is more than anything else the Party's private security firm and for obvious reasons it wields more power than, say, the GRU, the military intelligence service. It is divided into a number of Chief Directorates and Directorates, each with a specific role. For example, one Chief Directorate looks after operations outside the Soviet Union. It will have different departments or smaller directorates. Department or Directorate V would be responsible for sabotage operations. Department A for disinformation. The Scientific and Technical Directorate X looks after the gathering of scientific intelligence. There is even a department, the 12th, in the First Chief Directorate which is given the job of talent-spotting foreign students.

Another Chief Directorate's main function is counter-intelligence in the Soviet Union as far as subversion goes – and it can go far. This 2nd Chief Directorate will perhaps have some liaison with the 5th Chief Directorate which is particularly interested in the intelligentsia. The 3rd Chief Directorate is responsible for counter-intelligence in the armed forces. As we have seen, most units will have some form of KGB cell. It will also monitor the workings of *Glavpur*, the Main Political Directorate of the Soviet Army and Navy. It keeps track of the political structure within the armed forces, including the Party organisation, the Department of Military Sociological Research and the expanding Warsaw Pact Liaison Department.

Working on occasions with, but more often than not against, the KGB, is part of General Ogarkov's General Staff in the form of the Chief Directorate of Military Intelligence, the GRU. It gathers military intelligence, organises some unconventional operations and completes its analyses from intelligence of its own or from other sources. Instinctively, the KGB and the GRU are rivals and, because of its sheer size of operation, its wider range of activities, its obvious importance to the Party and to the State, and the importance of its Chairman, the KGB usually comes out on top in any battles that are fought – rarely in the open. There is a popular image of the KGB – and it is not confined to Western comic books – of the cloak-and-dagger KGB men plotting the downfall of some foolish diplomat, working against the CIA, pig-sticking unsuspecting émigrés on the Paris Métro or emerging from one of the various training schools such as that at Gaczyna to melt into Western society until needed. All this may of course be quite true and it would be a pity to spoil any images. But there is a larger and certainly more public sector of the KGB under Yuri Andropov's command, yet it is one quite often overlooked by Western travellers. The frontier regions of the Soviet Union are divided into nine border areas. Within these areas the KGB has control. To exercise this control there are something like 190,000 KGB border guards and it is, as we have seen, into this force that the politically sound youngster may find himself conscripted. As a reminder, they can be distinguished from other troops by the green backgrounds to their shoulder-flashes. Apart from the borders, the KGB troops may also be seen guarding Lenin's Tomb in Moscow.

Again contrary to popular opinion, the KGB does not run the labour camps, the Gulags, made famous by Solzhenitsyn in his *Gulag Archipelago*. These are run by the MVD, the Ministry of the Interior (the equivalent in Britain would be the Home Office). Like the Home Office, the MVD is responsible for law and order and runs the civilian police and the fire services. In all, the MVD controls more than a quarter of a million internal troops and they are considered part of the military institution.

In any war, these forces (the KGB and the MVD between them control nearly half a million men) would be utterly essential. Unofficial movement within the Soviet Union would have to be severely restricted – as it is in peacetime. Lines of communication would have to be guaranteed, potentially disruptive elements would have to be watched and if necessary interned.

However, the West is more exercised by the immediately recognisable aspects of the Soviet military system.

The Soviet Union is divided into four regions: European, Central, Southern and Sino-Soviet. And those four regions are further divided into sixteen Military Districts. They are as follows, with each Military District's headquarters in parenthesis: Leningrad (Leningrad), Moscow (Moscow), Odessa (Odessa), Carpathian (Lvov), Baltic (Riga), Belorussia (Minsk), Kiev (Kiev), Volga (Kuybyshev), Transcaucasus (Tbilisi), North Caucasus (Rostov), Central Asia (Alma Ata), Ural (Sverdlovsk), Turkestan (Tashkent), Transbaykal (Chita), Siberia (Novosibirsk) and Far East (Khabarovsk). From Lvov in the west to the most Eastern headquarter Khabarovsk, each of the sixteen Military Districts has an importance that cannot be judged simply by its proximity to the European border with the West.

The Transcaucasus headquarters of Tbilisi overlooks Turkey (a sometimes wayward NATO member state) and Iran. Tashkent, the Turkestan headquarters, is north of Afghanistan. Alma Ata, Chita and Khabarovsk all but overlook China. It is here in the Military districts where the enormous mix of nationalities that exists within the Soviet forces is best seen. Although an Asian may find himself posted to a ship, the impression should not be given that every single national is drafted away from his region although he may well find himself out of his home area. Furthermore, because of the vast turnover of conscripts there is a very large reserve force and many of them are highly, or at least recently, trained. It was the use of trained nationals that highlighted the initial military action in Afghanistan. Within two weeks of the action beginning around Christmas 1979, there were more than 50,000 Soviet troops in Afghanistan. The majority were reservists from the Soviet republics bordering Afghanistan. The Military District therefore is responsible for more than the day-to-day running of the regular army. The district commander has to make sure that his troops are not simply up to speed, he must be prepared to reinforce his district at very short notice, because not all Soviet divisions are at full strength – some of them are very much below this. Furthermore, a district may take on a new importance at relatively short notice and so Western Intelligence spends a great deal of time on its personalities file. The sort of thing that might happen is the move of somebody such as General Petrov from his job as First Deputy Commander of the Ground Forces (a very senior post) to become Chief of the Far East command. This signals to Western Intelligence analysts that the command has been upgraded by the General Staff and therefore probably by the Soviet Union's Politburo. It could also be a pointer that Petrov is destined for much higher things after the Far East posting.

There are four other major army territorial commands apart from the sixteen Military Districts. These are the four Groups of Soviet Forces that are not based in the Soviet Union. They are important for two obvious reasons. The first is their locations in Poland, Hungary, Czechoslovakia and East Germany. The second reason is their very size. Of the Soviet Army's 173 Divisions, there are about thirty-one stationed in those four countries. The vast majority, certainly the equivalent of twenty divisions, are based in East Germany. This is, in effect, the Soviet Union's front-line force and, when it is considered that the Soviet Union's mobilisation and reinforcement programme may not be so straightforward and rapid as many Western analysts believe, the importance of these front-line divisions becomes doubly obvious. (And see footnote on page 60.)

In sheer numbers and equipment, the strength or certainly the muscle of these Groups of Soviet Forces lies in East Germany.

Although troops and tanks were withdrawn from the Group of Soviet Forces Germany (GSFG) during 1979 and 1980, the overall number may remain close to the original equivalent of twenty divisions. It would seem at the time of writing that the GSFG is made up of nine tank divisions, an artillery division, and what are called, in the Soviet army, motor rifle divisions and an air army. In terms of numbers, this comes to more than 380,000 men (at least if the air force is included), about 5,500 tanks and some 900 available aircraft.

The Commander in Chief of GSFG has been, since 1980, General Mikhail Saizev. His headquarters is located just south of Berlin at Zossen-Wunsdorf and it is assumed that in the case of war it would also form the headquarters of a fighting front. The general has under his command five different armies. For those who would wish to plot these huge forces on a map, here is where to find them. In the north there is the 2nd Guards. It consists of two tank and two motor rifle divisions at Neustrelitz, Perleberg, Vogelsand and Schwerin. Further south there is the 20th Guards Army with three divisions headquartered at Bernau, Döberitz and Jüterbog. Again south and towards the East-West border with its headquarters at Magdeburg is the 3rd Shock Army. It has four divisions, the 207th Guards at Stendal, the 10th at Krampnitz, the 12th at Neuruppin and the 47th at Hillersleben. Towards the Czech border with its headquarters at Dresden is the 1st Guards Army, this time with almost five and not four divisions. The remnants of the 6th Guards are based on Wittenberg. The other divisions are at Dessau-Rosslau, Riesa, Halle and Dresden itself. Finally there are the 8th Guards at Jena, Grimma, Naumburg and Ohrdruf.

(The terms motor rifle division, guards division and shock army may be confusing to Western eyes. A motor rifle unit is best equated with a Western infantry unit. Guards does not have the élitist meaning in the Soviet Union that it might in the West, especially in the United Kingdom. It is a simple term for a unit which would have been formed and fought during the Great Patriotic War. A shock army does not consist of 'shock' troops armed with little more than an assault rifle each and buckets of adrenalin. It, again, is a fairly standard term.)

There have been some changes in the make-up of the GSFG during the past couple of years. On 6 October 1979, President Brezhnev announced that some 1,000 tanks and 20,000 troops were to be withdrawn from the force during the next twelve months. The Soviet statement was, predictably, treated with a certain amount of cynicism among NATO officials and the military in general. There were a number of reasons for this cynicism which even the more charitable now feel was partly justified. To begin with, although nobody in the West was certain, East-West relations generally and those between Moscow and Washington in particular were due to take a steep dive before the year was out. Some believed Brezhnev recognised this and the 6 October announcement was a softener for what he knew was to come. This is something of an over-simplification. It does not take into account more concrete factors. Two in particular stand out. A third is not so obvious.

Firstly, the long-running and long-winded talks taking place in Vienna to reduce the numbers of troops in Central Europe were stalled as usual. Known as MBFR (Mutual and Balanced Force Reductions), these talks were making no progress partly because neither side could agree on the number of Soviet troops stationed in the region anyway. Although it was not until the following year that the Soviet Union linked Brezhnev's speech with what was going on in Vienna, there are many who believe the planned withdrawal was all part of MBFR. This does not seem likely. What does is the second possible reason for the announcement.

It was made just a few weeks before European members of NATO were to be asked to make up their minds on the basing programme for a mixture of 572 Cruise and Pershing II medium range nuclear missiles. The Alliance's Nuclear Planning Group was to meet in The Hague and this was to be followed a month later, in December, by a full meeting of all NATO's Defence Ministers in Brussels. That the missiles, built, paid for and operated by the United States, would be based in Europe was not in doubt. This had virtually been decided at a meeting of the Nuclear Planning Group earlier that year at Homestead Air Force Base in Florida. Even the then British defence minister, Labour's Fred Mulley, had no doubt they would be deployed. The American Secretary of Defense, Harold Brown, was 'confident'. But there were some doubts about the numbers because not all countries were as compliant as Britain and West Germany.

The Soviet Union, not unnaturally, believed it could stop the Western Theatre Nuclear Force Modernisation programme as it was then called. After all a couple of years earlier Moscow had mounted a successful propaganda campaign to prevent the Enhanced Radiation and Reduced Blast Weapon (the Neutron Bomb) getting the go-ahead. Much to the military's annoyance, Washington had to back down. And so, in October 1979, it was obvious to everybody, including the Soviet Union, that not every country was one hundred per cent behind the Cruise project. The most hesitant were the Dutch. The Hague government would have liked to agree, but it did not believe it could get such a decision through the Dutch Parliament. All eyes were turning towards the Nuclear Planning Group meeting in the Netherlands. Brezhnev's announcement was perfectly timed. The message to the Dutch and, as it turned out, the politically unstable Belgians, was clear: here were the Soviets demonstrating their willingness to talk arms control at a time when the West was apparently thinking along other lines. So, on 12 December, the Western allies agreed to go ahead with the deployment, but it was without the full support of the Dutch and the Belgians, at that stage at least.

The third part of the reasoned equation is the size of Soviet military formations. Soviet divisions are smaller than Western units. Certainly until quite recently it has been accepted that a Soviet tank division had between 10,500 and 11,000 men. The motor rifle divisions have 13,000 men. British divisions for example average out at some 12,500 men. An American division is about 16,500 men. There is every sign that the Soviet Union has decided to enlarge many of the tank and infantry divisions. If one looks at what goes on in many of these units, a reason can be seen for this enlargement. For example, some maintenance now needs to be done on site as more equipment becomes technically advanced. The suggestion is not that men of the 6th Armoured Division moved out to make way for replacements. It is simply that, although 20,000 men and tanks have indeed been withdrawn from East Germany (including the 6th Armoured Division), other troops who were coming in anyway have arrived. So, until it can be seen what other moves in the GSFG are to be made, there does not appear to be any real reduction in manpower and certainly not in overall military strength and efficiency. If some of the Intelligence assessments are to be judged correct, then efficiency during the second half of 1980 actually improved in spite of the fanfares announcing the completion of the withdrawal of 20,000 troops and 1,000 tanks. The announcement neatly coincided with the end of the summer session of the Vienna MBFR talks. To the general public's mind, it might well have been that the exercise had a suitable result. The Cruise and Pershing II missiles programme may not have been cancelled, but there were those in Europe during the summer of 1980 who were openly saying to their governments that the withdrawals from East Germany warranted some Western response. While this was going on, there was speculation in the West of a different kind. The unrest in Poland, especially the strikes centred on the Lenin shipyards, had caught the imaginations and the politically dry nibs of Western leader-writers. There was, in some cases, speculation about the possibility of Soviet tanks rumbling into Poland. But there was no need to speculate, they were already there.

The Soviet Northern Group of Forces (NGF) has its headquarters across the other side of the Sudeten Mountains and into Poland at a place called Legnica. It is difficult to find on many maps, but from there the Soviet army controls two tank divisions and major elements of a Soviet tactical air army.

After East Germany, the country with the biggest group of Soviet forces on its territory is Czechoslovakia. There are perhaps as many as 70,000 Soviet troops in Czechoslovakia, a permanent fixture since 1968 with their headquarters at Milovice, north-east of Prague. There may be a further 4,000 men with the Soviet air force based in the country. In Hungary, at Budapest, is the headquarters for the SGF, the Soviet Southern Group of Forces. It controls about 76,000 men in two tank divisions, two motor rifle divisions and a sizeable tactical aircraft element.

As a joint force, the Soviet Groups of Forces amount to more than half a million men, perhaps closer to 600,000 when all the support elements are included. Their equipment is the most modern, especially as the more up-to-date tanks such as the T-72 are being used to strengthen the GSFG. (These T-72s have probably replaced some, but not all, the tanks that were withdrawn from East Germany following Brezhnev's 6 October announcement. As a front line it is impressive when the equally modern armies and tactical air units of the three most Westerly Military Districts in the Soviet Union are taken into consideration. Nor have we considered the relative strengths of the forces of the indigenous armies and air groups in Poland, Hungary, Czechoslovakia and East Germany. But of immediate interest to the would-be analyst is the composition of the huge Soviet armies, air forces and navies.

If the virility symbol of any army is its tanks, then the long-range rockets with their nuclear warheads have become the national virility symbols of the two Superpowers. This is particularly apparent in the United States where the major public debate has not been on the need for the MX Missile, but rather on where it should be based.

If the ICBM (Intercontinental Ballistic Missile) really is what terrifies us all, to the Soviet mind there is no doubt that it is something to be feared and, if necessary, used. The final section of the Moscow work, *Armiya Sovyetskaya*, has this to say:

'The appearance of intercontinental missiles . . . necessitated the creation of an entirely new fighting service, the Strategic Rocket Forces. Today this is the main service of the Armed Forces, the basis of the Soviet Union's defence capacity.

'Soviet strategic missiles possess a virtually unlimited range; they can carry thermonuclear charges of tremendous yield; they can hit targets with high precision; their flight paths are such as to make nuclear missile strikes sudden and inexorable; they can be used at any time of the day and in any weather . . .

'Whereas formerly the United States, feeling safe on the other side of the ocean and possessing bases on foreign territories, could count on waging wars at the expense of its allies, assuming that all retaliatory blows would fall on European or Asian countries, now it has lost its position of relative invulnerability.

'If a war starts American territory will become a theatre of operations within minutes . . . only a few bombs are needed to wipe out whole states.'

Few would doubt the Soviet claims of having unlimited range for their missiles, partly because the targets they might one day wish to attack are within the range of most rocketry. And, although some feel it necessary to question the last statement, there is every reason to doubt those who argue that any East-West confrontation would be confined to Europe. It is also a useful reference for those who maintain that such a war would begin with a conventional phase and only gradually move towards a nuclear exchange. Admittedly the

Soviet claim has been removed from its original context, but at the very least it does show the Soviet writer is perfectly happy to cast enormous doubt on the Western value of so-called flexible response doctrine – of which more later.

The Soviet Union has about 6,000 strategic nuclear warheads. Three-quarters of them are carried in Intercontinental Ballistic Missiles. The United States has far more warheads than the Soviet Union, more than 9,000. The tactician, especially the strategic tactician, would rightly argue that this is yet another example of the misleading numbers game. But it does not matter how many warheads a commander has, he must have a means of getting them to the target. There are three types of delivery vehicles in service: the ICBM, the submarine and the manned bomber.

When looking at the world of missiles, it is often difficult to get close enough because of the wood of jargon that disguises it. Rocketry is the world of acronyms and code names so filled with mumbo-jumbo that the casual reader will surely be tempted to resort to the simplest question, 'Is it pointed at me?' ICBM, IRCM, MRBM, MIRV, MARV, MRV, Throw-weight, CEP, Hot launch, Cold launch, SS-this and SS-that. The Soviet Union has other names and acronyms. Most of those we hear or read about are NATO designations. All Soviet missiles start with the letter S, and so they have all been baptised by the West and converted into Savage, Scapegoat, Scaleboard, Sandal and, at one point in the 1950s, even Shyster. To make it all a little easier to understand, there follows a poor man's guide to the terminology.

An ICBM, as we have seen, is an Intercontinental Ballistic Missile and by that is meant one that if fired from the Soviet Union would hit, for example, the United States. When the two Superpowers sat down to work out a Strategic Arms Limitation Treaty, one of their problems was to agree on a definition of an Intercontinental Ballistic Missile. Finally they agreed that ICBM launchers '. . . are land-based launchers of ballistic missiles capable of a range in excess of the shortest distance between the north-eastern border of the United States of America and the north-western border of the continental part of the territory of the Union of Soviet Socialist Republics, that is, a range in excess of 5,500 kilometers'. Most of the bigger ICBMs have had ranges of between 5,000 and 7,500 miles. The IRBM is the Intermediate Range Ballistic Missile. The best-known IRBM is the SS-20, a rocket which can be fired from a land-based mobile launcher and which has a range of somewhere between 3,000 and 4,000 miles. (Ranges are complicated by the fact that they may be increased by adding another booster rocket or by reducing the number of warheads and therefore the weight the rocket engines have to carry.) MRBMs,

Medium Range Ballistic Missiles, go back some time. The SS-4, the Sandal, is being replaced and understandably so. It has been around since the early 1960s, although there are supposed to be a number of them still in service.

MRV and MIRV are acronyms that refer to the actual nose of a missile – the warhead. The stark graphics that display the hitting power of a missile often show some long and often thin rocket soaring and then swooping on its target; which is far from what actually happens. Soviet and American strategic missiles may have different ranges, warheads and guidance systems, but basically ICBMs have relatively common characteristics. Before going on to discuss different terms and before taking a look at the Soviet (and later the American) strategic arsenal, it is worth describing exactly what is an ICBM and what it does. The American Minuteman III missile perhaps incorporates most modern design features and is as good an example as any.

It is white and about sixty feet long and, at its widest point, approximately six feet in diameter. It is not unlike the rockets that sent men into space and, in the crudest of terms, the theory is not dissimilar. Looked at at the bottom, there are three big nozzles whose mechanisms go up about four feet or so. The next eighteen and a half feet is the first stage motor. As with those space shot rockets, this falls away in flight. Above the first stage, the rocket narrows slightly to give it 'shoulders'. Above these 'shoulders' is the second stage motor and that is about nine feet high. Then there are another three feet of exhaust. Above that is the third stage motor which is only about five feet high. Above that is the rocket engine which is only about seventeen inches tall. On top of that is a section that is just over thirteen inches tall. It is the all-important guidance system. Sitting on top of all this is the lethal section – the re-entry vehicle which contains the nuclear warheads. It is not quite twelve feet tall and its point, the nose cone, comes off. By the time all the stages have fallen away we are left with a tubular re-entry vehicle inside which are three warheads. This rocket, sixty feet tall and weighing 78,000 pounds, is propelled by three motors up to about 700 miles at a speed well in excess of 15,000 m.p.h. It is the final section, the re-entry vehicle, that causes military men to start muttering about MIRVs. MIRV stands for Multiple Independently Targetable Re-entry Vehicle. All it means is that the warheads are able to leave the re-entry vehicle and independently seek out separate and, if necessary, widely spaced targets. (Many also use the term re-entry vehicle to describe the warhead.)

But will it all hit the target, or targets? When estimating this likelihood, missile men use the term CEP, or Circular Error Probability. Taking a target as the centre of a circle, the radius around that target is the area in which at least fifty per cent of the warheads will hit. It is, simply, the accuracy of the system. The latest American warheads would give Minuteman III a CEP of about 700 feet. Modern Soviet systems are thought to have a CEP of not less than 1300 feet.

According to American evidence, the Soviet Union has 1,398 Intercontinental Ballistic Missiles, ICBMs. This is the figure mentioned in the SALT II Agreement, the Soviet declaration, signed on 18 June 1979, admitting that there were 1,398 fixed launchers of ICBMs in the USSR. Although the Soviet Union has been known to dismantle some of her ICBMs, there have been suggestions by sources in Washington and Brussels that, in spite of modern verification systems, this figure of 1,398 was rather on the low side. It is thought the Soviet Union may have as many as seventy more ICBMs. There is of course the possibility that this higher figure includes test rockets.

But where are these ICBMs? Scattered across the USSR are twenty-eight ICBM sites. This number includes the two test sites, one in the north at Plesetsk and the other south-west of the Aral Sea and north of Afghanistan at Tyuratam. Again for those who would wish to trace these missile sites on a map of the Soviet Union, the twenty-six other sites are (going from east to west) at: Svobodny, Olovyannaya, Drovyanaya, Gladkaya, Uzhur, Itatka, Novosibirsk, Aleysk, Zhangiztobe, Omsk, Tyumen, Imeni Gastello, Verkhnyaya Salda, Kartaly, Shadrinsk, Perm, Dombarovsky, Yurya, Kashkar Ola, Kostroma, Teykova, Yedrovo, Tatshevo, Kozelsk, Derazhnya and finally Pervomaysk which is just over 110 miles in a northerly direction from Odessa.

It has often been said that the USSR got into the strategic rocket business after she had to back down over Cuba. There certainly appears to be an argument for saying that the programme accelerated, but, just twelve months before the Cuban missile crisis, the Soviet Union had at least fifty ICBMs, a comparatively large number for twenty years ago. The United States had only sixty-three, although she was about to introduce her major ICBM programme and by 1967 had reached her present level of 1,053 missiles. Another piece of evidence which suggests that the Soviet leadership was already moving ahead before 1962 was the formation of the Strategic Rocket Force under Chief Marshal of the Artillery, Nedelin. It was not then considered on a par with the rest of the army and the navy, but by the middle of 1960, two years before Cuba, Marshal Moskalenko had taken over and it was not only given equal status, it was very quickly recognised as the most important element in the Soviet armed forces. All rockets with a range of more than 1,000 kilometres, with the exception of the air defence missiles, were placed under Moskalenko's command.

The Soviet Union became a nuclear power in 1949, at the end of the summer. But she already had rockets. The first was developed shortly after the war and was little more than a revamped V-2, the weapon used by the Germans during the Second World War. For good measure, the Soviet Union had some of the scientists who had worked in rocketry and so they were put to work. The rockets were given the name Scunner by the West, and so began the long process of giving every Soviet major weapon system a recognisable English name. Scunner was followed by Sibling which had a longer range though nowhere near those developed by the late 1950s and 1960s. Next came Shyster and, in 1958, Sandal, which is still deployed, mainly in Central Asia. It is bigger than a Minuteman, probably about sixty-eight feet tall, has a range of approximately 1,100 miles and carries a single one-megaton warhead. The Sandal is remembered mainly because it was at the heart of the Cuban missile crisis. Sandal was classified as an MRBM, a Medium Range Ballistic Missile.

Today most attention is paid to perhaps five Soviet ICBMs, although one of them is banned under the SALT agreement. In the West, these ICBMs are known as SS-11 or Sego, SS-17, SS-18, SS-19 and SS-16. The Soviet Union does not have the same serial numbers for these weapons as the West, nor are they using the numbers that some Western experts say they are. In the Soviet Strategic Rocket Force, the SS-17 is known as the RS-16, the SS-18 is RS-20, the SS-19 is RS-18 and the SS-16 is the RS-14.

A correct equation with Western and Soviet serial numbers is necessary when trying to draw an accurate picture of the Strategic Rocket Force, especially as an appreciable amount of information about their deployment may be picked up by reading open source material, if the reader knows which missile is being written about.

The Sego, the SS-11, is ineresting because it is the most widely deployed of all the ICBMs in their various forms. Many of the earlier Sego ICBMs are being replaced by SS-17 (RS-16) and SS-19 (RS-18). These two rockets have been tested with four warheads on top and, for the RS-18, six warheads, or, to use the official jargon, four and six re-entry vehicles.

There is also evidence to suggest that some of the warheads in the Strategic Rocket Force are armed not with nuclear weapons, but with chemical payloads. This last point will be examined at a later stage.

The particular interest shown in the SS-16 (RS-14) is twofold. Firstly, the rocket is a three-stage missile, but in the two-stage form it is better known in the West as the SS-20, the mobile IRBM (Intermediate Range Ballistic Missile), cited by the United States in her reasoning for the deployment in Europe of Cruise and Pershing II missiles.

But perhaps the most important point of interest is whether or not the SS-16 is in service. According to the SALT II agreement, the

SS-16 was banned. Article IV, sub-section 8 of the Treaty is quite clear. It says that during the term of the Treaty the Soviet Union will not 'produce, test or deploy' the SS-16.

During private conversations, it has been suggested that the Soviet Union has deployed as many as thirty-five SS-16. It is further said that the White House was given evidence of this deployment before SALT II was signed in Vienna on 18 June 1979. There are three explanations for what is a serious allegation. To begin with, of course, it may not be correct although those who believe it is are well placed to discuss such matters at the highest levels of Intelligence gathering. Secondly, because of the difference in descriptions of Soviet missiles outlined above, the SS-16 may indeed be the RS-16 and therefore known in the West as the SS-17. In other words, they have got the wrong missiles. Or thirdly, the need to get an agreement on SALT II was so great, that Washington chose to ignore the information.

SALT II has not, of course, prevented research and development on new missile technology, especially in the areas of guidance systems for the warheads. Perhaps this is the future of missile development although it might be thought that more Soviet time is being spent on launch techniques, particularly for mobile launching systems. The present chief of the Soviet Strategic Rocket Force, General V. F. Toubko, has something like 378,000 men under his command, six major types of ICBMs (some are being phased out) and virtually the highest priority treatment from the Politburo and the resources of *Gosplan*, the State Planning Ministry. But what of other forces?

It is generally accepted that the Soviet Ground Forces are the next most important part of the armed services. However, based on information not only from Western sources, but also from Soviet, a case can be made out for believing that this Number Two spot may be occupied by the National Air Defence Command, known as *PVO Strany (Protivovozdushnoi oborony strany*, the abbreviation should be pronounced Pay Vay Oh Strarny).

PVO Strany is commanded by an air force marshal, A. I. Koldunov. He has 550,000 men, 7,000 warning radars, his own air force of more than 2,500 aircraft, more than 10,000 surface to air missiles (SAMs) and, furthermore, the only Anti-Ballistic Missile (ABM) system in the East-West military balance.

A protocol to the US-USSR Treaty limiting ABMs came into being in May 1976 and restricts either side to a hundred such missiles. The Soviet Union has sixty-four ABMs, called Galosh, deployed around Moscow. The United States has none. Galosh has a range of more than 200 miles and is probably armed with a nuclear warhead. There is no claim that Galosh effectively protects the Soviet capital or more importantly, the ICBM sites near Moscow. What is certain, though, is that an increased number of Western ICBMs would be needed merely to penetrate the Soviet ABM system, and therefore it follows that the chances of the West being able to keep a strategic nuclear attack to a minimum level is that less likely.

The eyes of PVO Strany are the thousands of radar systems. Backed up by early warning satellites, these radars with names such as Dog House, Hen House and Try Add have tasks which range from spotting an incoming attack thousands of miles before it reaches Soviet territory to transferring target data to the ABM units. But these units are put a part of the air defence system. Western names for the 10,000 or so SAMs include Guideline, Goa and Gammon. Gammon or SA-5 (surface to air – 5) is generally thought to be a high altitude missile. There have been claims that it may be used as an anti-missile missile. However, although not much is known about it, there would appear to be some doubt that it could be very effective against a super-fast missile. To look at, Gammon is about fifty-four feet long with four large fins at the tail, smaller ones in the middle and four medium-sized fins in the middle of the top section. Guideline is shorter, about thirty-five feet long, but looks very much the same, with tiny stabilising fins just behind the sharply pointed nose. It has been around since the late 1950s and was used against American bombers in North Vietnam. Goa or SA-3 may be found in all sorts of places other than the Soviet Union. The Egyptians had them, the Syrians, the Iraqis and the Libyans. It is also seen in Soviet ships, which immediately suggests that it is not very big. It is indeed only about twenty-two feet long and is designed to be used at close range, supposedly against low-flying aircraft.

Air Marshal Koldunov's air force consists of eight different types of interceptors including Foxbats, Floggers, Firebars, Fiddlers and 850 or so Flagons. Again, these names are all Western. The West tends to give interceptors or fighters names beginning with F for fighter, and bombers B-names. The Foxbat, one of which was flown to Japan by a defecting pilot, is also known as the MiG 25. In the PVO Strany it is used as an interceptor, but it also has a role as a reconnaissance jet. It will often be found in conjunction with an aircraft called Moss. Moss is the Soviet Union's version of the West's AWACS (Airborne Warning and Control System). It is a big, four-engined turbo-prop aircraft with a large circular dish mounted on top of the fuselage. Although it does not look unlike the Western version, the Boeing jet is considered far more sophisticated. Moss will, with its crew of twelve, cruise at about 400 m.p.h. for anything up to six hours before having to refuel. Its roles include spotting, enemy tactics, battlefield command and direction of other aircraft. Its biggest problem is that it is vulnerable to anti-aircraft fire and interceptor attack by enemy forces.

If the missile systems and the confusing aircraft types remain for the Westerner somewhat shadowy aspects of the Soviet war machine, then the ground forces, the army, have become the recognisable standard-bearers. During most people's life-times, Soviet soldiers with their tanks, armoured vehicles and rifles (can there be any better-known weapon than the infamous AK-47?) have been seen far further afield than the sharply-stepped May Day Parades through Moscow's Red Square. In post-war history, there have been the newsreel pictures from Budapest in 1956. In 1968, the world saw the uncertain faces of the tank crews as they moved into Czechoslovakia (Soviet sources say that the Soviet troops, at least many of them, really did believe they would be welcomed by the citizens of Prague). More recently there has been Afghanistan. While strategists argue about the intentions of Soviet military thinkers and planners, nothing has better demonstrated the Soviet ability to move and to move quickly than their ground forces.

They are, today, composed of 1,825,000 troops, not counting reserves. They are split into 173 divisions and not 168 as is sometimes thought. They have more than 50,000 tanks, 20,000 artillery pieces, more than 9,000 anti-aircraft guns, nearly 1,500 surface to surface missile launchers, 56,000 armoured fighting vehicles including armoured personnel carriers and scout cars; and they are, as they claim, getting stronger, faster and more sophisticated every year.

The ground forces are commanded by General of the Army I. G. Pavlovskii (although this could shortly change). As we have seen, the equivalent of 31 of the 173 divisions are permanently stationed outside the Soviet Union in Poland, Hungary, Czechoslovakia and East Germany. If one ignores for the moment those divisions in Afghanistan (partly because it remains unclear how many will remain there), the other 142 divisions are scattered throughout the sixteen Military Districts.

The bulk of the divisions, sixty-six of them, are in the seven districts which make up European USSR. About a third of them are tank divisions. Forty-six divisions are in the Far East, some right on the Sino-Soviet border. Three of them are in Mongolia. In the southern USSR, which includes the Turkestan Military District north of Afghanistan, there are twenty-four divisioons, and the final six are in the two southern Military Districts of Volga and the Urals.

Of the 173 divisions, 47 are tanks, 118 are motor rifle (mechanised infantry), and the other eight are airborne. As with most forces, the airborne are the élite of the army, or at least consider themselves to be so. Their bright blue berets and shoulder flashes distinguish them from other troops, they get the pick of the conscripts, and they incorporate the special diversionary groups – perhaps to be equated with the British Special Air Services (SAS).

The diversionary groups are sometimes called diversionary brigades (although brigade does not mean the same thing in Russia as it does in Britain where it might be a formation of 6,000 or so men). These groups are trained to operate as small units, from a handful to as many as fifty, although the latter would seem on the high side for the operations they are trained to carry out. French sources say there are about 800 groups stationed in Europe. They would be infiltrated into NATO countries before hostilities and be ready to attack strategic targets and so disrupt the enemy behind their lines.

In the United Kingdom where is a remarkable reluctance even to acknowledge the existence of these forces. True to form, the British Defence Ministry, which has a habit of classifying information about the Soviet Union except when it is such common knowledge that everybody else has forgotten about it, has said it is not willing to talk about the groups. It will not even admit the nomenclature. However, in a home defence exercise during 1980, mock attacks were made on so-called strategic installations, such as government buildings, ammunition dumps, underground command posts, power stations. These attacks against Key Posts (known as KPs – but of course they do not exist) were not apparently carried out by specially trained troops and it is not thought that any adequate defence system exists assuming any of the diversionary groups got through.

There have been suggestions that they would be parachuted into NATO countries such as the United Kingdom. However, according to many NATO sources, other means of entry are considered more likely. For example, given a good time span, there is little reason why such operators should not enter Britain with assumed passports. Closer to any conflict, they could come ashore from many of the Eastern-bloc fishing boats in the Channel, North Sea and Irish Sea. It is even said that the diversionary groups' technical branch has developed a coated canvas material, which is perhaps sealed in a polythene bag but, when opened out and dampened with sea water, hardens into a concrete texture and could be used for disguising a small boat or beached equipment. Perhaps this is going too deeply into the realms of gadgetry, but nobody doubts the efficiency of the groups.

However romantic, exciting and frightening the special forces of any army may be, it is the tank that best symbolises its strength. The newspaper graphic has done more in the West to perpetuate the almost invincible image of the Soviet tank than any rousing speech from the political platform. And perhaps the only disappointing thing about this tracked monster is that the Soviet word for tank is *tank*.

The Soviet tank division consists of about 10,500 men. (This may be in the process of revision. Certainly those forces in Poland,

Hungary, Czechoslovakia and East Germany may be increasing their divisional sizes by as many as 1,000 men.) In addition, it has 325 tanks and more than 300 armoured vehicles, though this last figure may sometimes be as high as 350. The organisation will be very simple, 3 + 1, in other words three tank regiments plus one motor rifle regiment. It will have its own artillery including surface to surface missiles, helicopters for reconnaissance, frogmen, chemical warfare troops with a series of decontamination vehicles and, a vital element usually overlooked in the West, bridge-laying equipment. The importance of this is usually lost on all but enthusiastic reservists. But, when looking at a map of Europe, especially the area between the Warsaw Pact lines and the Channel ports, it is easy to see the lacework of canals and rivers any advancing army would have to cross: hence the need for laying bridges and pontoons in rapid time.

The Soviet tank division is being modernised at a very impressive rate. At one time it was a fair guess that any tank seen was either a T-54 or a T-55. This 36-ton, 30-m.p.h. weapon went into service as the T-54 during the late 1940s and early 1950s. By 1961 the T-55 was rolling into the divisions and can now be found not only in the Soviet, but also in more than twenty other armies. The Soviets are gradually replacing them and although they have done remarkable service they have always had a few major faults. They tend to shed their 'shoes' or tracks, their fuel tanks are vulnerable, and by today's standards their armour is very thin. But they are still seen on the newsreels and it is possible to have a fair stab at differentiating a T-54 or T-55 from other Soviet tanks if it is remembered that it has a smooth gun with a 'sleeve' at the muzzle end. It also has five big wheels, the back three of which are closer together than the front two.

There may be some visual confusion with the more modern version of the T-55, the T-62. That too has five main wheels in the earlier models although this time the *front* three are closer together. Later models have six large road wheels. But the 'sleeve' of the T-62's gun appears to be a third of the way back from the muzzle. The T-62 is a larger tank, but hardly noticeably so to the casual observer, and it too has problems with keeping its tracks in particularly rough ground; and, since it came into service in 1965, it has not had the advantage of improved armour-plating.

Contrary to popular belief, the Soviet Union rarely produces what the Americans call a quantum jump in tank production. There is a tendency to modify existing equipment, as with the T-54, the T-55 and the T-62, although the last did have a new turret and gun unit. However, perhaps the biggest fighting problem of these three tanks is that they had to stop in order to fire at a number of targets, in spite of the T-62's stabilised gun.

But, when the T-64 appeared, the design changes were obvious to the untutored eye. The large wheels were smaller and there were six of them. Another identification feature is the definite slope to the hull top. It was the fighting quality that was the main difference for the soldier. A new gun system with an automatic loader meant that for the first time the Soviet army had a tank which could truly fight on the move. It also meant that, instead of a four-man crew, the T-64 would need only three. In theory at least, a division of T-64s and the later T-72s would then release 266 men for other duties. The other advantage of the T-64 is that it is better protected.

The T-72 has reverted to the large road wheels, six of them. (The T-62s are almost miniature compared with the T-72s.) It weighs thirty-nine tons, can travel at fifty m.p.h. and is said to have a special sandwich-type armour-plating not so unlike the Chobham armour developed in Britain, but only shortly to go into service with the Royal Tank Regiments.

It is not necessary to go into detail about the Soviet army's various tracked and wheeled vehicles such as self-propelled guns and personnel carriers, nor its extensive range of other infantry equipment. But it would be wrong to leave the army without mentioning the AK-47 rifle, the Kalashnikov.

Mikhail Kalashnikov was not an infantry soldier, he was a tank commander and a designer. Right at the beginning of the Second World War he was wounded fighting with Yeremenko's army to hold Bryansk and the well-trodden road to Moscow. He was evacuated and it was while he was recovering that he sketched and designed his first weapons. They were not successful. Then in 1947 he produced what was to be known as the AK-47, although it did not go into service until 1951. Eight years later he modified the weapon to produce the AKM, which to the casual eye looks very like its elder brother. It is the AKM with the easily recognisable Kalashnikov trade-marks, the pistol grip and above all the curved magazine just in front of the trigger, that is the personal weapon of most of the Warsaw Pact troops.

Kalashnikov's original design is sometimes called the most successful rifle the world has ever seen. Either it, or sometimes the Chinese version, is found with practically every self-respecting guerrilla group in the world. It has two great advantages over every other similar weapon. It is easy to get hold of and there is plenty of ammunition for it to be found anywhere in the world. Secondly, it is the simplest rifle to use and look after; in military terms the Kalashnikov weapons are 'soldier-proof'.

The sturdy design of most Soviet equipment has been commented on elsewhere. Much is made of the fact that the Soviets never seem to throw anything away. It is certainly true that a great deal of their equipment is modernised, re-modernised and improved upon rather than replaced with new designs. This pattern is less obvious in services known above all for their major equipment programmes. It would apply for instance to Admiral Gorshkov's navy. The Soviet navy is split into four main fleets, the Pacific Fleet with its headquarters at Vladivostok, the Black Sea Fleet at Sevastopol, the Baltic Fleet with its headquarters at Kaliningrad, and the biggest and most important of all, the Northern Fleet based at Murmansk.

Admiral Gorshkov has more than 430,000 men under his command, although 80,000 of these are in the naval air force, shore-based troops and the marines, the *morskaya pekhorta* – naval infantry. But it is the ship and the submarine that time and time again claim the front pages and headlines of Western journals and newspapers. In 1980, for example, the attention given to the passage of the Moskva-class helicopter carrier through the English Channel was out of all proportion to the strategic value of the ship. It was as if there had not been a Soviet ship in the area before. Today there cannot be an ocean or major sea in which Soviet warships and submarines do not sail. But, although the Soviet navy has a very impressive list of ships and submarines, once again the numbers are misleading. A typical figure often quoted is more than 1,500 surface ships and 450 submarines. What is not pointed out on these occasions is that of those 1,950 vessels less than 300 could be classed as major surface ships; and, of the 450 or so submarines, something like twenty-five per cent are in reserve. Some authorities put the number of major fighting ships in active service at less than 200.

What is important is the way in which these ships are used, and their capabilities. Instead of bemoaning the West's reduced circumstances for matching what is normally referred to as the 'Soviet Naval Build-up', perhaps more time should have been spent on watching the form of that build-up. The advancement of the Gorshkov navy began under Nikita Khruschev. Again it has been said that Cuba was a turning point because Khruschev realised that his navy did not have the power to rival the US fleet. But, while Cuba did nothing to harm the argument for providing unusual financial and industrial resources for Admiral Gorshkov, it is more likely that the Kremlin's major rethink of its naval policy was based on something the Americans started before the events of 1962.

At that time the United States had set out her policy of sending part of her strategic missile force to sea. This was the era of the Polaris nuclear ballistic missile-firing submarine. The Soviet Union needed to match it and, equally important, needed to be able to stop it performing in wartime. This latter point is interesting in concept because it meant that the Soviet fleet would need to go further afield, or further to sea, if it were to shadow and, in the event of war, destroy the American and later the British systems before they could get into position to fire their weapons at the Soviet Union. It also meant the Soviet navy would have to spend more time developing anti-submarine systems. However American technology was developing at a speed which the Soviet Union could not hope to match. It must be remembered that the Soviets were relatively backward in much of their design and planning work. Some of it has certainly been innovative, but many of the systems have simply been catching up with the West rather than anticipating them in design technology. Furthermore, there were building projects, involving major expenditure, which simply did not work as planned.

There are those who would say that the folklore surrounding Gorshkov as the father of the modern Soviet navy is decidedly shallow. He and his naval think-tankers were on many occasions found wanting. Given the openness of Western, especially American, building programmes, it is difficult to see how he misread the military signs. The development in the late 1960s and early 1970s of a new pack of hunter killer submarines by the US navy appears to have caught the Kremlin by surprise. The much-vaunted Moskva-class of helicopter carrier, designed for anti-submarine warfare, does not seem to have been the success it promised to be. Indeed the *Moskva* and the *Leningrad* are the only two ships of their type, yet the original programme was for twelve vessels.

However, there now seems little doubt that the Soviet planners have sorted themselves out. Their naval research teams have done remarkably well and the products now at sea are just the beginning of what must, by the middle of this decade, be a navy far removed from the type and role even envisaged at the beginning of the 1960s.

In the not too distant future, the Soviet navy will have four 40,000-ton aircraft carriers of the Kiev class with their jump jets and helicopters, They will be on the verge of introducing bigger carriers, more of the size of the American classes. Around these carriers will be built the modern Soviet surface fleets, probably consisting of a number, five maybe six, of independent battle groups. The *Kirov*, a nuclear-powered command ship, is already at sea on its trials. A former Royal Navy officer, Michael MccGwire, now a Senior Fellow at the Brookings Institution in Washington DC, believes such vessels could become the flagships of a series of these battle groups.

One of the major problems facing the Soviet navy is similar to that suffered by the United States fleets outside the NATO areas. To keep a group of ships at sea needs a massive support system. During the early months of 1980 there was a great deal of comment on the size of the Soviet fleet then patrolling the Indian Ocean. Sometimes, it was said, there were twenty-five or twenty-six Soviet ships in the region on any one day. What was not highlighted was the fact that often as many as half those ships were supply vessels. In spite of its reported influence, the Soviet Union has limited facilities throughout the world. Even if she had more, warships are not doing their job if they are for ever sailing off to port for supplies of oil, spares and food. The supply ship can and does run these errands for them. It is interesting that it is only during the past decade that the Soviet Navy has perfected the art of transferring these supplies at sea. At one time, for example, most Soviet warships had to refuel 'line-astern' from their oilers. They soon learned from watching Western navies that the best technique was to replenish abreast, and further learned that, by doing so, it was possible for a supply vessel to replenish more than one ship at the same time.

If one looks at all the fine ships now in service, vessels such as the *Kara* and the *Krivak*, one question remains unanswered. Do they work? Some experts believe they have too much equipment on board, too many weapon systems. Others say the Soviet navy does not practise firing its weapons, although there is evidence that it goes through the motions at very regular intervals – but they do not actually fire their missiles. (This is a growing trend also within Western navies where it is considered too expensive to have no more than a handful of live firing exercises a year.)

While the introduction of new ships, especially aircraft carriers,[1] has attracted the West's attention, the main interest has centred on the vessels we rarely see – the submarines. The West has named Soviet submarines after the common communications alphabet (A = Alpha, B = Bravo, C = Charlie, D = Delta, etc.). They may be divided into three groups.

The first group of ninety or so carries the strategic ballistic nuclear missiles. These are Deltas, Yankees, Hotels and Golfs, and it is known that a new one is being built codenamed Typhoon.[2] At the

1. The term aircraft carrier may be misleading. The name implies something like the old *Ark Royal* with aircraft on board to be used in strikes against enemy territory. Today, there is a second style. The British Invincible-class is one, the Soviet Kiev-class is another. With the increase in anti-submarine warfare techniques, it was found necessary to have a platform for helicopters to search out submarines, using among other things a device called dunking sonar. In its simplest form, dunking sonar is a microphone on the end of a wire lowered from a helicopter into the sea. There, it listens for the sounds of a submarine. Many means of attacking shipping rely on reconnaissance aircraft telling the missile firer where the fleet is located. The jump jets of both the Royal Navy and the Soviet Navy would be used in war to knock out those recce aircraft.
2. Because there is already a Soviet submarine called Tango, the new class was christened Typhoon.

moment the most important of these is the Delta, because the latest versions are able to sit in the Barents Sea and fire their missiles at the United States. This is, at first glance, impressive if not frightening. Each Delta III carries sixteen missiles known in the West as SS-N-18s and in the Soviet Union as RSM-50s These submarines, generally called SSBNs (Submarines Ballistic Nuclear), have one role and that is to remain undetected until called upon to fire their missiles. This may, of course, be argued as the role of any submarine whether it is hunting another or tailing a surface ship. The main difference perhaps is that other types of submarines put themselves at risk by going after a target which may have the means of defending itself, whereas SSBNs will loiter until the word comes to launch their long-range rockets at a static target, say, a city. For years, there has been a Yankee-class SSBN loitering off the east coast of the United States. Some Intelligence analysts maintain that the Yankee is moving to different waters. It is possibly losing its missiles in order to become a so-called attack submarine.

But some remain. They are not as invincible as many people say they are. They have great problems in keeping in touch with the surface commanders. Their missiles have a limited range, therefore they stand more chance of being detected. When the Delta was introduced it overcame these problems to some extent, but like many Soviet submarines was very noisy and so again became vulnerable to enemy detection.

One step down from the SSBNs, the nuclear bombers of the Soviet navy, is a class of submarine fitted with cruise missiles. Apart from possible use for knocking out a naval base, their main potential has been seen as a weapon against the big American carriers. A new vessel, the Oscar-class is being introduced, but the main classes are the Charlie and the Echo II. But they too have their problems. The Charlie is not very accurate by itself and would probably have to rely on a surface ship to tell it what to do, to hit the target.

The Echo II's missiles have a longer range, perhaps 180 miles, but it too would have to rely on satellite communication, an aircraft or another ship for target data. Its biggest drawback may be that it cannot fire its missiles while it remains submerged. It has to sit on the surface for as long as twenty minutes in order to launch its weapon. Obviously while it does so it is vulnerable and presents a substantial headache for any submarine commander. Although it is not that easy to detect in, say, 20 minutes.

Seventy per cent perhaps of submarine crews are conscripted, but the officers are thought to be of a very high standard and many of them will have been to the only naval academy for submarine officers, the Leninskiy Komsomol Academy in Leningrad. From there they will go either to a training flotilla such as the one in the Caspian Sea or to one of the four fleets mentioned above.

Fifty per cent of the Soviet submarine force is in the Northern Fleet where there are ten important bases. For the map reader with a chart of the area around Murmansk and the Kola Inlet these bases are: Severodvinsk where they build nuclear submarines, and Rosta where they build conventional (diesel) boats (a submarine is a boat, not a ship). The other bases are at Litsa Bay, Olenya Bay and Saida Bay where there are warhead and missile stores, Ura Bay, Penchenga, Iokanga and Polyarniy.

The Baltic Fleet has mainly conventional boats. However at Leningrad there is a certain amount of important nuclear construction. The other bases are at Baltiysk, Riga, Leipaya, Tallin and Kronstadt.

The Black Sea Fleet is not an important submarine fleet, but the Pacific is growing in relevance every month. Half the submarines there – and there are more than a hundred of them – are nuclear-powered. The headquarters is at Vladivostok with bases at Petropav-lovsk, where there is a missile store, at a place called Sovetskaya Gavan (literally, Soviet Harbour), Magadan and Vladimir-Olga. This fleet, along with the Soviet surface ships in the region, is expanding, and is of particular concern to Japanese Intelligence. In any future war there is every likelihood that Japan would find itself under attack from this area.

Every submarine, whatever its fleet, is in potential control of the Naval Headquarters in Moscow. Obviously some submarines have more difficulties than others, but they all have Very Low Frequency (VLF) receivers. Most of the VLF traffic to submarines goes through the main transmitters at Minsk, Kudma, Arkangels on the White Sea and Khabarovosk. Although the majority of submarines come under the command of the different fleets, it is natural to believe that the strategic submarines are commanded by the Defence Ministry.

Each fleet will break down its submarines into four commands. The major command and control unit is an *ehskardra*. The sea-going command could well be exercised in a surface ship or a shore base. It is possible that the Soviet Union may be building a super-sub to do this job in the future. The *diviziya* consists of between twenty and twenty-four submarines, usually with a junior admiral in charge. A senior captain commands a group half that size called a *brigada* and a commander will have charge of an even smaller unit of about four or six submarines, a *divizion*.

In spite of good organisation, the Soviet submarine system has many weaknesses. It is, for example, thought by some Western Intelligence agencies that less than 15 per cent of the SSBNs, the big ballistic missile firing boats, are simultaneously at sea. This figure is improving with the introduction into regular service of the Delta III.

Others believe that only 12 per cent of the anti-shipping submarines are at sea on any one day. It is not clear whether this affects their performance, but it is known that, for some time, Soviet submariners were not good at keeping their depths.

The big SSBNs spend a deal of time using what is known as Bottom Contour Navigation systems. As a consequence they follow the shape of the sea-bed. It also means that they have to use very noisy echo-sounders for this purpose, and that means they can be detected much more easily. Generally, then, the Soviet submariner drives a sometimes noisy boat, that might spend more of its time in port than on patrol; he is getting new detection systems that will improve his ability to fight; the SSBNs can hit the United States without going out of their backyard, the Barents Sea; to some extent he suffers the same problem that many Western navies live with – too many of the boats in the fleets are getting old and in some cases dangerous. There have been cases reported of radiation sickness in the older nuclear boats such as the November class. But, as one Western Naval Intelligence officer has pointed out, most of the weaknesses are made up for in sheer numbers. However, it should be remembered that it can take at least thirty days to get a Soviet submarine ready for sea, depending upon its state alongside. Furthermore, as with many of the army's 173 divisions, not all submarine squadrons are up to full strength with equipment and men.

If the submarine is fairly simple to hide from the public, then the aircraft is not. Regular sightings of most if not all Soviet aircraft have led to a steady flow of pictures and information in the Western press. For that reason alone, it is not perhaps worth considering in great detail this part of the Soviet military machine.

Two points, though, are worth considering. The Backfire bomber was excluded from SALT II because the Soviet Union said that it could not reach the United States without refuelling. The Soviet Union said she would not fit the Backfire with a refuelling probe. Two days before SALT II was signed President Carter received from President Brezhnev written assurance that a refuelling capability that would allow Backfire (the Russians call it Tu-22M) to reach the United States and return simply did not exist. Many believe that President Carter was wrong to accept this assurance. During 1980, the Soviet Union started to fit Backfires with air to air refuelling probes. There does not appear to have been any official reaction to this, although Washington Intelligence sources, and some on President Reagan's staff have known about it since May 1980.

The second point to bring out concerns an aircraft called the Fencer. While the Backfire has claimed the stage, the Fencer (named the Su-24 in honour of the design bureau of Pavel Sukhoi) made a brief appearance in the 1970s. It has been in service since the mid-1970s and there are now 250 or so Fencers in Air Chief Marshal Kutakhov's air force. Armed with nuclear warheads, they would be a formidable foe for Western European air defences.

Many more details of all three Soviet services could be given: their improved use of helicopters; the development of a marine landing ship, the *Ivan Rogov*, which would allow the naval infantry to go further with more equipment; the increase in support vessels to allow the navy to operate further afield; the development of new radar systems. But this book is not for the analyst; and this chapter is designed to give the reader a feel for the size, the organisation and the people who one day may have to manipulate this military machine. And, when thinking about the Western equivalent, it should be remembered that the Soviet military organisation also includes the other members of the Warsaw Pact, Hungary, Poland, Romania, Czechoslovakia, Bulgaria and East Germany.

Footnote: At the time of the Western concern for the events in Poland during 1980, Western governments briefed their media on the '30 or so' Soviet divisions 'surrounding' Poland. The impression was given that Soviet forces had gathered about the recalcitrant ally. As may be seen on page 39, these troop formations have been there for years. What did happen, was that many of them had been brought to a higher state of readiness. Nevertheless, the presentation of the 30 or so divisions, served its purpose as far as some Western administrations are concerned.

FOUR

The Warsaw Pact and Nato

There are seven nations in the Warsaw Pact. There used to be eight. The Pact was formed as a counter-force to the Western Alliance which already existed and as a sure way of consolidating the not inconsiderable territorial gains made by the Soviet Union by the end of the Second World War. (It was the Belgian Prime Minister, Paul-Henri Spaak, who in 1948 observed that the USSR was the one Great Power that emerged from that bloody conflict having conquered other territories.) One of the problems facing the Western nations during those post-war years was what to do about the new Federal Republic of Germany, West Germany. After much discussion and planning, West Germany became a member of the North Atlantic Treaty Organisation, on 5 May 1955. Nine days later, in Warsaw, eight socialist European countries signed an 'Agreement on Friendship, Co-ordination and Mutual Assistance'. The signatories were the Soviet Union, Albania, Bulgaria, Czechoslovakia, East Germany, Hungary, Poland and Romania. At a later meeting of the heads of state of those eight countries, the term Warsaw Pact was adopted.

But that was only the first stage. Two months after the events in Hungary during October 1956, a series of bilateral agreements were initiated. Among other things, these mutual declarations allowed for the basing of Soviet troops in Poland, Hungary, East Germany and Romania. By the middle of the following year, these countries had signed separate treaties with the Soviet Union. Yet the Pact was already a troubled alliance. Romania was showing signs of being reluctant to allow herself to be dominated by the Soviet Union, and, during 1958, just twelve months after the bilateral treaties had been concluded, allowed her agreement to lapse. Soviet forces were withdrawn in June of that year, though Romania did not leave the Pact.

Czechoslovakia had not agreed a bilateral arrangement with Moscow. It was not until two months after Soviet troops intervened in Czechoslovakia during August 1968, that such an agreement was drawn up and signed. Soviet formations remained in the country and the Central Group of Forces was established. Another of the original signatories to the 1955 Treaty, Albania, used the intervention in Czechoslovakia as an excuse to leave the Pact. The Albanians quit in September 1968 although they had been nothing more than sleeping partners for the previous six years or so.

In theory, it is now difficult for any member state to do what Albania did. The first agreement lasted until 1977 and today it is supposed to be renewed every ten years. There remains a clause in the contract which says that no member may leave without making a declaration to do so during the final year of the Treaty's life.

That means that if anybody does wish to leave, 1985 would be the next official opportunity. Very few people believe this could happen, however independent some nations might be, although Western diplomats have for some time been interested in the way ahead for Romania. Apart from letting lapse the agreement for stationing Soviet troops on her territory, Romania has also refused to bow to Soviet demands that all Pact nations increase defence spending by considerable amounts.

There is also a marked nervousness in the West, that any one of the Pact states should wish to withdraw because very few believe this could ever happen without a violent reaction by the Soviet Union. Any attempt by one state to achieve political and military independence would be considered dangerous for the West. As was seen during 1980, Western countries were very slow to react when Polish workers went on strike. Ever since 1968, there have been speculations that another 'Czechoslovakia' would demand a response. Poland was not another Czechoslovakia and, while it was clear countries such as the United Kingdom, West Germany and the United States were sympathetic to the demands of the Polish strikers, it was equally clear that those same countries did not wish to show more than polite interest. As Britain's Foreign Secretary declared at the time, during a visit to Finland, the events in Poland were an internal affair and should remain so. Perhaps this was also a warning to the Soviet Union that Moscow too should treat the strikes and political unrest in the same way. But, no doubt, there were sufficient advisers in London, Washington and Bonn, who were saying that any overt reaction could be used as an excuse for the Soviet Union to use force to 'settle' the matter.

It remains clear that the West does not wish to see any Warsaw Pact state withdraw from the Eastern bloc alliance. However, an undercurrent of opposition and disenchantment with the Moscow line has always been the ambition of the West. In time of war, if there ever should be one, this disenchantment would be invaluable to the NATO states. The Soviet Union recognises this and, in its War Plan, there exists a contingency operation for 'looking after' any unrest that should show itself as a disruptive element.

Apart from any political cohesion within the pact, of vital interest to the Soviet Union is the physical muscle of the other members of the 1955 treaty. This interest also applies to the territorial integrity of its members. The Soviet Union does not have a border with NATO except in the very north with Norway and in the south with Turkey. The vital East–West European border is braced by the other six members of the Warsaw Pact. Poland, East Germany and Czechoslovakia lie between the Soviet Union and the West. Soviet troops would have to cross through Rumania and Bulgaria to reach Greece. From this it can be seen that the Groups of Soviet Forces described in Chapter Three are of vital military significance. Many in NATO believe these Soviet forces, especially those divisions in East Germany, could be on the move within forty-eight hours of being given the green light.

And the troop sizes of the Warsaw Pact members, other than the Soviet Union, are by no means insignificant. Taken in alphabetical order and not in military importance, the non-Soviet Warsaw Pact is approximately as follows:

Bulgaria: Three Military Districts of Pleven, Plovdiv and Sofia are occupied by more than 150,000 forces. About 95,000 of these soldiers, sailors and airmen are conscripts. (Two years except for the navy when it is three.) Most of these conscripts are in the 115,000-man army which has between 1,700 and 1,800 tanks, the vast majority of which are old or very old. The navy has 10,000 men to run an assortment of Soviet hand-outs which include a couple of submarines and two frigates. The air force has 24,000 men, 170 aircraft, and includes a parachute regiment.

Czechoslovakia: Two Military Districts of Slovakia and Bohemia-Moravia are covered by the army (140,000 men and the air force of more than 50,000 men). There is a small river unit which is more of a para-military force than a navy. The army has nearly 3,500 tanks and the state has its own tank production lines building Soviet machines. The air force has more than 450 aircraft, the majority of which are not front-line jets, as is the case in most air forces. But they are being equipped with later versions of the Soviet MiG 23 and a large proportion of their aircraft are modern.

East Germany: There are five Military Districts, nearly 160,000 regular forces including more than 90,000 conscripts. The army (about 100,000 plus) have more than 2,500 tanks and production appears to have begun of the modern Soviet T-72. The navy is quite big (something like 16,000 men) with mainly patrol and fast missile boats. The air force is well equipped with some 330 combat planes, and the fairly recent build-up of its assault helicopter capability should not be ignored considering its closeness to the NATO front lines.

Hungary: There are two Military Districts covered by an army of 85,000 or so men and a 150 combat plane air force. The Hungarian forces are not in very good shape and they look better on paper with their 1,200 tanks and surface to surface missiles than they are in reality. It is doubtful whether many of their forces measure up to full strength.

Poland: Here there are three Military Districts with perhaps more than 300,000 troops. Poland is not only politically in the red, she is financially crippled. However, she has shown willing to go along with Soviet calls to step up military spending, though for how long is uncertain. Poland's 210,000-strong army is the biggest in the non-Soviet Warsaw Pact, it has a small but respectable navy and a large (about 700 aircraft) air force. It also has a para-military organisation of about 100,000 troops.

Romania: The two Military Districts are lightly organised with 140,000 troops, a 30,000-man air force and a 10,500-man coastal navy. Her determination to resist the idea of spending on defence until the domestic economy can afford it is reflected in the obsolescent military structure and equipment (some of which is ex-Chinese).

It can be seen from this extremely brief look that once again there is far more to totting up the East–West balance than drawing up a list of who-has-what. Furthermore, just because the overall picture of one particular country does not look so powerful, it should not be forgotten that the contribution of one particular unit to the total Warsaw Pact force may be of vital importance. It could well be that Moscow is reasonably happy with one of the member states having only one up-to-speed element in its armed forces. That unit, whether it be an air squadron or a specialist armour unit, may be earmarked in the future as an essential part of a joint battle formation.

Two further points are worth consideration. The Warsaw Pact armies, navies and air forces would come together as one fighting unit in wartime. The peacetime commander and the chief of staff is always a Soviet officer. However, it must be remembered that there is no peacetime Warsaw Pact Army. Moscow could not, for example, order a Czech unit to Afghanistan or to the Chinese border. Only the East Germans are directly controlled by the Soviet Union, through the commander of the Soviet Group of Forces Germany.

Secondly, in time of war, it is unlikely that a non-Soviet general or marshal would be allowed to command his own country's armies. In the Soviet scheme of things, nothing must be left to chance. There must be no possibility of rebellion. Nobody, and no country, should be in a position to opt out. What is not known is whether this uncertainty in the Moscow mind is similar to the one which exists in NATO towards some of its members.

In considering the other side of the Military Balance, the West, it is just as easy to draw the wrong conclusions from the numbers in the

Western armies, navies and air forces as it is when assessing the true strengths of Warsaw Pact forces. In the West it is perhaps a greater intellectual crime to make such mistakes; there is far more information readily available, especially in the United States where the job of presenting the public with details of defence policy and equipment is considered an important aspect of political and commercial operations. The same might be said of a number of NATO government organisations, although it is equally true that the French and British still have a great deal to learn in this area. An American researcher's descriptions of the French official information system as 'disdainful', and of the British as 'a whole bunch of deadbeats', are considered by many to be approximately correct. However, it should be pointed out that, at the higher levels in Whitehall, there have been efforts during the past few years to change this condition, and some of those efforts have been successful. It is often argued in the United Kingdom that, as long as there is little interest in defence among the general public, little information will be forthcoming. Considering the highly technical aspect of defence and the complicated machinery of NATO and the different governments within the Alliance, it is understandable that defence is something that is generally left to government to get on with. That has more or less been the case since 1949.

It was in that year that the North Atlantic Treaty was signed, on 4 April. In many respects it was an acceptance on both sides of the Atlantic that, in any future conflict, it would be unthinkable for Europe, Western Europe that is, to go to war without Canadian and American allies from the very outset. During the years between the end of the Second World War and the 1949 signing, the military and political structure of the West had changed dramatically. The allied armies, for example, had not only returned to barracks, but they were less than 20 per cent of their wartime strengths. Allied forces in Europe numbered some 880,000 men whereas, at the end of the European war, they had stood at something like five million.

Furthermore, the Soviet Union and the Western Allies were no longer facing a common enemy – Hitler's Germany was defeated and the somewhat tenuous unity with Moscow was lost. The Soviet Union had fought Nazism because it threatened not just the Homeland, but also the still toddling socialist system. If anybody in the West believed the Second World War would open the barriers between East and West, he was sorely mistaken. There were many Western generals who would have dearly loved to continue the war and take it into the Soviet Union. Meanwhile, the apparent victors of the war saw a way to carving up their territorial spoils and, after great difficulties, putting their pens to a series of peace treaties. It was also clear that the 1945 signing of the United Nations Charter was not going to help resolve any of the problems to be faced during those post-war years. The great difficulty was to get a peace treaty which would cover the old enemy, Germany. As early as 1945 a framework agreement was reached, but it did not come to anything. All through 1947, telegrams were sent back and forth, ministerial meetings were held and then abandoned.

But it was quite apparent that no agreement was going to be reached that year, the next, or in the then foreseeable future. From the West's point of view, all this was going on against a background of disturbing land and government grabbing by the Soviet Union. By the end of the war, the Soviet Union had control of parts of Romania, Czechoslovakia, Poland, East Prussia along the Baltic, Latvia, Lithuania and Estonia. By 1948 Moscow controlled the complete territories that now make up the Warsaw Pact and Albania. It was during that year that Europe, without the United States and Canada, established its own defence union of sorts. On 17 March 1948, Belgium, Britain, France, Luxembourg and the Netherlands signed the Brussels Treaty, pledging mutual defences and economic ties. (Seven days before the Brussels Treaty was signed, the body of the Czech Jan Masaryk was found on the path beneath his window. He had favoured Czechoslovakia's acceptance of aid under the American Marshall Plan. He was earnestly a nationalist and never wanted to see his country run by anybody but his own people. There are many who believe Masaryk was murdered and it was against this sombre background, a background of assassinations, political pressures, brutishness and unsmiling demands from both sides of what Churchill had by then called the Iron Curtain,[1] that the Treaty was signed.)

The Brussels Treaty was the forerunner to the setting up of NATO. It did not have the determination nor the vigour of the later agreement. It could not go as far as saying that an attack on one signatory was an attack on all. But it was an essential start and it attracted the observations of the United States and Canada. From the Treaty came the Western Union Defence Organisation. But that was not until September 1948. In June of that year, the Berlin blockade began. It was becoming more obvious that Brussels could be nothing but the embryo for a much larger alliance. A glance at the European map clearly marked East from West. The different camps were staked out and it was now the moment to see who would join. The United States and Canada recognised that it was only a matter of time before their flags would be flying along with the original members of the Brussels Treaty, but for them it was a major constitutional effort. The

1. See Churchill's telegram to President Truman, May 1945.

European countries had taken the lead. Yet the side of that lead crossing the Atlantic came not from Europe, but from Britain's Commonwealth partner, Canada – officially at least. Five weeks after the Treaty was signed, an all-embracing defence pact was proposed in the Canadian House of Commons.

Meanwhile with the help of Tom Connally and Arthur Vandenberg, two American Senators, the United States administration was paving the way for a truly trans-Atlantic bloc. On 11 June 1948 what became known as the Vandenberg Resolution was adopted by the Senate and the way was clear for the Americans to join in. If there had ever been any doubts about the Soviet attitude they were dispelled when, in an attempt to stop the Treaty going ahead, Moscow warned the intending signatories that the formation of such an Alliance could only be seen as an aggressive act. The North Atlantic Treaty was signed in Washington the following year on 4 April by Britain, Belgium, Canada, Denmark, France, Iceland, Italy, Luxembourg, the Netherlands, Norway, Portugal and the United States. One year later, on 19 December, General Dwight D. Eisenhower became the first Supreme Allied Commander Europe (SACEUR) within NATO and four months later the headquarters of the command was established just outside Paris at Rocquencourt. Eisenhower meanwhile had decided to run for President and it was the American General, Matthew Ridgway, who was appointed to succeed him in May 1952. Also in 1952, Admiral Lynde D. McCormick of the US Navy became the first Supreme Allied Commander Atlantic (SACLANT), Lord Ismay became NATO's first Secretary General, and the Alliance's provisional headquarters opened at the Palais de Chaillot in Paris.

During the first few years, there was constant friction in the Alliance, especially over West Germany. The role of West Germany was a sore point for many nations, especially the French. There had been an idea, agreed in Lisbon, for the establishment of a European Defence Community – a sort of military Common Market or EEC. But, in August 1954, the French National Assembly refused to ratify the Lisbon Treaty. Twelve years later, relations with France were coming to a head. President de Gaulle, suspicious of the way NATO was heading and even more critical of the so-called reliance on the United States, announced in March 1966 that he was going to pull France out from the military side of NATO. That meant that the NATO bureaucracy had to move. Accordingly, the following year, the Supreme Headquarters Allied Powers Europe (SHAPE) moved from Rocquencourt to their new home at Casteau Mons in Belgium. The Secretary General and his staff, the diplomatic representatives and the Secretariat moved to the Brussels headquarters.

It is often said that France left NATO in 1966. She did not. NATO is basically a two-fold Alliance – military and political. France opted out of the military side, but is still an active and equal member of the political Alliance. In spite of some impressions, France is still closely involved in military operations. There are few, if any, military NATO staffs without a French liaison team. France still takes part in many NATO exercises and deploys three divisions of a total of about 34,000 men in West Germany. Whether or not they could be counted upon in time of war remains another matter.

The whole of NATO is run by the North Atlantic Council which lives in Brussels. Its chairman, at the time of writing, is a Dutchman, Dr Joseph Luns. Luns will be seventy this year and for some time there has been a great deal of pressure for him to go. He is a tall, witty man with a voice which gives the impression that he is always gargling. It is said round the NATO bazaars that, among others, the Americans would like to see the back of the Secretary General partly because of what they believe is a 'seen it all before' attitude adopted by Dr Luns. Anyway, it is up to the Secretary General to announce his own retirement and nobody else. During the past couple of years there has been much speculation on a successor; but there are not many men with the demanding qualifications for the job.

NATO's Secretary General has to be at least bi-lingual. He should have English and French, but this is a minimum requirement and both languages should be *truly* bi-lingual. With fifteen nations having fifteen different attitudes on occasions of major importance, there should be no possibility of anybody getting the wrong interpretation of what is being said. He should also have some military background, although it is not necessary for this to be a service career. A distinguished defence minister might fill the job or, indeed, a former NATO ambassador. Ideally he must not be an American. The United States tends for obvious reasons to dominate the Alliance; they hold two of the three major NATO military commands on a permanent basis. As with the United Nations there is a tendency to edge towards a representative of one of the more non-aligned states in the organisation, especially as he may be called upon to act as a conciliator. The Secretary General chairs the two most influential bodies in the Alliance. The most important, the North Atlantic Council, meets twice a year under his chairmanship in ministerial session with foreign ministers of all fifteen nations get together in late spring and early winter. But, at least once a week, the fifteen NATO ambassadors, known as Permanent Representatives (the local jargon is 'PERM REPS'), will meet in Brussels where they have their offices at NATO headquarters not far from the airport. There is also an annual presidency of the Council. This is held by a foreign minister and he is chosen according to the alphabetical order of the member states.

The Secretary General will also chair the Defence Planning Committee (DPC). Instead of foreign ministers, defence ministers meet, and again the Permanent Representatives have their own sessions. It is the Defence Planning Committee that discusses military policy. As might be expected the DPC works to its individual political briefs.

Both the council and the DPC have committees to prepare the background for policy decisions, most of which have to be ratified by individual governments. Some of these committees and study groups are becoming more important. For example, the Nuclear Planning Group will meet at ministerial level, and it was such a group that started the ball rolling on the deployment of Cruise missiles in Europe. Not everybody has been happy with the way in which NATO affairs are run, especially on some of the working groups. Inevitably there is a feeling among some member states that too many major decisions are forced through by a small clique which includes the United States, the United Kingdom and West Germany. An illustration of this frustration is the new composition of the Nuclear Planning Group. The nuclear planning of NATO has been greatly influenced by the United States and Britain since the early 1960s and, when it is considered that these two countries are the only two nuclear powers within the military side of the Alliance, this is perhaps understandable – from their points of view. (Following their meeting in Nassau towards the end of 1962, President Kennedy and Prime Minister Macmillan put forward the idea of a NATO multilateral nuclear force as well as assigning part of their combined nuclear forces to the Alliance.)

However, there is far more to nuclear planning than simply owning nuclear weapons. Medium-range missiles and aircraft armed with nuclear weapons have to be based in non-nuclear countries. So, it was argued that the host nations should have more of a say in the way in which NATO planned its nuclear policy. All members were invited to join a new body called the Nuclear Defence Affairs Committee. But of more interest was a spin-off from this committee – the Nuclear Planning Group. Originally it was a seven-nation group, controlled by an inner cabinet of ministers who would invite other NATO members to its meetings on a rotating basis. Clearly this was an unsatisfactory system and it needed a major issue to bring matters to a head. This issue arose in the spring of 1979 at the meeting of the NPG in Florida, where an agreement in principle was taken to go ahead with what was then called Theatre Nuclear Force Modernisation, or TNF Modernisation. Some of the countries, notably the Netherlands, rebelled, and made it clear that in future the rotating invitation system should be scrapped and that all interested parties should be allowed to attend all meetings. The Big Three – the UK, the USA and West Germany – along with Italy, agreed.

In 1968 another group was formed which is promising to become increasingly more important. Called the Eurogroup, it is open to all the

European members of the Alliance. Handled correctly, it should during the coming years be in a position to present the European case for the running of NATO. It is not meant to be a separate power bloc against the United States, yet there is a very good case for the European members of the Alliance clearly defining their very considerable contribution to NATO. Many are more than concerned that in the United States there is a belief that only the Americans make any major contribution to the defence of the Western world. Perhaps it is not necessary to explain the very real value of the European contribution to the Department of Defense in Washington nor to the White House. But there is a clear, and so far unresolved, need for the European countries to convince the American people and their representatives in the Senate and House, of the part played by those countries much closer to the East–West border. In doing so, it may be that many of the American deficiencies will be highlighted, but that will not be a bad thing. The defence of the Alliance is not going to get any cheaper, and so it will be even more important for Congress and the American people to realise that in many, although by no means all, cases the Europeans are pulling their weight.

Unfortunately, the Dutch and Belgian decisions not to support fully the Cruise decision of 12 December 1979 does not help the cause. But it does go to show that the Eurogroup needs to be the driving force in explaining the political, economic and, in some cases, the diplomatic realities, which are rarely appreciated outside Washington.

It is perhaps natural that the political element of the Alliance is full of frustrations, and on occasion these frustrations are reflected in the workings of the highest Service body within NATO, the Military Committee. The Committee is the North Atlantic Council's and the Defence Planning Committee's advisory body. NATO Chiefs of Staff meet never less than twice a year, but the real strength is the permanent representatives and their Chairmen of the Military Committee. It is said that this chairmanship can make or break the military case inside the Alliance which is dependent upon the political climate and the inability of many member Chiefs of Staff to get through their defence recommendations at national level. There is no standard requirement for the type of officer in this vital job. For example, the 1970s saw two totally different men. The British Admiral of the Fleet, Sir Peter Hill-Norton (now Lord Hill-Norton), was considered to be flamboyant, aggressive almost to the point of bullying. Later, the recently retired Norwegian general, H. F. Zeiner Gundersen, was quiet and, according to some, a more cautious politican.

But NATO's biggest problem will always be the fact that it remains a multi-national rather than a truly international force. For this reason, political disharmony is rarely far below the surface although the so-called NATO splits that show up in headlines every couple of years or so are usually blown up out of all proportion. But a look at the composition of its membership explains a great many of the problems faced by the Secretariat, the diplomatic element and the military.

NATO is fifteen nations, but very different ones. They all have differing loyalties to the Alliance, differing political systems, differing economies, differing values. Put the lot together and it is some wonder that the organisation has held together for so long.

Belgium, the 'capital' of NATO, has so many political problems that they go almost unreported elsewhere in the Alliance. The Belgians can go without a government for months on end, as they have done in recent years, without anybody taking much notice.

The Canadians have well-publicised leadership problems, confusing standards on unity within the Provinces that have in the past overshadowed the desperate economic difficulties, and armed forces which have never quite recovered from the questionable decision to merge all three into one all-in-green group.

Denmark at one time looked 'safe' with its modest but stable long-term defence plan, but this stability has also crumbled.

France continues to go the way of France and in spite of her liaison with all major bodies shows only occasional signs of rejoining the military end of the Alliance. However, France's willingness to operate further afield than the NATO boundaries could in some circumstances be welcome to other members of the Alliance, particularly the United States. Relations with the United States continue to be on the very low side. During the 1980 Venice Summit, a French observer was moved to remark that President Valéry Giscard d'Estaing had nothing but contempt for the then President Carter.

West Germany has gone through her election drama and little has happened that will make her position in NATO any different from that of previous years. The West Germans, perhaps more than any other NATO nation other than Norway, have good cause to believe that the United States simply does not understand the European end of the Alliance. President Carter did little in 1980 to make things better. The West German economy has not been able to avoid the overall world recession, yet it still fares better than most. It is clear that Germany is fed up with being taken for the rich uncle of Europe.

Greece through its economic and political depressions is in a worse state than most in the Alliance. The Athens government withdrew from the military side of NATO in 1974 following the Turkish invasion of Cyprus, and has rejoined, but as a cautious ally.

Iceland has no armed forces in NATO and her position as the home of the largely American base at Keflavik is a source of some political discontent. Iceland's position is crucial to the West for the monitoring of Soviet ships, submarines and aircraft. Consequently, the Icelanders realise they are on the number-one target list held in the Kremlin. There have been occasions when Icelandic feelings have tended towards opting out of NATO.

Italy has a ruptured economy, one of the most unstable political systems in Europe, enormous social problems, a high crime rate, seemingly constant and uncontrolled terrorism and a burning desire to be at every important conference as an equal party. Nobody doubts Italy's loyalty to the Alliance although there have been doubts about discussing sensitive issues with the Rome government partly because of the Italian Communist element. In spite of all this, Italy continues to provide vital Mediterranean facilities for, among others, the US 6th Fleet, and reliable support during the most sensitive Alliance discussions. Italy is one of the four permanent members of the NPG.

Luxembourg spends about one per cent of its GNP on defence and, with a population of 360,000 and an army of less than 700 men, it cannot be expected to do more than that.

In the Netherlands, there is a growing movement among some of the 14 million population against the idea of nuclear weapons. This feeling was illustrated during 1979 when the Dutch government wanted to go ahead with the Cruise missile programme but could not get the political opposition's support. There is also a trend towards further economic problems and these will be even more pronounced when some of the Dutch natural resources begin to dwindle. Natural gas for example will be no longer a major asset before the end of this decade.

The Norwegians have an official understanding with the Soviet Union that any stationing of nuclear weapons or other NATO forces on her territory would be seen by Moscow as an aggressive act. Forces such as the British Royal Marines get round this by carrying out regular long training exercises. Portugal is still an uncertain political factor in NATO. Top secrets have in the past been withheld from the Portuguese. The country's financial position is far from stable.

Turkey is to be loosely described as broke. When U.S. Secretary Alexander Haig was the Supreme Allied Commander Europe he said that NATO should not think of solving Turkey's problems in military terms, but in economic ones. Along with Greece, Turkey makes up what is sometimes called the soft underbelly of Europe. It is an overplayed phrase, but between them they do constitute an enormous area of political, financial and military uncertainty which, in its present state, NATO cannot afford.

The United Kingdom is on a military high under the government of Mrs Thatcher. But it should not be supposed that only a Conservative government is good for Britain's and NATO's defences. In spite of the memorable occasion when the Labour Defence Minister, Fred Mulley, fell asleep during an RAF fly-past in the presence of the Queen, Mr Mulley was very well thought of by many defence chiefs. It was he who represented Britain at the Florida meeting of the NPG and agreed to go along with Cruise missiles. It was a Labour government (under pressure) that instituted big pay rises for the armed forces and it was a Labour government that kept going Britain's Polaris nuclear missile modernisation programme. Whatever government is in power during the next three or four years, it is going to be difficult to justify the continued priorities given to defence spending, unless of course the nation's economy takes a decidedly better turn.

The United States has been through one of the more traumatic decades in her history. She has, during the past ten years or so, suffered defeat in South-East Asia, the ignominy of Watergate, the consequent rejection of political leadership, the vulnerability of her economy, humiliation in Teheran, wretched disappointment in the Iranian desert and, perhaps above all, a general loss of confidence in her leadership, both at home and abroad. Her relations with other NATO members have been less than inspiring and on occasions it has been left to the British Prime Minister to give the only public support to a White House which too often has displayed little professionalism, little diplomatic skill and even less understanding of the realities of being a European member of a sometimes shaken Alliance. The ultimate humiliation must have been in 1980 when many in Europe, normally loyal to the American system, came to believe that the saddest comment on the United States was that the country could not come up with a higher calibre of Presidential candidate.

The frustrations the United States inspires are reflected in similar frustrations felt by Washington towards her NATO allies, and the whole state of affairs is in some part an indication of the complexities within the Alliance. There is perhaps a further gap in trans-Atlantic relationships. The Europeans are more used to dealing with one another on a number of different levels and matters. One obvious example is the fact that only the Irish Republic, of all the members of the European Communities, is not a member of NATO. Yet the fact that the Alliance is often under remarkable stress should be no surprise.

Put fifteen nations together and there are fifteen different economies, fifteen histories, eleven different languages, as many cultures and different political procedures. Stretch those cultures, economies and political systems from Asia, through central Europe, along the Mediterranean to conservative New England, to the near edges of the

Far East, add to them bilateral obligations in the Middle East, the Pacific, Africa, South-East Asia and even Central America, and it is little wonder that on occasion such an organisation as the Western Alliance begins to bend at the knees.

In spite of the various problems, the West's military legs are, however, remarkably muscular: close on five million men under arms, more than 24,000 battle tanks, more than 34,000 combat aircraft and close to 700 major warships of which 270 are submarines – many of them nuclear-powered and some of them ballistic missile-firing.

During 1980, it is very likely that NATO countries including France and Greece, will have spent around 240 billion dollars on defence.

How much actually is being spent is remarkably difficult to estimate, and to some extent it is just as valueless a statistic as are tank, jet and missile numbers. It needs a great deal of qualification. However as a bald figure it is an indication of the political will of any country. Britain, for example, has about 900 main battle tanks. She has had 900 for many years and so, when it is recorded that in real terms the British army has maintained its tank strength from one year to the next, all that is being said is that Britain is still running her tanks and has not thrown them away. But, when it is announced that Britain is increasing her defence expenditure over the previous year by as much as 20 per cent allowing for inflation, then the political inference is that Britain is committed to defence and honouring NATO pledges. And, when it is being done in Britain and other countries during the tightest of economic circumstances, this is further indication of a country's commitment to the Alliance.

The general way of looking at how much of its overall budget a country is willing to devote to defence is by taking defence spending as a percentage of that country's Gross National Product. Even then, it may be a misleading figure, because an accurate picture of GNP may not be painted for some time after any given year. By the time outstanding receipts are gathered and matched to the national currency for the year in question, as many as five or six years may have elapsed. During the second half of the 1970s, the average spending on defence by NATO countries was more than 3.5 per cent. (During the same period the Warsaw Pact countries appeared to spend an average of 4.5 per cent of their combined GNPs on defence. Lack of accurate information makes this figure nothing more than a guide.)

There are some interesting figures in both Western and Eastern bloc sets. In the Warsaw Pact, the bulk of the percentage is made up from Soviet spending. She is variously estimated as spending between 12 and perhaps 15 per cent of her GNP on defence. In the West, the major partner, the United States, spends about 5.5 per cent which compares favourably with a number of other NATO states, although some of them, perhaps Turkey and Portugal, have shown a rapid decline during the past five or six years.

However dangerous the figures become in the wrong hands, they are generally a consistent indication of the nation's willingness (not necessarily its desire) to spend money on its own and the Alliance's defence.

What it does not show is whether the money is wisely spent, not in moral terms but in utter value for money. The new American Defense Secretary Mr Caspar Weinberger is determined to get more value for money from his defence budget and his efforts will be watched with interest on both sides of the Atlantic, and elsewhere. The American expression, 'more bang for the buck', is still to be heard in NATO circles, and well it may be. NATO's military budgets are often unwisely spent. Yet, contrary to many political and military observations, the mighty Warsaw Pact war machine, with all its central control and rapid advances over the past decade, has yet to be built up into an unassailable force, in spite of NATO's many weaknesses and because of the Alliance's many strengths.

FIVE

The Western Military Machine

The United States has thousands more strategic nuclear warheads than the USSR, a fact worth considering for two reasons. Firstly, just as the West is fearful of the vast Soviet nuclear arsenals, so the Eastern bloc respects the enormous destructive power of those held by the United States, the United Kingdom and France. Secondly, it has become almost a convention to portray the Soviet strategic weaponry as certainly equal, if not superior, to that of the West. Nuclear and strategic parity is a confusing term and only *begins* to make much sense when it is put in the simple context: if there were to be a war, how much of the bang would get through to the target. With more wisdom, the argument might be: will the nuclear weapons actually deter as they are supposed to?

Leaving aside the British and French nuclear weapons, partly because the British system is supposedly independent and because the French really is, it is noticeable that the American systems have made steady if not spectacular advances in recent years. Today the USSR has little more than 6,000 warheads. The USA has 9,200. The 1970s were designated by the United Nations as the Disarmament Decade. During those ten years, the United States increased her number of nuclear warheads by more than 5,000 and the Soviet Union by more than 4,000 warheads. Furthermore, today's warheads are far more accurate than they used to be. The United States has 1,053 Intercontinental Ballistic Missiles. More than half that number are accurate enough to stand a very good chance of getting within about 600 feet of their targets in the Soviet Union. Each missile carries three warheads, all with this capability. Shortly, 300 of these missiles will be fitted with more powerful, 335-kiloton warheads and an even better guidance system will get most of those to within 500 feet of their targets.

The American ICBMs are deep in silos at nine bases throughout the United States. The older rockets, the 53 Titans, are at Davis-Monthan in Arizona, at McConnell in Kansas and Little Rock, Arkansas. The Titan has been around since 1963. It is a big missile, about 103 feet tall and ten feet round the girth. It may have the biggest warhead in the American arsenal, but the Titan is a liquid fuel weapon and it is best described as a plumber's nightmare, certainly for those who have to maintain it.

The modern Minuteman missile is based at Minot Air Force Base in North Dakota; F. E. Warren AFB near Cheyenne in Wyoming; Grand Forks, North Dakota, and Malmstrom, Montana. Earlier models of the

Minuteman series are at Ellsworth AFB in South Dakota, Whiteman AFB in Missouri and again at Malmstrom. The missile sites are spread across large areas of land. They do not, as some have imagined, consist of a number of closely-linked silos which will immediately fire off a missile each as soon as the President presses a button beneath the ledge of his Oval Office desk.

Each silo is some eighty feet deep. They are in clusters spread over perhaps many square miles and the launch control may be three, four or many more miles away from the weapon. The launch control is seventy or so feet below ground. All that can be seen from the surface is something that looks like any other single-storey hut, which in fact houses a canteen, rest room, television and guard facility. It also has the elevator entrance to the underground launch control capsule. The elevator is likely to be quite large, rather like a service lift, because it has to be big enough to carry equipment as well as personnel. At the bottom of the shaft, there is a thick steel blast door which opens to an inner chamber for machinery and stores. There is a further door, about three feet thick, which leads to the launch control itself. This room is narrow and long, maybe eight feet by twenty. It is banked by computers and launch panels. Inside, for one day at at time, live two missile officers. It is their job to be ready to go through the book procedures and turn their keys. When they move into an operational stage, they are strapped into chairs, rather like airline seats, twelve feet apart. The theory is that one cannot possibly get to the other's key in time to set in motion a launch. The keys have to be turned within two seconds of each other. Their orders have to be confirmed by a second team which may be many miles away at a command post. If other posts are knocked out, it is possible for the Minuteman missiles to be fired from a flying command post, an airborne battle room in a converted Boeing jet. With a ranking general in charge, such a plane will be in the air for every minute of every day of every year, in case all else fails and there is nobody left to take decisions.

As yet there is not a large enough fleet of these special aircraft. Present aircraft known as E-4As do not have the special low frequency and very low frequency communications, nor can they pick up air force satellites, and they do not have the necessary launch facilities on board. However a more modern version of the National Emergency Airborne Command Post, the E-4B, is flying. It will be joined by other jets by 1984 while the present fleet will be updated by the second half of this decade.

There are 2,400 officers and men crewing the Minuteman and Titan missiles. It takes more than 5,000 further officers and enlisted men to maintain the 1,053 missiles. Naturally, it is the actual button-pressers who are in the limelight, and it is interesting to see how their age groups are falling. A few years ago, the two-man missile team on a Minuteman would probably have been majors or even lieutenant-colonels. Today they are likely to be no more than junior captains and perhaps young lieutenants. Nobody would doubt the efficiency of these young men, most of whom appear to be in their early twenties. The fact that they are there is certainly a reflection on the inability of the air force to attract and keep sufficient officers and men. The nine strategic missile wings come under the control of the Strategic Air Command, run at the time of writing by one of the air force's more brilliant generals, Richard H. Ellis. His headquarters is at Omaha, Nebraska. From there he controls about 120,000 people, more than 400 long-range bombers, the 600 or so air-to-air refuelling tankers vital to the nuclear and conventional bombing force and more than fifty bases, including the missile units and the nuclear bombing squadrons. Perhaps every one of those bases is a classified target for the Soviet Union. Not all of them are in the United States and the significance of this is something to examine when we discuss civil defence in a later chapter.

The importance of the SAC element in the American nuclear arsenal can be gauged by the fact that it carries fifty per cent of the 9,200 warheads. One of the weaknesses in the American system is that 76 per cent of the warheads would be carried either by submarine-launched missiles or by bombers. As yet, neither system has the accuracy of the ground-launched and fixed missiles. The larger part of the American Minuteman system would be virtually unstoppable. The submarine system, which carried 50 per cent of the warheads, is being improved, but is not yet fool- or foul-proof. The bombers, the giant B-52s and the F1-11s, are vulnerable as any aircraft must be. At the same time, the fixed silos are vulnerable in themselves. They cannot hide, as can bombers which would disperse to other airfields or remain in the air at the first sign of an attack, or submarines which if at sea would possibly be the least vulnerable of all the systems.

The problem with estimating the numbers which might survive is that the answer depends on where they are and in what state they are in when the warning comes. It takes, for example, two years to give a major overhaul to a nuclear submarine. If a boat happens to be undergoing one of these refits when the warning comes, there is no chance of getting it to sea. (The British Royal Navy with its four Polaris boats would be lucky to have more than two at sea in an emergency.)

The American strategic bomber force is old. It needs a considerable amount of maintenance and there is a major problem with ground crews. The standard needed to maintain those aircraft is not present in the Strategic Air Command. If there were to be a war, aircraft might well fly below the peacetime safety standard. If the United States wanted to fly a convincing number of B-52s, then she would have to fly them below that standard. It would be quite possible for a series of false alerts leading up to a war to 'wear out' so many of the B-52s that, come the day, less than 50 per cent of the total force would be airborne.

The toll taken on an older aircraft, when it has to scramble, fly about and return, and then repeat the process on a number of occasions, is demanding to an extreme on the machinery and avionics. Few are certain that the United States SAC would be able to cope with such a sequence of events. Furthermore, nobody is certain of the effect on the aircrews. The Strategic Air Command is no different from any other part of the American system. It has manpower problems. It would like to keep more than two-thirds of its personnel after their first enlistment period. The actual figure is much less than 30 per cent. For a nation given over to all things technical, it may not be surprising that the US armed forces' most fundamental weakness is its manpower.

There are more than two million men and women in the American forces. During 1980, about 30 per cent of the recruits were in the lowest intelligence brackets. An army joke running the rounds had a recruiting officer telling a new entrant, 'As a high school graduate, you will be entitled to go on the army computer training course.' The recruit replies, 'What's a computer?' And the joke sums up the problem for the US Services. Today's forces are stuffed full of modern and sometimes staggering technology. The army is no longer something that can be polished, painted and saluted, and then expected to run efficiently. According to one source, six out of every one hundred recruits accepted for the army were illiterate in the true sense of the word. Before they could continue with any Service training they had to be taught to read and write. This was in 1980. Another source claims that only one per cent of the tradesmen who maintain US army gun systems passed their basic skills test. Perhaps more frightening, only ten per cent of the army's nuclear weapon fitters were able to pass their basic trade tests.

Again during 1980, the US Navy was looking for an extra 20,000 technical petty officers but was unable to find them. Not long ago, the author asked the captain of the American aircraft carrier, the *John F. Kennedy*, what his main mission was. The answer was very simple, to retain as many men as possible after their initial enlistment period. The problem of getting spares and people to fit them also extends to the air force, although they do not yet have the shortfalls of the other services. But it has been estimated, at the higher levels of the Pentagon, that American aircraft spend half their service life out of action. But there are even worse problems for service manpower management.

A Presidential task force has discovered that more than 50 per cent of American enlisted men admit to taking drugs. Many believe that the figure is considerably higher. Those forces serving in Europe tend towards hard drugs, partly, but only partly, because the so-called softer narcotics are less freely available. But the drug-taking and the low educational standards are not symptoms of the way in which America runs her services. It is very much the attitude in the country at large. Since Vietnam, the United States has had an all-volunteer army, and it is not working. To some extent this is not surprising, since the mark of the military must have reached an all-time low after Vietnam. The problem, though, is not unlike that experienced by the British. Recruitment has in the past been difficult enough, but the biggest headache was keeping the recruits in once the initial enlistment had been completed. For the dedicated man, there will always be a good life in the Services, but for many others, say, infantrymen, the experience of a disrupted home life, discipline in an increasingly ill-disciplined society, poor pay and the opportunity to get on first-name terms with every pine cone in Fort Bragg, have little attractions for the modern young American. If the American armed forces are to improve their manpower problems, three things have to happen.

Unemployment in civilian life must continue to rise. People do turn to the military if they cannot get a job elsewhere. Unfortunately that does not mean the people the Services need will be signing on the dotted line. Secondly, the American people must be willing to pay their forces far more than they do. Officers working as forecourt hands at gas stations, and sergeants driving cabs are not good advertisements for the services. Yet this type of thing is happening in the United States just as it did, and sometimes still does, in the United Kingdom. It took a pay rise of more than 30 per cent to satisfy the British serviceman. If one looks at the 1981 pay rates in the United States, a further 20 per cent is needed to attract and keep the calibre of manpower needed to cope with the increasingly technical military. The irony is that, with all the technical advancements and scientific research, not enough has been done to make the faster, bigger, more lethal machinery easier to operate and maintain. There are, admittedly, signs that this is happening in the air industry. (A good example is the McDonnell Douglas F/A-18 twin tail jet for the navy. It does have the potential for easier – but not necessarily easy – maintenance, but at a price.) Furthermore it has to be remembered that it is not enough to reduce the technical expertise required simply by being able to remove a part and replace it. In time of war,

The Soviet Union's recently-built battle-cruiser *Kirov*, seen from the stern by a photographer in a helicopter operating from HMS *Newcastle*. It is said to be nuclear-powered, although this picture shows smoke exhausts, which may be for auxiliary machinery. The mass of radars, wireless aerials, hatches, spars and booms provide hours of analysis for Western maritime intelligence officers. Even old ships are examined in some detail in case new equipment has been installed. A slight bump, or section of angle iron, could, for example, indicate some development in the Soviet navy's electronic counter-measure system.

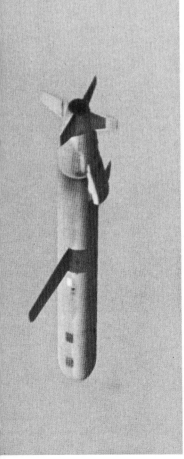

The Cruise missile shown here is the system built by General Dynamics and is known as the Tomahawk. It will be carried on low-loading trucks in groups of four, and in war would be scattered away from its peacetime base. Missile engineers say its strength is that it does not need pre-survey launch sites and that it is able to fly quickly beneath the Soviet radar system. A typical launch truck is seen above with the missile in flight (top). On the right, the missile goes through its various launch stages. Similar systems are due to be based in the United Kingdom, Italy and West Germany during the next two or three years. The governments of Holland and Belgium have avoided requests by Washington to base the US-built, -financed and -operated system in those two countries.

The so-called Spy Trawler. The West calls these little ships AGIs (Auxiliary Gatherer Intelligence). With an impressive array of aerials, they monitor signals and frequencies at shore-based or seaward units. There are certain areas of the world where these Soviet AGIs are on constant station. For example, there has for many years been such a vessel standing off the coast of Ireland near Malin Head. It is in a good position to monitor British and American nuclear submarine operations. Some trawlers have been used to pick up communications between England and Northern Ireland. Others are sitting off American bases on a year-round timetable.

Here the West gathers intelligence. An RAF Nimrod from 120 Squadron shadows an old Soviet Kotlin-class destroyer which had been 'inspecting' an oil rig in the Orkneys area. (This picture was taken by another intelligence-gathering aircraft.)

A Soviet Krivak-class guided missile destroyer patrolling in the English Channel. Note the ship's company gathered on the after-deck, watching themselves being photographed from a helicopter flying from HMS *Daedalus*. Also note one of the after-guns trained on the photographer . . . many of the crews regard the intelligence-gathering game as fun.

Nobody waving here. This is a Soviet photograph of one of their nuclear-powered submarines. It first came into service towards the end of the 1960s.

The F-15 Eagle built for the American Air Force by McDonnell Douglas. It has been called the finest interceptor in the world. In spite of some problems that produced crashes in some of the jets based in Europe, the Eagle is still said to be the most agile aircraft of its type.

The McDonnell Douglas F-18A Hornet development aircraft. One problem for any Navy or Air Force squadron is the complicated technology used to maintain modern jets. A great deal of thought went into making the Hornet as simple as possible to maintain. Turn-round time may be crucial for an operational squadron.

A Soviet soldier takes the Oath of Allegiance. During his pre-service training and certainly during his conscription, he will undergo political and ideological education and is likely to have a better idea than his Western counterpart of the system to which he owes his allegiance.

Perhaps a set-piece lecture, but these Soviet soldiers are supposed to be having a study period on World Affairs. It is an indication of the importance of such training.

A Soviet jet about to take off for an exercise. There is some doubt in Western Intelligence circles as to the flying time given to Soviet pilots. Some sources believe the Soviet pilot does not get sufficient hours in to maintain a high standard. However, shortages of oil and economic restrictions may force Western air forces to cut flying training.

An older, but nonetheless effective, Soviet Surface to Air missile.

there may be few if any spares getting through and it will be the skill of the line engineer and fitter that keeps an aircraft in the air – where, after all, it was designed to be, rather than on the ground waiting for somebody with enough skill to let the pilot get on with his job.

The third and longer-term answer to many of the manpower problems is fraught with political pitfalls. It is of course conscription, the draft, No matter how much the government is willing to pay its troops, and whatever the conditions they are given, there are only limited numbers of people who are willing to join the peculiar life the Services can offer. It is a fact of life that, if a country wishes to maintain large forces – and by any standards the US maintains large forces – then an all-volunteer system has few chances of producing the constant quality needed. Even more crucial is the question of who should be exempted from the draft. A two-year draft should include college candidates; certainly, universities should not be havens for draft-dodgers. A two-year draft period would have two results. It would increase the standard of recruits and it would also give the United States a much-needed pool of reserve soldiers. The draft would not work in some countries, notably the United Kingdom where not even the military would want to go back to conscription. But in the United States it would be at least a short-term answer to what can only become an increasing problem, especially if more jobs become available as the economy recovers. President Carter's Draft Registration was a political gambit that had little military value. It did show, however, that many young Americans were not so violently opposed to the system as perhaps some had thought they would be. Whether or not this was in the safety of knowing the scheme was a registration and nothing more, or whether it was sheer bravado for the occasion, is another matter.

There is a tailpiece to the question of the draft. Conscripted soldiers are not paid as much as regular servicemen. It might then be argued that conscription would reduce to some extent the American military wage bill which includes pensions and facilities for dependents. The defence budget will be heading towards the three hundred thousand million dollar mark by the middle of this decade and, with the cost of major equipment programmes escalating every month, this is easily understood. The American budget does not have time to stand still. There are so many different equipment projects simultaneously in the pipeline, that it is impossible to believe that the military could ever pay for them all if the defence manufacturers decided to call in their debts.

Considering that a modern jet will cost the air force at least twenty million dollars a copy, it is understandable that an argument exists for building cheaper products and buying more of them. The counter-argument must be that an aircraft, say, is only as good as its ability to take out an enemy system. There is no sign that the Soviet Union is moving away from qualitative improvements – rather the reverse; therefore the US cannot afford to drop her technical standards. It is also doubtful under present circumstances whether the air force could find very many more pilots to fly extra aircraft. The answer lies perhaps in the method the Americans use to arrive at the acceptance of a new system. There are, for example, far too many brilliant resources competing for the same military market. It would be interesting to see by how much the cost of aircraft and their avionics and weapon systems would be reduced, if the Department of the Air Force had more control over, say, one or at the most two research and development projects. At the same time there are those who say that bureaucracy never managed to do anything but increase the cost of a paper clip.

What is important is that the US air force must have its full resources and not an empty hangar of promises. This applies equally to all NATO nations. In any future war, it would be a matter of come-as-you-are. The chances are that there would be no time to go into production once the war had begun. It was possible during the Second World War for the Americans to produce a good aircraft from drawing-board to in-service operations in under four months. If there is another war, there might not be four days to get things together. US Air Force advances have been considerable, especially with the introduction of the F-15 Eagle and the too-often maligned F-16. But there are still major weaknesses.

There has been far too much vacillation over the decision to go ahead with a new large transport aircraft. NATO needs the US Air Force Military Airlift Command (MAC) to produce a heavy trans-port plane with two basic qualities. It needs to be able to lift a big cargo load and it must be able to put it down on the shortest and roughest of air strips. It will be no good relying on smooth 12,000-feet runways in wartime. They will not be there.

There is also a need to update reconnaissance aircraft. Indeed, it is a desperate requirement if the United States still believes she may have to fight a war in Europe. Europe is not known for its brilliant weather conditions. It is one thing exercising aircraft and attacks in the Nevada desert, it is something else to plan for an operation along Europe's central front. Very few of the United States Air Force aircraft are able to carry out vital reconnaissance missions at night. A commander cannot fight with any form of certainty unless he has good intelligence from reconnaissance flights. Along with the rest of NATO, the US Air Force is stuck with a massive delay in getting photo-reconnaissance back to that commander. More money and effort need to be spent on giving the air force a direct data-link between the commander and the intelligence gatherer. If this is not done, then the air force's ability to give the commander the information he needs and to cover him during the battle will not only be militarily unsound, it will waste lives. The air force has built an operations intelligence centre at its European headquarters, Ramstein in West Germany. But this is only the start. There is still no effective method of transforming the unevaluated intelligence into the reliable information a commander needs in time to fight his battle.

Although the F-16 and the F-15 Eagle both boost the air-to-air combat strength of the air force, there remain some distinct doubts about other American aircraft and the policy surrounding them. The chances of US jets being able to carry out tactical ground attacks at night, and in foul weather, are slim. They are simply not fitted with the necessary avionics to turn them into night owls. Furthermore, the chances of existing runways surviving for long in a future war are, as already explained, remote. Therefore the argument would be for the introduction to the United States Air Force of a jump jet aircraft, or a jet which needs only very small lengths of runways, runways which may include grass strips and converted highways. That is the reality of modern battle concepts.

The enemy would have the same problems. To safeguard their aircraft on the ground, the Soviet Union have for some time built shelters giving massive protection. There now seems every reason to suppose that more would be gained by attacking not the aircraft, but the runways. To do this, new weapons would be needed by the air force. The chances are that an attacking jet would have but one chance at its target, therefore the weapon systems have to be the most effective available. When a war starts, there is going to be another problem not only for the US Air Force, but for other NATO and ground troops: communications. The chances of being able to carry out preplanned assaults are very slim. Attacks and defensive operations would have to be conducted with the co-operation of other forces. The existing communications system is inadequate. It is doubtful whether it would survive more than the initial stages of a war in Europe. Until 1980, General John W. Pauly was Commander, Allied Forces Central Europe, and recognised as having been one of the more far-sighted American air force generals to hold that post. In his opinion, the need for secure, survivable, jam-proof communications is one of the highest priorities.

The problem with most communication set-ups is that they have to be fixed and therefore easily targeted. Even the more advanced airborne command posts such as the Boeing E-4 have limited value. Because of their mobility and ability to operate to some extent out of reach of attacking missiles and aircraft, they could survive for some time. But they cannot stay up for ever.

This vulnerability applies just as much to the more strategic systems such as ICBM warning units as far afield as Australia and Colorado as it does to battlefield command and communication posts.

None of this should give the impression that US forces are about to fall apart for lack of men, equipment and policy judgements. New systems are coming into operation. The present anti-aircraft missiles based in Europe, Hawk and Nike, could be easily jammed by Soviet electronic counter-measures (ECM). But a new missile, called Patriot, would not suffer the same problems to the same extent. More than 7,000 new tanks are being produced for the army, although there is some very real doubt about many of its components. The navy's Trident submarine-launched missile force is expected to be good – but late. It is hard to detect and its missile is not only accurate, it has room for development, which is an essential requirement for any new weapon system. The Aegis missile cruiser will be able to fight in all weathers and engage a number of targets, including the Soviet navy's Backfire jets, at the same time. There are also very good hopes for the Cruise missiles to be carried in converted B-52 bombers. One particular feature of these Air Launched Cruise Missiles (ALCMs – pronounced Alkums) is the computer guidance systems. It is thought to be better than those scheduled for Ground Launched Cruise Missiles (GLCMs – pronounced Glikums). The legitimate question may be, therefore, why is it that the more advanced system is not being used elsewhere?

Probably the biggest debate for some time will revolve about the MX-missile. The MX is a mobile missile, based on land and, like the Minuteman, it has an ability to hit targets in the USSR when fired from the United States. That is the theory because the MX is still in the development stage although mock-ups of the rocket as well as of its transporters can be seen. It has therefore reached the stage where it is possible to go along and kick the tyres – there is something visible. What is difficult to see, is how President Reagan can agree the proposed MX basing system. The great debate has centred on where it should be based. Ideally, said the experts, it should be in Utah and Nevada. There have been environmental objections and those should be left to the people of the United States. Proposed basing systems have included the wrongly called race track system. This term was used to describe an idea whereby the missile would be stored in a shelter and then every few months be pulled out and run about a track, perhaps over many miles of road, before being 'hidden' again in another shelter. This would be happening throughout the missile sites. It is the strategic missileman's version of Find The Lady. And the best description of what is supposed to be going on is that, instead of shuffling cups about and betting the punter that he cannot guess under which cup the pea is hidden, the United States proposes to do the same with missiles and the bets are being placed by the Soviet Union. The reason behind this almost bizarre idea is that, because modern guidance systems on Soviet ICBMs have become so accurate, the permanent Minuteman and Titan silos have become unacceptably vulnerable. In fact if some of the calculations are correct, by the second half of this decade less than 20 per cent of American intercontinental ballistic missiles would survive a first strike by the Soviet Union. So the idea is simple: hide the missiles by shuffling the strategic weapon deck. But it is impossible to believe the MX will be any less vulnerable if the shuffle takes place even immediately an attack warning is sounded – there would be little time. The cost of all this is said to be in excess of 56 thousand million dollars. But by the time the cost of the warhead and the support operation is included, even at the present dollar rate, the total will be more than double that 56 thousand million.

A further problem is that too much blinkered thought is contributing to the final decision on MX. Firstly, a lot of time is spent arguing over the basing programme and not enough examining the real needs of the US strategic force. By the time MX is ready for deployment it should be clear that US guidance technology will be sufficiently advanced to make submarine-launched missiles more accurate, and perhaps good enough to take over the role of some of the traditionally land-based weapons. The submarine is the least vulnerable of all missile platforms. Its ability, in spite of new detection systems, to hide in the sea is its greatest asset. There are good arguments against the idea of submarine-launched missiles to replace a land-based MX. Not least of all is the cost. Thousands of millions of dollars have already been spent on developing MX and nearly thirty major associate contractors have been involved in the project. Secondly, there would have to be an enormous capital outlay to build sufficient submarines and systems to take MX missiles, and it is not certain whether the US Navy would be able to find the qualified manpower to operate them. Then there is the matter of communications. In spite of major advances in communication technology, it is still very difficult to keep in reliable communication with a submarine system. Finally, only a fraction of the submarine force would be at sea at any one time and when, as we have considered, a nuclear-powered submarine might take two years to refit it would be impossible to get every boat to sea in an emergency.

Whatever happens, the MX is a programme that should and could have gone into operation in a much shorter time than is now envisaged. Ironically, there are those in Washington who believe it is the missilemen themselves, the US Air Force, who are partly to blame for the delay. There has not been sufficient co-ordination on the basing plan. Perhaps, though, the final irony of MX, a missile project designed to hide from the enemy, is the inspection system. Under SALT, the Soviet Union has the right to be able to be certain that the limitations on the number of missiles has not been exceeded. There are a number of ways of doing this. The most obvious is for experts from the United States and the Soviet Union to be based in each other's countries for on-site inspections. The Soviet Union is predictably not enthusiastic about this idea. Instead, the most likely method to be used is satellite observation. At a prearranged time, satellites would be flown over the missile sites. To make sure the Soviet systems can see into what are supposed to be strengthened missile shelters (the jargon is 'hardened' against nuclear attack), inspection panels, or ports, would be built into the roof. It would seem, however, that this system would weaken what are supposed to be tough shelters.

None of this matters, of course, so long as there is not a war. If there should be and 'it goes nuclear', then the warning of an attack by ICBMs would come through the North American Air Defence Command, NORAD. NORAD achieved certain publicity between November 1979 and the summer of 1980 when it came up with false alarms of nuclear attacks. On the first occasion, an exercise programme was fed into the system and few people realised it was nothing more than an exercise until it was double-checked. But, by that time, the Strategic Air Command had gone to its first alert stage. In June 1980 there were two further alerts triggered off by malfunctions in the computer software. Again nuclear bombers and missile crews went to the Alert stage. There were many red faces. Some were red through embarrassment, others through anger. In the British parliament there were demands to know what had happened, the matter was described as serious and there were mutterings about the American malfunction taking the West to the brink of war. These reactions were quite understandable in a society which allows, quite rightly, all shades of political opinion. What happened at NORAD did leave the whole system open for political and military criticism.

Yet the system failures might also have been better exploited by the military. There may have been a breakdown in the technical process, but at the same time there was a golden opportunity to demonstrate how difficult it is to go to war by accident. What did not fail was the system of checks and balances that exists to guard against such malfunctions resulting in the wrong buttons being pressed.

The headquarters of NORAD is inside Cheyenne Mountain, just outside Colorado Springs in Colorado State. It is approached from the main highway by driving up a winding road and then through a third-of-a-mile-long tunnel into the mountain itself. Inside are nearly three miles of cavities and chambers, and in those chambers are fifteen separate buildings, eleven of them three-storeys high. Each building is balanced on massive thousand-pound springs. The idea is that, if the mountain were attacked, then the buildings and their valuable contents would ride the nuclear punch. Before an attack came, three three-foot-thick doors, each weighing twenty-five tons, would be shut. When that happened many of the 1,700 Americans and Canadians (NORAD is a joint US–Canada command) who keep the place ticking over would be set to ride out the war. They say they could stay there for thirty days in the hundred-million-year-old Rocky Mountain.

NORAD has three main purposes. It is there to give warning of any penetration of North American air space by unidentified or enemy aircraft. However, the change in American strategic thinking considers this eventuality unlikely and there is not much of an air defence system even if it did happen. Some at NORAD believe it possible for a low-flying aircraft to penetrate American radar. One officer has explained to the author that, as long as there were few aircraft flying in, it would be possible for them to reach any major strategic or national target.

NORAD's second role is becoming more important. Cheyenne Mountain houses the Space Defense Operations Center, known locally as SPADOC. There are nearly 12,000 space objects recorded in the SPADOC log. Today there are more than 4,500 objects flying about, from big satellites and space stations down to small bits of space junk left over from earlier experiments. All this is monitored by SPADATS, the Space Detection and Tracking System of telescopes and radio, radar and camera monitors. And it is a busy operation. There are something like 30,000 observations made every day of the year. The future of space monitoring is assured as the likelihood of nuclear weapon systems high in the sky increases.

The best-known of the three roles is missile warning. If the Soviet Union launched its land-based ICBMs at the United States, they would take about thirty minutes to reach their targets. However, the Soviet Union also deploys nuclear submarines with ballistic missiles. If, for example, one of those boats fired at the United States, the time to target could be as little as five minutes. In theory, NORAD should be able to pick up a missile within a minute of lift-off. The first indication should come from a series of early warning satellites in synchronised orbit some 23,000 miles above the earth. This information would be checked out and perhaps confirmed by a series of radar systems. The more modern one, known as PAVE PAWS, might take about two or three minutes to confirm or reject the satellite report.

Once an attack had been confirmed, NORAD's job would be all but over. Its last function would be to pass on this information to the National Command in Washington and at the same time to Strategic Air Command's headquarters at Omaha, Nebraska. What is rarely talked about is the series of double-checks that exists outside the launch warning system. One of them is a constant computer update on the whereabouts of top Kremlin figures. If, say, there is a period of tension, the United States will have a detailed account of the Soviet leaders' movements. A report that Mr Brezhnev and his Chief of Staff are sunning themselves at some Black Sea resort might cast doubt on the seriousness of the so-called tension transmitted by the military. Another check is the celebrated Hot Line. While US and USSR people do communicate directly, the Hot Line itself is not a red telephone at the President's right elbow. There are telephones, but the nerve centre is a telex-type machine. The Western end is in the National Military Command Center which in turn is in the Pentagon. Furthermore, it is not meant to be used simply in an emergency. Every hour, during every day, American and Soviet technicians talk to one another by making test transmissions on the machine. It is said that, if the Soviet Union did not reply and the machine was functioning correctly, then that would be answer enough.

All this sounds as if the United States *is* NATO. Obviously it is not, but the preceding pages do illustrate the major part the USA has in the Alliance and that it is far more than a political domination. In fact, because of developments during the past four years or so, American political influence is less than ever. The European end of the Alliance is the area where most would imagine that any future war would be fought. Indeed, apart from a sea battle, the terms of the Alliance would not allow its members to come together as one force to fight anywhere outside its boundaries. Many countries have interests far removed from the NATO area and regularly deploy troops, aircraft and ships throughout the world, often in concert with roving American forces. It seems likely that the United Kingdom does this more than any other European NATO nation.

During 1980, British forces were to be found not only in West Germany and other NATO countries, but also in Cyprus, Gibraltar, Belize, Hong Kong, Brunei, Diego Garcia, the Falkland Islands, Oman, Saudi Arabia, Antarctica, the Caribbean, the Pacific and even China. For those who believe the British pulled away from every part of the world except north-west Europe during the 1960s, it is interesting to see how determined were the chiefs of staff to man-oeuvre round the political instructions handed down when the withdrawal from East of Suez took place. One ruse was to set up what the Royal Navy called a group deployment. Every year, a group of ships leaves the United Kingdom during the late spring and makes a global tour that takes until about Christmas to complete. Consequently the flag is still flown in places whose people had imagined they had seen the last of a British presence. But Britain's main contribution to Western defence remains in north-west Europe. Spending around five per cent of the GNP on defence and maintaining her efforts to increase spending by three per cent in real terms, Britain has come a long way in a very short time as a loyal member of the Alliance. It is less than a decade since Britain was being chastised for not pulling her weight. It would be easy to believe this reformation has come about because of the 1979 change of government. But there was every sign that, under the Labour administration of James Callaghan, Britain was determined to be senior member of the Alliance. Britain's position is important for a number of reasons other than political popularity.

As a non-continental member of Europe, the United Kingdom's forces have the same problems as two other members, the United States and Canada, that in time of emergency a major effort has to be made to move her reinforcements on to the continent and then to join up with those already there. The size of this problem can be seen when it is considered that the British Army of the Rhine would have to be at least doubled in size during wartime and that those reinforcements would be mainly reservists. There is no way in which this crucial element can be fully rehearsed. The 1980 series of exercises known as Crusader 80 may have been the biggest peacetime reinforcement exercise since the Second World War, but it could not simulate either the numbers or the conditions that would surely be faced during a war build-up. Take one expected problem, that of refugees. There could easily be millions of people trying desperately to get away from what would be the war-zone, while heading in that direction would be soldiers trying to meet up with their parent formations and, equally important, much of their equipment.

Another factor in Britain's importance is that the islands would become the major rear base for other NATO troops and aircraft, mainly American. Up to 40 per cent of NATO's offensive aircraft could be based in the UK. Furthermore, the existing American base facilities in the United Kingdom, together with the proposed Cruise missile basing, makes it very unlikely that Britain's tactical position will ever be downgraded.

As a military organisation, Britain has been reasonably successful in maintaining an efficient fighting force, in spite of many criticisms to the contrary. Yet although huge amounts are spent on defence there are problems, some of them serious.

The weaknesses in Britain's air defence system have been well-documented. Although the Alliance works collectively, Britain remains responsible for her own air defence; it is called UKADR, or United Kingdom Air Defence Region. It is estimated that the Soviet Union has up to 600 aircraft earmarked that could easily reach the United Kingdom. What may be surprising is that it was not until 1974 that Britain's defence planners reconsidered that a danger existed of a manned aircraft attack on the United Kingdom. To those who are reminded of the Battle of Britain this may sound ludicrous.

The difficulties for the RAF are clear. Most of the existing aircraft are old, there are too few of them and the control element is inadequate. If, in 1981, the Soviet Union wished to render the RAF air defence system useless, it would be possible to do so without a shot being fired. Using a tactic as simple as that described earlier, Soviet 'probe' aircraft could simply fly into the UK Air Defence Region (not Britain's Air Space which is something quite different) and almost demand to be intercepted on every occasion. Interception does not mean attack. If there was no state of war, they would not be attacked. But the Air Defence Region extends for hundreds of miles towards the north, and Soviet planes could fly in every day, in ones or twos, and the RAF would be obliged to scramble to check them out. One senior fighter controller has estimated that it would take not much more than two weeks for Britain's elderly Phantom and Lightning jets to be 'exhausted'. In other words, the wear and tear on both aircraft and crews would be enough to render the Air Defence System nothing more than a skeleton of what it should be.

New aircraft are on the way. The interceptor version of the Tornado, a jet built by a consortium of British, West German and Italian companies, is due to go into service later in the decade. The radar system is being revamped and the British Aerospace Nimrod early warning jets will make all the difference. But to bring all this together takes time and it is not so certain that the ensemble will be able to cope with what many strategists see as an increased air threat during the mid-1980s. Finding aircraft is to some extent simply a matter of finding a good design and the money. What is more difficult is manpower. To produce an *extra* three squadrons – which is what the RAF needs – would mean not just fifty or so jets. It would also mean finding about 2,000 extra men. Once the RAF had the aircraft it could hang on to them for the next twenty years, assuming of course they were not shot out of the sky or did not crash in training flights. But men are not only harder to find, they are harder to keep.

All three services have had their problems in retaining trained personnel, but the big wage increases awarded by Callaghan's Labour government did a great deal to attract recruits and to keep some of those who were thinking of leaving. Rising unemployment has played its part. This means that pay is a big item in the British defence budget. It is worth repeating that one advantage of having a conscript army is that many of the men are cheap to come by, consequently more money may be allocated to equipment programmes. In the 1980–1 British Defence Estimates, the total expenditure was £10,785 million. Of that, £4,527 million went on personnel, £200 million more than was spent on equipment.

There are, of course, ways of reducing that figure. It might be argued that the Services should not have to pay pensions. Why should they not come out of the civilian budgets? It would be a complicated operation, because some Servicemen 'retire' before they are forty, whereas the earliest a State pension begins is at sixty and, for men, sixty-five. What the difference would be if the State took over the payments at the standard reitrement age is unclear, but it is almost certain that the administration needed would make it a worthless operation.

The outstanding problem in the region of manpower, according to some senior military men, is the standard of some of the officer candidates. During the 1970s it was recognised that the army could not struggle along with its old system while the country was eagerly trying out new ones. Social attitudes and educational systems and standards were changing, although in the latter case not necessarily in the right direction. The most obvious result of the rethink in army officer recruitment and training came when the long course at the Royal Military Academy, Sandhurst was reduced from two years to just one year. Although this has been slightly adjusted, it is sometimes difficult to see how this could have been a successful move. True, it was necessary to get young officers out to their regiments and corps as quickly as possible. The units needed them and it was believed that a great deal of the early training could be done once they were at the 'sharp end'. Furthermore, some believed it was better for the young men to get to their units rather than dally at Sandhurst where a great deal of time was perhaps taken up with more social and sporting events. What might, only might, not have been recognised, is that the two years in which the young man was steeped in the army before being let loose was to his and the army's long-term good. At the same time, with more people going into the army from the universities and with the army trying to attract more people with that further education, it is possible that an extra two years at Sandhurst on top of their three years might not have been so beneficial. The British army is believed by many to be the most professional in the Western world. Yet it would be interesting to predict the long-term effect of a two-year course based on, but not necessarily at, Sandhurst.

The Royal Navy has had its share of manpower problems. Technical training, as in the RAF, is extraordinarily high. Keeping the qualified technician has been just as much a problem as in other navies and air forces. But, as well as pay, conditions for the sailor have improved. An interest taken in the 1970s by the then Commander in Chief Home Command, Admiral Sir Terence Lewin, did much to improve welfare arrangement for sailors and their families, and the navy had managed to maintain its rather democratic tradition. Furthermore the navy spends far more time at sea than many imagine.

For many a year, it was fashionable to criticise the Royal Navy for its lack of ships. Yet the existing fleet of more than seventy major surface ships and nearly thirty attack submarines is being modernised at a steady rate and is probably as big as any future recruiting programme will be able to handle. There is no point in having so many ships that the navy cannot find sufficient men to sail them. The Royal Navy's strength is in its Anti-Submarine Warfare (ASW) capability. New ships, some new equipment and a good research programme have made the navy not only the biggest in European NATO, but also one of the most efficient in the world. It is elsewhere that the shortcomings are so obvious.

One of the navy's jobs in time of tension would be to move a large section of the Royal Marines to Norway. Although modern thinking is in favour of pre-positioning equipment in Norway for the Marines to pick up when they arrive, nevertheless they would still have to take a great deal with them, especially as, come the day, they would not be able to pick and choose where they landed. It would be better if the Royal Marines could have more than the two out-dated assault ships now at their occasional disposal. To rely on such things as roll-on, roll-off ferries does not seem reasonable. But then in European defence terms very little is reasonable and some countries have far worse problems than those of the United Kingdom.

Taking just two, at the extremes of the Alliance boundaries, is sufficient to see how these can vary. During 1980, NATO was much exercised by the Danish government's refusal to increase its defence budget along with other NATO nations. It was estimated that, by not increasing the budget by the promised three per cent, Danish defence spending had in truth been reduced by as much as 30 per cent when inflation was taken into account. It prompted the Chief of Denmark's Operational Forces, Lieutenant General Christian Vegger, officially to warn the ruling Social Democrats that, in the event of an East–West confrontation, reduced Danish forces would be overrun before the NATO allies could reach them. It is said that the general told the government that one precondition for being reinforced from outside was that Danish forces had to be able to hold large enough areas for those reinforcements to secure a foothold. It is also his opinion that so-called superior equipment cannot make up for lack of manpower and that further cuts will mean exactly that. Although Denmark is modernising some of her forces, it is not without some difficulty. Along with the Netherlands, Norway and Belgium, Denmark is buying the F-16 jet from the United States. But financial arrangements, which included agreements to build up the Danish aerospace industry so that some of the cost could be recouped by increased job prospects and co-production, have not met expectations.

In Turkey, beset by political, social and economic torment, the problems are more complex. Her geographical position is of vital importance for the rest of the Alliance. In wartime Turkey would have a massive job to perform, but in peace she is still a vital link in the Electronic Intelligence system of the West. It is no wonder that, when assessing Turkey (and especially when adding Greece's name), NATO analysts become nervous. A recent US Senate Foreign Relations report believed that Turkey has turned some economic corner and that, properly supported by the rest of the Alliance with large economic hand-outs, the country could be back on its feet within four to five years. Part of this assumption was based on the proposition that Turkey's terrorist activity would go away as soon as the economy righted itself. This would appear to be a simplistic view. In the military, there is a desperate need for new equipment. Instead, the best that may be hoped for is a series of hand-outs, mainly discards from other Alliance members. One example is the fact that Turkey is to buy old F-104 jets from the Netherlands. It is the sort of deal that many Third World countries would never have entered into. Unfortunately NATO does not have the facilities to mount a diplomatic and financial rescue operation of the type that is needed not only for Turkey's sake, but also for that of the Alliance. When a political system hangs perilously by one or two factional threads, it is difficult for even a willing government to be seen to do business with outside influences that may be objectionable to those within the government and the country.

Even governments with apparently few internal problems and even fewer external differences often find it difficult to come to agreements which would without doubt benefit the Alliance and themselves in the long term. This is abundantly obvious in two vital NATO areas.

For years, NATO commanders have shaken their heads in despair over what is generally referred to as the lack of standardisation of equipment in the Alliance. Put simply, too many countries are using too many different types of equipment to do the same job. The Warsaw Pact armies use what is generally Soviet-designed military hardware. All Warsaw Pact nations use Soviet tanks, MiG jets, radars, armoured personnel carriers, rifles, field guns and ammunition. It is all standard, which means that to a great extent whatever the nationality, each one knows that the equipment is interchangeable, as are spares, training procedures, ammunition and communications.

This is not so in NATO. Even the most basic weapon, the rifle, is not subjected to NATO's standardisation rules, nor will it be for many years to come. The Americans and the British, for example, not only have different rifles, they have a different size of ammunition for them. A German tank repair unit could not fit a British tank regiment, because the British and Germans not only drive different tanks, their engines are different. Furthermore, one is petrol and the other diesel, so they could not even fuel each other. Some of the existing differences are so dangerous that it is remarkable they have not been corrected.

It is quite possible that, in time of war, an American anti-aircraft battery would shoot down a British jet because the Americans and British still use different identification call systems. The system is known as IFF, Identification Friend or Foe. The idea is a simple one. If, say, an RAF ground attack jet takes off from a base in Germany, fights and dodges its way through enemy surface to air missile systems, enemy interceptors, gets to its target, delivers its weapons, fights its way back, it needs to know that in the heat of battle if is not going to be shot down by its own side. The IFF system is supposed to reduce that risk by using a simple cockpit device which will allow the anti-aircraft unit positively to identify the incoming jet. There is nothing much wrong with the kit used by the RAF, it simply does not match that of other NATO units, and so the RAF pilot cannot guarantee that he will not be shot down by his own side. There now exists a study aimed at coming up with a joint system but, as one senior American officer has told the author, if there were to be a war tomorrow, it would be better if the British stayed clear of most friendly SAM units.

A great deal of energy is being devoted to getting standard equipment throughout NATO. The added problem is that the IFF standardisation attempt is perhaps only being tackled for national rather than truly international reasons. The Americans for example use what is known as the Mark 12 system which is more than twenty years old. Advances in Soviet technology have led some to believe that it is possible for Soviet aircraft to 'mimic' the cryptology. Following a NATO Summit in Washington during 1978, the American, the British and the West German governments officially started a research programme in 1980 to replace the Mark 12. However, there are major snags. The Pentagon wanted a new system developed and in service towards the end of this decade. Yet it is now clear that the United States does not want to share the programme, nor does she intend to allow the European members of NATO to have a share in the technological advances the Americans are making or might make in this area. It seems very likely that the project will end with the Americans once again going their way and the Europeans having to decide to buy American or build their own version. Whatever happens, it is yet another example of the lack of co-operation, whatever the fine words laid out in NATO communiqués.

Some projects are likely to go ahead in other fields and there is a general recognition that many of them will succeed. In some cases they have already done so. There is something called the NATO Family of Weapons concept. It sees a lot of the old animosities being set aside and both sides of the Atlantic getting together to build either the same weapon system, or complected systems. The biggest problem is likely to be the reluctance of some groups or countries to transfer the technology to others.

Another problem for NATO planners is the lack of cost control in any one country, which makes joint production that more difficult. Inflation in the United States, for example, has meant soaring costs in such projects as the Aegis cruiser, the XM-1 tank and the Satellite Communications system. Many countries have companies that are trying hard to avoid cost spirals and also to reach understandings with their opposite numbers in other nations. The American corporation, Martin Marietta, who are involved in the MX, the Pershing II missile and the Copperhead weapon programme, is a good example of a company recognising the need to tie in with European firms. But, too often, even people like Martin Marietta are bound by jealousies within their own country's administration and Services.

For all this, NATO is in much better shape than it was during the mid 1970s. The Long Term Defence Programme agreed during 1978 has at least presented guidelines for planners and governments alike. But it still has a long way to go in order to get basic concepts right. Communication systems that are unlikely to survive the first few hours of war, a supply line that runs north and south through NATO's front line and is therefore obviously vulnerable, a continuing reliance on long runways which will inevitably be badly damaged or even destroyed during a war, a weak electronic warfare system (including jamming and anti-jamming equipment) and a need for major reassessments on industrial co-operation are just a few of the problems.

Interestingly enough, one of the weaknesses so often reported is the lack of numbers compared with the Warsaw Pact's vast military machine. But those numbers are often deceptive for a reason not yet stated.

It is perfectly true that NATO is outnumbered in most areas. But, if one takes the Central Region of Europe, the area in which any conventional war would most likely be fought if for no other reason than that is where most of the forces are concentrated, the picture is not at all to NATO's disadvantage. For although NATO remains outnumbered, it is the one place where the numbers game becomes the most most questionable of sports.

If there were to be a surprise war, a 'come-as-you-are' affair, then it is doubtful if the Warsaw Pact forces would get very far. Overall, the Warsaw Pact would retain its advantage, perhaps a ratio of about 1.3 to 1. Yet military wisdom suggests that an attacker needs at least a three to one advantage if he is to win along a broad front. Now, as the Israelis have shown, it is possible to be outnumbered and win by launching surprise and concentrated assaults on one or two key areas, thus leaving the perhaps larger forces stranded and even impotent. It is also true that NATO's forces are scattered, perhaps too much so. Yet the broad European war that may be envisaged does not lend much to the argument that the Warsaw Pact forces could be *easily* at the Channel ports within days.

If there were to be a build-up of, say, a week or ten days, the picture might not alter that much from the Warsaw Pact point of view, although it would certainly test to the full the American, Canadian and British reinforcement plans. The biggest Soviet advantage might be in the gathering of their tactical air forces, and this could be crucial. But, even with two or three weeks' warning and build-up, there still might not be that much of a numerical advantage to the Eastern bloc nations. It is, of course, a complex tactical point of argument and one which should not be examined too closely without the analyses of each side's capabilities for reinforcement, movement, support and military philosophy. It is, however, a point that equally should not be left out when the stark graphics are drawn to illustrate the military balance.

And, today, it does not take into consideration what weapons might be deployed not only on the battlefield of tomorrow but high above it. And tomorrow might only be in the mid-1980s.

SIX

Future Weapons

Since World War One, military science has developed from a machine-gunning biplane, to the submarine fantasia of Jules Verne, to the controlled explosion of a nuclear weapon, to a journey to the moon and back without catastrophe, to the ability to send the deadliest of warheads into space and then back again to strike within a few feet of an enemy target. Yet it is the simple that seizes the imagination. For example, it is no longer remarkable that man can send a satellite into space. The fact that he can tell that satellite to eject a small package of film and then send up a plane to catch it in mid-air as it tumbles towards earth does seem extraordinary. But it is a technique used for many years.

If one considers the remarkable advances made in aviation, nautical and ground technology by the military, it may appear slightly ludicrous that any future war would begin in space. Yet it is precisely these more earthly technological advances that have made space battle not only more likely, but even necessary. The vastness of the East and West military blocs demonstrates that war might well be fought on a grander scale than ever before. Furthermore, the idea that such a conflict could continue for years on end, as was the case with the Second World War, seems outdated.

A major conflict, over a short period of time, relying to some extent on surprise and, initially, on rapid territorial and strategic advances, would need a great deal of management at every level. Nor would the course of the confrontation alter the almost inevitable clashes in space during the opening stages. It would make no difference if the war were fought in a conventional manner or opened immediately with an inter-continental ballistic missile attack. To grasp why this is so, it is worthwhile going over the obvious elements in any commander's Intelligence brief if he is to be fully prepared to attack or defend. He must have some good idea of his enemy's strengths, weaknesses, capabilities and readiness. He must know exactly where his enemy is and the size and composition of those forces. He needs to know where the tanks are, what supplies have been coming through, whether aircraft have left their normal bases and dispersed to alternative airfields, whether there is an unusual amount of signal traffic, what reserves are mobilised and where they are being sent. His naval staff will want to know if ships are putting to sea in unusually large numbers and what support vessels are going with them or being pre-positioned. He will also be interested in knowing if major towns are being evacuated, a sign perhaps that the authorities are preparing for air-raids. He will wish to have a good idea of the lengths of his enemy's supply lines and how much activity is going on in them. Are train services, for example, being cancelled to clear lines for military railway units? The commander will even wish to know what the weather is like; the immediate weather reports, the medium- and long-term reports, will be essential especially to his air commanders, many of whom will not have the aircraft capable of operating in bad weather conditions.

If a war does start, and it begins with a conventional phase, then the commander will need constant updating on all these vital matters and will want it quickly. The way in which a Soviet division moves provides a good example of how an area picture might change during a twenty-four-hour period – even before an engagement. A Soviet division of, say, about 12,000 men with tanks and armoured vehicles would probably advance along a front of something like twenty-five kilometres. It will do so perhaps along three different routes and the whole division could easily keep going for some time at about fifteen kilometres every hour. Some elements will move more quickly and other elements will be detached from the main force. Its reconnaissance unit, for instance, might be fifty kilometres ahead of the main group. The Western commander will need to know how far the reconnaissance group is ahead, how far behind are such tell-tale units as chemical warfare detachments, and whether the artillery groups are also well forward so that they can be quickly deployed. He will want to know how the enemy is protecting the advance by putting out patrols on the route's flanks.

He will also need information about his own units. This may sound far-fetched; after all an allied commander should be precisely briefed on where his own men and equipment are. But, in the preparations for a battle, this may be quite difficult. He will of course know the locations of the pre-positioned forces such as the US 7th Army in Europe and, let us say, the Fourth British Division in West Germany. But reinforcements may be experiencing all manner of problems joining up, supply lines may be broken through transport difficulties even before a conflict begins. The commander will need to talk to his own side, but securely, and he will need to negotiate the probable electronic jamming put out by the enemy.

All this is but a small part of the needs of the overall commander. Some of the information, especially on preparations, is easily come by. In the period leading up to any conflict, much of it would be readily available. Political tension, monitored radio broadcasts, countries closing air space to civilian flights, and diplomatic reports would give the commander a considerable amount of information. But, on the day, he and his staff would rely almost exclusively on electronic intelligence gathering systems – and most of these are airborne.

So we have the commander asking a few basic questions: how and where is the enemy deployed, what is he doing at this precise moment, what is he likely to do during the next twelve and twenty-four hours, what state are my own forces in to counter any attack, and will there be any unexpected reasons why I cannot enact the plans I have made during the past few years? On this last point, it could be that the weather would close in, making an air attack on enemy lines almost impossible. The intelligence picture needs to be as broad as possible and quickly obtained. To do all this, the commander, whether he be military or political, will rely on high-flying reconnaissance jets and, more importantly, satellites.

It has been estimated that some 70 per cent of the satellites launched have a military value. The first satellite was launched in 1957, but it had long been recognised that such a craft was the essential element in any military form of early warning and communications.[1]

The invention of the aeroplane meant that man no longer had to climb the highest tree, clutching an eyepiece, for an assessment of an enemy's positions. Yet it was not until the shooting down of Gary Powers' U-2 jet during the 1950s that many people realised that spying-in-the-sky was considered to be an essential peacetime as well as wartime occupation.

Today the United States operates three types of aerial reconnaissance aircraft. The RC-135 flies at 600 m.p.h. at a height of more than 40,000 feet. By using air-to-air refuelling, it can stay aloft for long periods, sending back information not only to the Department of Defense in Washington but to its guardian, the Strategic Air Command in Nebraska. Once analysed, that information is used to draw up such things as target lists. The Strategic Air Command also runs two other aircraft, the U-2 and the SR-71, known as the Blackbird. The U-2 is not a fast jet by any means, it operates at speeds of little more than 400 m.p.h., but then speed is not the prime requirement. It has an almost glider-like capability and its prime function might well be to loiter some 70,000 feet above an area while its pilot gathers intelligence data. Faster and high-climbing interceptors and surface-to-air missiles make the U-2 vulnerable, as Gary Powers discovered. So did Major Rudolph Anderson Jr. In a less well known

1. See documentation produced by the Stockholm International Peace Research Institute, in particular research by Dr Bhupendra Jasani.

U-2 incident, Major Anderson was shot down over Cuba by surface-to-air missiles towards the end of October 1962. He had been monitoring the area at the time of the Cuban missile crisis.

The most spectacular of the recce aircraft is the SR-71. It has been in service since 1966 yet is still classified as the most advanced aircraft of its kind. It flies at more than 2,000 m.p.h. and at heights in excess of 80,000 feet. (To give some idea of what it means to travel at these speeds at altitude, a rifle bullet is not so quick.) It does, however, need forward bases, which is why the Blackbird is a frequent visitor to Europe, where it operates from British air bases run by the United States Air Force.

Impressive and valuable as these aircraft are, they do not match the gathering power of the satellite. The aircraft are flying up to 80,000 feet. A reconnaissance satellite will be nearly 500,000 feet, or something more than ninety-three miles, high. As the man with his eyeglass would point out, the higher the tree, the more you might see. However, the increased height may give a broader field of vision, but it does present problems when it comes to focussing and recording the earth. Yet, given the right conditions, the photographic satellite can obtain a good picture of thousands of square miles of the earth in one photographic frame. Some platforms, such as the American Skylab system, have returned good pictures from more than 270 miles high. By good pictures, we are not simply talking about clear definitions of runways and cities. Aerial photo-reconnaissance began with what the Services still wish to refer to as the Mark I Eyeball. A pilot would come back and say what he had seen. If he was lucky, he would be able to photograph the ground. Of major importance was the introduction of the stereoscope which allowed the interpreters to measure heights of buildings by using nothing more than what may easily be described as a pair of stereo spectacles mounted in a wooden or brass frame. A known object, for instance, a lorry or a well-documented building, was picked out and, with that as a scale, everything else in the picture was related to the height of the known object. Having built the stereo, or 3-D picture, a reasonably accurate intelligence dossier could be established. It would, for example, be important for a bombing mission to know the height and therefore perhaps the thickness of an enemy hangar, or an undercover dockyard where a submarine or a frigate might have been built or fitted out. Knowing the strength of a target determined to some extent the types and number of bombs to be carried; this in turn could determine the numbers of aircraft needed on the mission.

Satellite observation allows for the same information to be gathered but, as we have seen, it increases the range of intelligence, especially when more modern techniques are used. Satellite sensors are able to operate in what is commonly known as the electro-magnetic spec-trum. They pick up electro-magnetic wave-lengths and infra-red wave-lengths.

Being able to monitor heat or energy has tremendous advantages for aerial intelligence analysts. It is even possible to tell whether or not a missile is armed with a nuclear warhead. Fly a satellite across an enemy airfield and it can, of course, record the number of aircraft on the base. If its ability to pick up heat radiation is used, it can do far, far more than that. What may appear to be an empty runway or parking apron may reveal quite important intelligence. An aircraft parked on an apron or at the end of the runway with its engines running will 'heat' the concrete on which it stands. For some time after the aircraft has left, the concrete will remain 'warm', not necessarily to the touch but certainly to the satellite's eyes. As it scans the empty runway, the satellite will record the white outline of the aircraft where it it has been standing before take-off. Therefore the intelligence man knows how many jets are normally parked, where they park, and to some extent how long ago they left. The sensitivity of the satellite instruments is further demonstrated in tests that have been going on in the United States for some time. For the MX ballistic nuclear missile to be successfully hidden from the Soviet Union, part of the programme calls for an empty missile casing to be trundled along the site roads. The idea is that the Soviet Union's reconnaissance satellites will not know for sure that the big transpor-ter is carrying a missile or an empty case, and therefore will not know which silos contain the armed missiles and therefore will have difficulty in working out a Soviet targeting programme to destroy the MX before it can be fired. According to the engineers at the MX Test Bed at Lathrop Wells in Nevada, the Soviet satellites are so good they would be able to tell if the case were empty or not because they could detect the difference a full case would make on the pressures on the tyres of the transporter, the strain on the engine, and the heat pattern left on the roadway as the loaded transporter goes along. Conse-quently, they are having to carry out tests to disguise tyre pressures and engine strain in an attempt to fool the satellite sensors.

It is claimed that a satellite can tell if a building is occupied or not because it can pick up the increased heat, or energy, radiation from human bodies. All this may be very impressive, but the problem is to get that information back to the people who need it, usually in a hurry. A satellite is able to take in signals and photograph areas and then develop them, read the signals and transmit them to ground stations.

This process only seems normal in such a technologically advanced system. But for some years ground commanders have been able to recover the photographs taken by the satellite's cameras through canisters ejected by the space craft. The Americans have a satellite called Big Bird. The advantage of Big Bird is that it does the job of what used to be two satellites. At one time it was necessary to have one satellite taking pictures over a wide area, with all the intelligence limitations, and a second craft to photograph the particular detail that was of interest to the ground controllers. Big Bird manages to carry out what are known as area surveillance tasks and send the broad information back to earth by radio signals. But Big Bird also carries six capsules for the film, containing the information requiring perhaps closer examination. The ejection operation is relatively simple. The satellite remains in orbit and, as it passes a predetermined point, often over the sea, it ejects one of the capsules containing the film. The capsule, using its own propulsion, will re-enter for its descent to earth, signalling as it does so and being closely monitored along the way. When it is about nine miles or so above the earth, the capsule opens its own parachute and continues to 'flash' its radio beacon which is not only identifying it to the ground control but allows the control to monitor the line of descent. Just above the surface, a specially-fitted cargo plane, often the Hercules, will fly to meet the signal and a twin cable will be paid out from the plane. It is this cable that will catch the falling capsule and its important cargo. For an ocean drop, there is a ship and helicopter on stand-by; recovery may be similar to the technique used for returning astronauts with the helicopter picking up the capsule from its splash-down point.

But a satellite has to do far more than take pictures. Just as it was necessary for the bomber commander to know the strength of the target so that he could plan his raid with greater accuracy, so the intelligence officer must play his part in making as sure as possible that the bomber will stand some chance of getting through. Spotting enemy surface-to-air missile sites is relatively simple. Picking out their associated radars is not more difficult. What is more of a problem is to establish the effectiveness of those radars. A surface-to-air missile is virtually worthless without its radar which picks up the target and than tracks it for the missile. Therefore the intelligence officer wants to know how far out the radar can effectively 'see' and what signals it uses. Once he knows that, the analyst is able to help the technical experts design electronic counter measures (ECM). A modern bomber pilot does not simply go for a target given him by the raid planners. He will have on board a series of gadgets which will attempt to jam, among other things, enemy radars. When the enemy turns on his radar, it shines just like a torch. As mentioned earlier, the trick is to put out that 'light'. (Looking at a picture of a bomber, even the older type, many of the bumps and small pieces of angled metal on the fuselage will be ECM fittings.) The satellite's ability to identify or double-check known information about radar frequencies and bands is essential to the military planner.

These are specific tasks for the satellite. It will also provide the commander with the broader picture, which is equally important. Establishing that the Soviet armoured division is deployed in a certain position is relatively simple. Equally, the Soviet commander will have no problem establishing where the British or American counter-division is based. Both sides will have a very accurate idea of the hardware in the opposing divisions. They will, long before, have made up their own minds as to the efficiency of that equipment, the manpower and the efficiency of the division as an operating unit. Both sides keep records of opposing units. When, for example, the Royal Air Force newspaper records that such-and-such a squadron has achieved peak efficiency and has won some bombing trophy, this is immediately recorded. The fact that, during the 1980 reinforcement exercises, British reserve forces were said to be extremely tired by the time they arrived at their forward units on the Continent will have been noted in Moscow just as keenly as it was in Whitehall. In all, the Soviet commander will want to have some idea how capable the Western soldier is to operate the equipment given him and for how long. Both sides, therefore, will have had the opportunity to build up a reasonably sound picture of the deployed troops and equipment. What the satellite might be able to tell at any one time is what back-up those forces have available. The first indication that reinforcements are being moved towards the battle area may well come from a satellite. More importantly, it may also be able to tell, from the composition and route of the reinforcing group, for which front line unit it is heading.

Gathering this information is not the difficult side of the operation. There are restrictions on the satellite sensors, some of which are not easily overcome. Some sensors have problems getting through bad weather to photograph clearly what is going on on the ground. Certainly, infra-red photography, which produces what is called a line scan, is not the answer to every intelligence-gatherer's prayers. There is also an operational question mark over exactly where the satellite is going to be, although today the orbital dynamics present few problems and a satellite passing over the area of interest about every hour and a half will give good coverage. Furthermore, if the satellite is simply fired into circular orbit when it is at its furthest point away from the earth, the craft can be put into what appears to be the same position over the earth's equator. The technology, then, is not excessively difficult. What is a problem is getting the various ground agencies to analyse that information and then forward it to the military commanders in time for them to make good use of it. Which leads to the general matter of communications.

One of the most efficient ways for ground units to communicate is by bouncing signals from a satellite, as anybody who has ever watched live television coverage will have noticed. On the battlefield, or at sea, this is extraordinarily important. Naval commanders will get constant fixes of their positions, Cruise missile operators will rely on satellites for feeds to the missiles' brains, and battle commanders will be able to talk to their different units. It is worth remembering one of the favourite themes propounded by General Richard H. Ellis, as Commander in Chief of the United States Strategic Air Command. He has long believed that, if the West is to have a reliable means of communicating between the crucial commanders – those at the highest political and strategic levels – as well as those in charge of nuclear forces, then there is a vital need for a survivable system of command, control and communications (C^3) in space. The important word is survivable.

The world is moving more and more to rely on these satellite systems. To be able to identify the military problem, communicate that problem and then to relay the counter-action, has become the role of the so-called space-based unit. Therefore, the initial task of any commander at the outset of war is to knock out those satellites.

The theory is that satellites may be destroyed either from the earth or from space. As far back as the early 1960s, the United States looked at a programme for intercepting and then destroying enemy satellite systems. Working on the principle that it has long been relatively simple to match up two space-craft for a docking operation, the technique had to be developed to manoeuvre the American craft so that it could close on another space craft which might well be taking evading action. The crudest form of intercept would be to get another satellite to crash into the enemy instrument. It has also been considered that firing missiles armed with conventional or nuclear warheads would be a very capable way of dealing with the matter. Whatever the form of wizardry this may represent in the current art of missile engineering, it must be considered at the very best to be crude as a form of warfare. The future for outer space, and perhaps even the more earthly weapon systems, would seem to be in the research work now going on in the United States and the Soviet Union into laser and particle beam weapons. The more sensational reports of the development of Death Rays may be forgiven when the potential effectiveness of these systems is considered. If that appears to be a little arrogant, it is not intentional. The complicated science and engineering for laser and particle beam research defies most people's understanding of what appears to be the most important weapon development since the nuclear warhead. Without attempting to elaborate the technical progress, it is worth looking at the basic principles involved and to see why these weapons are not so far beyond belief as many have supposed.

Laser should really be written LASER. It stands for Light Amplification by the Stimulated Emission of Radiation. But like radar (Radio and Ranging) Laser is common usage and represents to most people a brilliant beam of light.[1] And that is, more or less, what it is. Laser beams work through the electro-magnetic radiation spectrum and show up as equal wave-lengths. The obvious difference – to the layman at least – between what might be called ordinary light and a laser beam is that the latter is more intense. In very simple terms, all the scientist and engineer has to do is produce a power source that will repeatedly 'energise' atoms and molecules. The atoms will throw out radiation including light for a very brief moment and then return to their original state. But, if they can be captured and agitated as soon as they are in this 'energised' state, the atoms will continue to throw out an energy beam of light, which of course is the laser.

The laser is normally produced in three ways, either through intense light exciting the atoms and molecules in a crystal; sending a current through a semi-conductor; or, thirdly, by passing a very high voltage through a tube of gas. Much of the work going on to test the military application is concentrating on rare gas halogen lasers (the halogens include chlorine, iodine and fluorine), hydrogen fluoride chemical lasers and what are known as free electron lasers.

The other weapon is the particle beam system. The most commonly discussed is the charged particle beam which is just about what it says it is – high-energy particles such as protons or electrons. The problem of inducing such high energy is just as difficult with particle beam systems as it is with lasers, perhaps more so. The machinery, the accelerators, needed to produce the energy supply tend to be enormous. They certainly do not add up to the gimmicky laser demonstrations shown at trade fairs. Future work in the United States on the laser and the neutral particle beam weapons should be pushing ahead as quickly as possible if the United States wishes to attempt to catch up with the work done in the Soviet Union.

It is clear that the Soviet leadership recognised some time ago the importance of space-based systems such as the intelligence satellites discussed earlier. It is equally obvious that the American leadership

---

1. The Romans, however, used the word laser to describe a particularly resinous gum – but not the chewing kind.

was not able to think clearly in terms of future weapons, otherwise they would have recognised the same pointers as had the Soviet Union. What is more disturbing is the fact that, even when the Washington decision-makers were given the signs, they did not accept them. Major General George J. Keegan, one-time head of US Air Force Intelligence, is said to have retired in protest against the Pentagon's refusal to accept the fact that his Foreign Technology Division was right when it presented intelligence evaluations pointing to a growing Soviet lead in the area of beam weapons.[1] The general, in many ways an uncompromising figure, was not out on his own in this matter; but his stand on what he believed to be the correct assessments from his intelligence system illustrates to some degree a tendency, in the more senior elements in Western military and political leadership, to ignore weather forecasts until they get wet.

General Keegan and others were trying to convince senior Pentagonians, and therefore those further up the ladder, that the Soviet Union was getting far ahead in the area of particle beams. They were also convinced that, unless the United States did something about catching up, then the US higher command would wake one morning to find they were still living in the comic book world of laser and particle beam battle stations in space, whereas the Soviet Union would be sitting up there cocking a snook – and possibly a trigger – at Washington. At the same time, there were various private and government research programmes in the United States and in other parts of the Western Alliance. But most of the work was, and is, concentrated in the United States. The inability to grasp the importance of the military implications probably meant that much of the defence research was really a spin-off from industrial applications, although the Navy's Chair Heritage and what the Army now calls White Horse were two excellent projects in particle beam technology. There has also been a question of funding. Not even the big spending of the US Department of Defense is able to cope with every single project, and perhaps the case for this kind of research was not presented with the right military, political and commercial options. The upshot was that the projects that did exist carried on producing excellent work, but slowly and without the necessary direction from Washington. What is extraordinary is that, until the end of the 1970s, few in the West were able to believe how far advanced the Soviet Union was and how far behind were the Western experiments.

It is now accepted that the Soviet Union has an operational carbon dioxide-based laser that could knock out the sensors on board the American Big Bird Satellite.

1. See in particular *Aviation Week & Space Technology*, 28 July 1980.

The American work is generally co-ordinated under the mantle of an organisation known as DARPA, the Defense Advanced Research Projects Agency. So, while the Navy has its Chair Heritage programme at the Lawrence Livermore Laboratory in California and the Army its White Horse project at Los Alamos, DARPA is the guiding hand. Their research, coupled with similar programmes and what is known of the Soviet project at the Kazakhstan test site close to the Sino-Soviet border, shows that the great disadvantage for anybody not up to speed in particle beam technology is that, as a weapon system, it produces so much energy that no counter-measure is yet possible.

While it is believed that lasers could be deflected, it will take decades to produce an antidote to particle beam weapons. Many believe that is a forlorn hope. So what has woken the American mind to the urgency to get into the laser and particle beam programme?

Of all the reasons put forward in Washington, perhaps three or four stand out. Having built a spectacular array of space-based early warning, reconnaissance and communication systems, the West now recognises that these same wonders of technology are not only priority targets but also vulnerable ones. In other words, space has become the front line. From that, it has followed that the realisation that the Soviet Union is already up to taking out at least part of the front line means that the potential enemy has the upper hand, which it would take an almost superhuman effort to better. There is also an understanding that these future weapons need not be limited to attacks on satellite systems.

A Directed Energy Weapon (DEW) orbiting in space may well be capable of knocking out manned bombers, certainly the rather slow and large American B-52s and even the faster F1-11s both of which, as we have seen, will carry a large percentage of the West's nuclear capability. Nor do ground-launched ballistic missiles escape the eagle eye of the Directed Energy Weapon system. It has long been recognised that ICBMs are vulnerable to attack in their silos, but it is also conceivable that they can be knocked out in flight. Finally, the gathering together of a number of different programmes under DARPA's roof has given the whole project a badly needed boost. Whether or not sufficient funds will be pumped in is another matter. At the same time, it should not be thought that the United States is so far behind that she is running about like some headless scientific chicken clutching an empty test-tube. One of the problems is producing a high energy source for these beam weapons. It is reported that the Lawrence Livermore Laboratory has designed a device that would have a small nuclear unit at the hub of a cartwheel of fifty lasers. The result is that the nuclear energy would be transmitted along the laser beam at the target. According to research carried out by Clarence A. Robinson Jr and Philip J. Klauss, these devices could be placed in orbit within two or three years of being given the production go-ahead. They would be used as a defence against ballistic missiles which, in theory, they could engage at distances of more than 4,600 miles.

The advantages of Directed Energy Weapons are obvious. Lasers can deliver their corpuscles of light at the speed of light, and particle beams transmit their energy at near the same speed. Consequently, once the target is spotted, a straight aim is all that is needed. There are no requirements to 'lead' the target, to anticipate where it will be when the 'bullets' reach the area. From this it follows that either beam is a supremely accurate weapon with a 'first hit' capability; consequently targets could be disposed of more quickly and with great economy. It might also follow that, once the system is space-based, then as long as the energy source could be maintained the directed energy weapon would have a greater number of shots in its 'magazine'.

One problem not often considered is that of giving the beam weapon a method of spotting, identifying and then tracking a target. In the United States work in this area is going on under the code-name of Talon Gold, and, once scientists have managed to get their claws into the monitoring and tracking difficulties, they will have eliminated a problem that has long dogged the more conventional processes of weapon design. It might be noted that it is not necessary for a space-based weapon to destroy a satellite or incoming missile; there is no need for a comic-strip-type blinding flash as the target vapourises or is turned into so much white space dust. However crude the ultimate mission of a satellite or missile, it must be remembered that the systems which control that mission are extraordinarily sensitive. So all that is needed is a weapon that can immobilise. An example of this is the Soviet laser unit. It appears to be quite capable of destroying the layered lens coating in an American satellite – and what good is a blind satellite? A beam switched to a missile should be capable of puncturing the missile's skin. Perhaps the guidance system will burn out. It is also possible that a sufficiently damaged skin will render the missile aerodynamically unsound, therefore unstable and therefore unlikely to fulfil its mission. There have of course been occasions when a damaged space vehicle has continued on its way even though part of its outer coating was damaged, so the prime requirement is to use the beam weapon for rapid military surgery on the weapon's brain.

The beam weapon must be able to identify a target very quickly. In the case of a missile, the Directed Energy Weapon must be able to spot the missile within seconds of its being launched, track it until it gets into range and then not only hit it, but also recognise when enough damage had been done so that the beam may be directed to another target. In an extreme case, there may be something like 2,000 missiles aimed either at the West or the Eastern-bloc nations. Beam weapons may be asked to cope with ten per cent of that number. Therefore a further requirement of the tracking and aiming system is that it can decide for itself the front-runners, those missiles represent-ing the more immediate threat. And the DEWs would not only have to deal with manned bombers, missiles and the need to knock out an enemy's conventional satellite systems, they would need to be capable of defending their own satellites and themselves. A space-based system for the West to attack and defend satellites would probably mean somewhere in the region of ten 'battle groups' of beam weapons in orbit. If they were to act as anti-ballistic missile units, at least twice that number would have to be in orbit.

This is clearly a massive project, especially when the difficulty of providing the energy supply is emphasised. It could of course be possible to base a laser power-pack on earth and perhaps reflect the beam from some orbiting mirror. However, the most desirable solution is to put the whole system in space, even with manned space stations to command and control the operation. The Soviet Union seems way ahead in this area and the importance to the American Department of Defense of the much-delayed space shuttle system is obvious.

Some experts believe the United States could have high energy chemical lasers in orbit to defend their satellites by the mid-1980s. To the military strategists what is disturbing is that because of the American failure to recognise the importance of this area of research, the so-called space battle stations they believe to be vital to the whole project, will not be ready for operation until the 1990s. They also believe the neutral particle beam programme to be about ten years behind.

There are those who say this is excellent news. Rightly or wrongly, some believe that none of these systems should be deployed because space should be retained as a neutral zone. Worse still, runs the argument, by placing all these systems in orbit – even the simple programme of satellite defence lasers during this decade – the chances of war are greatly increased. That reasoning is partly based on the understanding that satellites fulfil a desirable function if used to verify such things as strategic arms treaties, promises not to build new weapon systems, and the monitoring of nuclear tests and basic troop movements. The reasoning continues that, if a satellite is jammed by one side, as communications were in Europe shortly before the Soviet intervention in Czechoslovakia during 1968, then the opposing government may over-react. There is another argument put forward against the development of space battle stations. It is simply that some people believe it is wrong to extend military capabilities to yet another area. This is taken a stage further by the claim that, because it would be remote, war in space may become 'acceptable' and therefore likely and therefore may descend to earth. Some of the arguments are valid, and there have been occasions when international scientific and political bodies have refused to allow them to be raised during formal discussions on the uses of outer space. Whatever the objections and whatever the technical difficulties to be overcome, space-based beam weapon systems, although in their primitive state, are on their way. It will not be long before analyses such as the responsible International Institute for Strategic Studies' Military Balance will be listing them as legitimate weapon systems to be cautiously assessed by war-gamers and scenario-builders by the middle of this decade.

But, before they do grapple with these systems, there will have to be, perhaps within the next couple of years or so, a re-evaluation of a more controversial group of weapons: those coming under the loose heading of Chemical Warfare (CW). It may sound ludicrous to classify chemical weapons as future armaments, considering that they were used on such a large scale during the First World War. One hundred thousand troops died after chemical attacks during that conflict and it has been estimated that there were one million three hundred thousand casualties. The first recorded use of chemicals was not, as many believe, by the Germans, but by the French. Shortly after the war started in 1914, the French used a crude form of tear gas grenade. Although they did not get much further, this not only started the general use of these new weapons, it signalled the beginning of the development by France of CW weapons which continues to this day. However, within a few months of the French action, the Germans launched an attack using a chlorsulphate against British forces in France and then shortly after that a bromide form on the Russian Front. These were crude attempts and showed how important it was for anybody using this form of warfare to be able to contain the chemical agents in some easily handled form, to get the right 'mix', so that dispersal would not be overcome by extremes of temperature; and equally important, should pick the right wind conditions so that the agents would not be blown back on the attacking troops. It was in April 1915 that the Germans launched what is generally recognised as the first major chemical attack. More than 500 drums of a chlorine gas were released over a four-mile front close to the town of Ypres. There were about 15,000 casualties. A third of them died. Five months later, the British retaliated with a chlorine attack at Loos and then in December of 1915 the Germans introduced phosgene, a lethal agent which attacks the lungs.

Eighteen months later, the most infamous of the World War One chemical agents was used. Again at Ypres, the Germans launched a mustard gas attack. Mustard gas (dichloroethylsulphide) in many forms is difficult to see and smell. It burns the skin, irritates the lungs and, when the doses are large, at the very least produces incapacitating blisters and, at the other extreme, kills. By the end of the Great War, more than 100,000 tons of chemical agents had been used. During the aftermath of that war the world began to view the development of this form of weaponry with the same sort of alarm shown towards nuclear power in the 1950s.

In 1925 a protocol was signed in Geneva outlawing the use of chemical weapons. Some signatories declared their reservations by reserving the right to use CW if it was used against them. Some countries have treated the 1925 Protocol with a certain contempt, believing that, if it were felt necessary, chemical weapons would be used however the Geneva document read. (The United States, for example, did not ratify the 1925 Protocol until fifty years later.) The document did not stop people stockpiling such weapons and it certainly did not stop development work. By the 1930s, the Germans had made great advances in this area and produced a formula for nerve gases. Chemical weapons include nerve gases. Their main feature is their ability to attack the muscular system. Acetylchlorine renders the muscles useless to varying degrees and generally results in a failure in co-ordination and therefore a collapse of the whole body.

The first effect of a gas attack would be a distortion of the eyesight and at the same time vomiting and breathing difficulties. As the muscles are attacked, the victim would have no control over normal bodily functions such as bowels and respiratory muscles, and the result is asphyxiation.

Defenders of the 1925 Protocol claim that it prevented either side using CW during the Second World War. This may be so. It is also possible that tactically it never made sense; or equally that the Germans wrongly assumed that the Allies had developed nerve gases – which they had not. Possibly nobody wanted to initiate that kind of war.

By the end of the Second World War, both the French and the Americans were determined to continue with their experiments, work was going on in the United Kingdom, and the Soviet Union had captured a German nerve gas plant manufacturing an agent called Tabun. The Americans were concentrating on producing Sarin which had the doubtful advantage of being more toxic than Tabun. British laboratory work managed to come up with a substance 'better' than Sarin. It is now under the general heading of V-agent. There are six or so lethal chemical agents: the two nerve gases VX and Sarin; two which attack the blood, cyanogen chloride and hydrogen cyanide; phosgene which affects the lungs, and the blister agent, mustard gas. The chemistry and the engineering for these weapons is relatively simple. It is certainly easier to come by than information about who has what when it comes to counting the international chemical stockpiles. An indication of the political, rather than the military, sensitivity surrounding CW is the fact that more information is freely available on nuclear weapons than on chemical weapons. Considering the latter have been in use since 1915, this secrecy may seem remarkable.

It is generally accepted that the Soviet Union had a large chemical warfare capability. One estimate given to the author suggests that at least 100,000 Soviet troops are trained in the use of chemical weapons. Other estimates, some of them in official documents found in Washington, put this number at 60,000. It is very unlike the Americans to underestimate, for public consumption, Soviet capabilities, especially if there is a willing audience; it could be that this is nothing more than a ball-park figure. There may also be some confusion, over the role of these troops. There have been some pictures showing Soviet troops exercising in 'Noddy' suits – the protective clothing developed for troops caught in a chemical environment. The photographs have often shown the soldiers washing down tanks and other vehicles as if they had been subjected to a chemical attack. This does not mean, of course, that they are Chemical Warfarers. British and other Western troops are often seen dressed in similar clothing and going through similar routines, but nobody in the West suggests they are special chemical attack troops.

However, the Soviet Union does have special troops for CW actions and it does seem likely that Chemical Weapons are held at regimental level. To the Soviet higher command, with its often uncomplicated military thinking, chemical warfare is a legitimate part of modern battle planning. As CW may be used in some future conflict, it is inconceivable to that mind that preparations should not be made, not only to cope with any attack, but to initiate an attack if necessary.

The United Kingdom is showing active interest in Chemical Weapons, Perhaps this is a misleading statement inasmuch that Britain has never lost interest in them. She has always held limited stocks. Since about 1957, they have been largely if not entirely experimental as a means of developing protective clothing and warning equipment for troops in a battlefield. Britain is thought to be far ahead of the rest of the NATO members in this area and certainly far advanced in any antichemical warfare measures the Soviet Union has deployed. In 1980, the British government departed from its official line of CW development as a 'purely protective measure'. Gentle steps are being taken to prepare British public opinion for the United Kingdom's active participation in a NATO Chemical Warfare capability. This will take place in tandem with the United States, the only member of NATO holding large stocks of these weapons. There are something in the region of 42,000 tons of CW agents stockpiled by the United States. Most of it is old forms of mustard gas, the remainder is Sarin and VX nerve gases. Like the Soviet Union, the United States had deployed her chemical agents in mortars, multi-barrelled rocket-launchers, land mines, aircraft and missiles. One report in Washington, accepted by experts in the Pentagon, describes the total nerve gas weaponry of the United States as 'about 130,000 tons'. The greater part of the CW stockpile is three million or so nerve gas projectiles for 155 mm and eight inch artillery shells. Other weapons include 160-gallon spray tanks and 500 pound chemical bombs for aircraft. The same Pentagon experts agree that the best place for the deployment of these aircraft would be West Germany and the United Kingdom. The United States has been forced into a major reconsideration on her CW deployment, and Britain's backing, especially at the NATO discussion table, has been extremely helpful.

The result is that, during the next couple of years, a weapon system of the past will become very much a weapon system of the future. But where will it be deployed? At the moment, the vast majority of chemical munitions are based in the United States at Anniston, Alabama; Newport, Indiana; Pueblo, Colorado; Denver, Colorado; Lexington, Kentucky; Tooele, Utah; Hermiston, Oregon; Edgewood, Maryland, and Pine Bluff, Arkansas. One report from the Utah complex shows four miles of nerve and mustard gas containers. There are also limited stocks on Johnston Island in the Pacific Ocean, and in West Germany. The American capability in Europe is confined to bases in West Germany. However, within the next few years, probably before the middle of the decade, chemical weapons will be stored over a wider area of the NATO countries. Other countries will be asked to provide storage facilities and some countries, perhaps the United Kingdom included, will want to have some control over those weapons. It is possible that Britain will want her own weapons. The deployment of American chemical weapons in Europe is likely to be even more unacceptable to public opinion and to some governments than was the relatively simple exercise of getting American Cruise missiles into continental Europe and the United Kingdom. There are those in NATO who had contemplated the idea of deploying the chemical weapons without telling anybody. This was turned down on the grounds that people would find out sooner or later. Part of the campaign to prepare public opinion has been to take every opportunity to tell the public how big and how dangerous is the Soviet Union's CW capability. It is doubtful whether this campaign has exaggerated the facts. What it has not done, so far at least, is to outline in some detail the West's existing capability in this field, including the location of stockpiles and the fact, for example, that aircraft with a CW capability regularly use British and West German bases.

If NATO does decide to expand its limited CW capability, then for military reasons it will be necessary to increase the European stockpile and to produce further training for troops, sailors and particularly air force personnel. Gas weapons will not be one-off affairs. The Germans learned this during that first major attack at Ypres. The German High Command did not have much faith in the new weapon. Consequently, there were few if any reserves of CW to follow up the undoubted advantage created by the assault on the Allies. Those who decide to allow the deployment of chemical weapons in Europe will have to realise that it cannot be done in any small way. There will be a need, at least a military need, to make sure the stockpiles are big enough for the Allies to go to war without having to rely on supplies crossing the Atlantic. They will have to be treated as any other tactical weapon that may be used to create an advantage during a battle. During the present political climate, it may turn out that the initial stockpiling will take place in the United Kingdom and West Germany. Although the West Germans have declared they will not have the weapons themselves, it may be that no real objections will be raised to their being based at American sites at Mainheim, Viernheim, Hannau, Massweiler and possibly Ramstein.

As with the introduction of Cruise missiles, Britain seems to be willing to take something of a European lead in the matter. It would, therefore, be difficult for the present Conservative government to reject suggestions that British bases should be provided for stockpiling. This is the situation in late 1981. It is difficult to believe that this likelihood will be reduced during the near future. It may be that a decision will have been taken by late 1981. Whether or not it is announced is, as ever, another matter.

There are perhaps two public concerns: safety and revulsion. Safety may be assured by the development of what is now called a binary nerve or chemical weapon. It is simple in its operation. Two seemingly innocuous agents are placed in, say, a missile warhead or an artillery shell. (The British government is about to buy from the Americans a gun suitable for carrying such warheads.) While in the live shell, these agents are separated. Once the shell is fired, a diaphragm collapses allowing the two agents to mix. Separately they have been virtually harmless. Together they become highly toxic. The argument runs that while the binary weapon is stored it remains harmless. It is certainly easier to handle although the overall safety is doubtful and, considering the numbers involved, security will be a major headache. One shell in the wrong hands would be horrific and consequently a new area for safeguards against terrorist intruders is raised.

In spite of all the problems of handling, storage and security, the argument for deployment will be forcefully made. Military commanders are convinced of the need, and some go as far as to create the link between chemical and nuclear weapons. During a 1979 European exercise called WINTEX, chemical weapons were introduced. The results of the exercise have never been published but one of its aspects illustrates the concern of the military. When the Soviets 'attacked' with Chemical Weapons, the war-gamers were asked how they would respond. The answer was simple: a warning was sent to Moscow to stop using CW weapons. When no response was forthcoming, the West retaliated with a tactical nuclear weapon. In that game, it was the beginning of nuclear war. So the commander will argue that, as the only Allied response to a chemical weapon is a nuclear weapon, there is a strong reason for building chemical stocks in the West.

There are two further points worth considering. Firstly, there are some commanders who believe that chemical weapons could be confined to the battlefield and that therefore only soldiers would suffer. This seems a generalisation, especially if the effects of wind conditions are considered, when a vapour may be carried many miles from the fighting. Nor does it cover the moral point of view, which must be considered. Secondly, it might be argued that chemical weapons carry the stigma of sixty-five years of horrific tale-telling, dating back to to the Ypres trenches. It is possible that people view CW as a nastier form of warfare than even nuclear weaponry, yet there is no comparison when it comes to assessing the likely effects of their use. It may even be that those who would not normally bother to protest against the nuclear bomb would feel moved to do so over the deployment of chemical weapons. None of this implies that one is more acceptable than the other, nor should it. What may be considered is that the terrible, if incomplete, memories and tales from World War One do not put the use of chemical weapons during that period in perspective. Their use was seen as a horrid interlude during a particularly gruesome war. Until there is a miraculous advance in instant medicine and the treatment of wounds, it is difficult for some to believe that there is anything else but gruesome war, and that one interval might well be equally as horrid as the last. It has also been argued that Chemical Weapons may be more, not less, humane than some of the more conventional methods man chooses for his soldiers. This might well have been the case during 1915. As one historian has noted, the chemical weapon was novel and therefore labelled an atrocity by a world which condones abuses but detests innovations.[1]

The same might be said about another weapon which will almost certainly be deployed by the West during the near future, but which in principle has been around for some time. The neutron bomb might easily go down as one of the more inept politico-military public relations jobs of all time. If the powers that often be had spent as much time thinking out the presentation of their case for this weapon as they have done on far more dangerous weapons, it might now be deployed instead of falling into the category of future weapons. The more correct term for neutron bomb in Enhanced Radiation Weapon, and it is this more accurate description that explains exactly what it might do. It was developed back in the 1950s and not in the mid-1970s as many understandably believe, for it was not until the 1970s that the United States began her foolish programme to supply it to her own armed forces. It became dubbed as the bomb that kills people but leaves buildings standing. Consequently, it immediately aroused those paradoxical emotions the general public tends to reserve for what it choose to believe are inhumane, or even unfair, weapons. (It is understandable that, for example, new guidance systems or fusing devices, which increase by astronomical amounts the chances of a more conventional weapon killing more people than it could previously have done, are not met with such outrage, indignation nor revulsion.) Although the description that it could kill people while leaving buildings standing was a misleading one, it carried enough truth to make it unlikely to be forgotten, especially when the so-called experts, called to qualify the popular descriptions, too often began with a phrase similar to 'Yes, but . . .'

Simply described, the Enhanced Radiaton Warhead is a mini-thermonuclear weapon which would cause most damage by pumping out gamma rays and, more importantly, neutron particles – hence the popular name of neutron bomb. As with all thermo-nuclear explosions, there has to be a bang. However, because the weapon itself is so small – perhaps less than a kiloton – the blast effect from the explosion is small. If it were ever used, the weapon would be detonated perhaps 400 feet or so above the ground. The mini-bomb would have such a small blast that not much on the ground would be drastically affected; but the radiation would be intense, and it would be that

1. See B. H. Liddell Hart's *History of the First World War*.

which would knock out enemy formations. All thermonuclear weapons would throw out the same gamma rays and neutron particles, but because the blast would be so much bigger in a more 'conventional' nuclear bomb, the devastating effect of the bang in the immediate area would mean that these radiations would have but academic interest. The idea for their use is quite simple: the warhead would be fired from perhaps a field gun or the business end of a short range missile. It would explode over the battlefield, when the radiation would kill off the troops below. In military terms it has the advantage of being able to destroy tank crews on a comparatively large scale without having to tie up large formations to do so, as is now the case. The tanks would not be knocked out by the radiation, and in theory could be re-crewed.

The Soviet Union became extremely worried about the deployment of the weapon when NATO talked of doing so towards the end of 1970s. The Soviet commanders had very good cause to be worried because the neutron or enhanced radiation weapon would, in theory, be devastating against the huge armoured divisions of the Warsaw Pact. There have been Intelligence reports indicating that the Soviet Union is reaching the stage where she too could deploy such a weapon. There have been few assessments made of the likelihood of the West being able to change Soviet minds and those of their satellites with the ease with which the Soviet Union managed to get the West to shelve its plans. Development work on the engineering for the weapon has continued in the United States, and there seems little military reason why the enhanced radiation and reduced blast weapon, or neutron bomb, or whatever the West wishes to call it, should not be deployed within the next couple of years – certainly before the middle of the decade.

It is likely that the middle of the 1980s will see the appearance of many 'new' weapons. At least they will be new to the battlefield. Chemical weapons will be deployed in the West, tentative steps will be taken to get the US anti-satellite system working in space and neutron will be ready for deployment in Europe. Cruise missiles should be making their first appearance in Europe, command control and communications procedures and equipment will have been greatly enhanced, and the Supreme Allied Commander Europe may be on the way to getting his own military intelligence system instead of having to rely on outside sources as he does now. (It is preposterous that SHAPE does not have an autonomous intelligence facility, although this should not really be surprising considering the multinational rather than international nature of the force. As an example of the weakness which this omission shows up, the SHAPE assessment of what was going on in Afghanistan, prior to the Soviet intervention towards the end of 1979, was all but triggered off by an outside intelligence summary. But it was not an official, military or government, report, but one supplied as a supplement to a well-known British weekly magazine.)

Military commanders hope that major deficiencies, such as these in the West, will be rectified during the coming few years. If one considers the current state of NATO decision-making, this seems wishful thinking. In the Soviet Union and the other nations of the Warsaw Pact, there are similar decisions and battlefield advances to be made. The Soviet lead in outer-space warfare is considerable, although it is possible for the United States to accelerate her programmes. Weapon development tends to move at the same rate, whichever power bloc is drawing the blueprints. Consequently one side is catching up in one field while roaring ahead in another. What nobody seems to have on his drawing-board is a weapon system to make the outbreak of war between the two Superpowers less likely than it is today. As has been shown, the introduction of certain weapon systems, and their deployment in the near future, may even create the illusion among some that war is even acceptable, because it can be restricted in one area or contained in the ferocity of the weapons to be used. There are even some who have suggested that chemical weapons are an acceptable alternative to nuclear weapons. In whichever land of dreams, hypothesis or even reality we live, there are few people today who could honestly believe that some super-power conflict would not set off the biggest tragedy of all time. Whatever sales pitches are laid down for new weapon systems, new treaties or new problems, most people live in the shadow of The Bomb and what they imagine it would do if reason finally snapped and the nuclear hives scattered through the United States and the Soviet Union were disturbed.

SEVEN

Nuclear Effects

Within sixty seconds of a modest theatre nuclear weapon exploding, its fireball will be more than a mile wide, and it will have risen about four and a half miles from the point of the explosion. All this in under a minute. Perhaps it is worth looking at a few basic questions about what is grandly called nuclear physics. Most people went through elementary science lessons during their early teens, lessons that would have explained the majority of what is needed to understand exactly what lies behind a nuclear explosion and its aftermath. Probably, few have bothered to apply that fundamental teaching to anything so macabre as the military techniques of destruction. Strategists talk of missile and warhead capabilities and most accept what is said without really understanding what is entailed in the glossy examples often put over with all the enthusiasm of the launching of a new model from Detroit or Dagenham. So, what is an explosion? What is the difference between a nuclear bang and a conventional explosion? What is blast? What is a fireball? What colour is it? What is radiation? What can it do to people – the tax-paying customer?

To get a bang, an explosion, all one needs to do is blow up a paper bag and hit it hard, or sharply enough to burst it. However, there is no way in which the junior physicist will get his or her very own mushroom cloud from bursting a paper bag; yet the fundamental principle is the same for all explosions. An explosion is nothing more than energy within an extremely confined space being released remarkably quickly. Without continuing too far with such a simplified explanation, the instant the bag is burst, there is a satisfying bang. That is the explosion.

Whether we are talking about a nuclear explosion or a so-called conventional explosion, the important common factor is energy and the key is the way in which the energy is released. A conventional explosion is a chemical reaction. A nuclear bang produces energy by the formation of different atomic nuclei. Once the energy is released, and because it all happens so quickly, the pressure rises, everything gets hotter; everything, therefore, is converted into hot and compressed gases.

Because these gases are under pressure and *exceedingly* hot, they do what humans tend to do when they are hot and under pressure – they lash out. In other words, they expand, violently. This expansion sets up what are called shock or blast waves. It does not matter whether it is a nuclear bomb or a conventional weapon made of TNT, both weapons destroy things, mainly by this blast effect.

But the idea that conventional and nuclear weapons are more or less the same cannot be pursued too far. And it is at this point that the differences are obvious. Nobody doubts the destructive power of a high explosive weapon but, in Strangelove terms, nuclear weapons do the same thing and so much more. Nuclear weapons are often *millions* of times more powerful than the *biggest* high explosive warhead. To get anywhere near the amount of nuclear energy released by, say, a tactical warhead, a conventional weapon would have to be massive. A tiny nuclear weapon can do more damage than a huge conventional warhead, and the method of releasing the nuclear energy is different. A nuclear explosion will also result in thermal radiation, a concentrated display of heat and light. But, to many people, the main difference between a nuclear and a conventional explosion is *nuclear* radiation.

But how to get the nuclear bang in the first place? Most people know uranium is needed to make a bomb. Uranium is an element. Everything is made from one or more elements. Iron, copper, oxygen, hydrogen, nitrogen, they are all one of the ninety or so elements. And the smallest part of any element is its atom. Some are heavier than others. Uranium elements are the heaviest of all, hydrogen elements the lightest. But the atom itself can be divided and it too has a heavy and a light part. The nucleus of the atom is the middle and the heaviest part. That heavy nucleus is surrounded by electrons which are masses of light particles. Again it is possible to break down this atom, even though it cannot be seen. The heavy nucleus consists of protons and neutrons. As their names imply, protons and neutrons are easily distinguishable. A neutron is electrically neutral, it is uncharged. A proton carries a positive electrical charge.

Because the proton carries a positive charge – and remember that these protons are in the middle, the nucleus – then the electrically-inclined proton *charges* the nucleus. But, those electrons surrounding the nucleus are *negatively* charged, so they balance each other. The important thing is that scientists know exactly how many protons and neutrons there are in every nucleus in every atom of every element. To distinguish between one atom of an element and that of another element, it is necessary to identify the number of positive charges, the protons, in the nucleus. That is how scientists have arrived at the so-called atomic number of an element.

The atomic number is nothing more than the number of protons in the nucleus. Using the physical jargon for weight, which is 'mass', there is another important factor in this muddle of neutrons, protons, electrons and nuclei. It has been shown that the nucleus is made up of a known number of neutrons and protons. The neutron and the proton have almost the same mass. But, although all nuclei of any element have the same number of protons, they do not necessarily have the same number of neutrons. That means that, if one atom has more neutrons than another, then its mass must be greater. This will not alter its atomic number because the number of protons is constant. Atoms of an element, having the same number of protons (and therefore the same atomic number) but at the same time having more neutrons than another atom of the same element, have different masses and have to be identified. This is where the well-known, but often little-understood, word isotope comes in. Isotopes of an element are nothing more than atoms, which have the same atomic numbers but different masses. And, to recognise an isotope, scientists give it a mass number. This is done simply by adding together the number of protons and neutrons in the nucleus.

Hence, Uranium 235 and 238. Both forms have (in their nuclei) 92 protons. But one has 143 and the other 146 neutrons. Add 92 to those figures and you get Uranium 235 and 238. There is more Uranium 238 than Uranium 235. In fact when the element is mined, or rather when it is extracted from the basic ores, about 99 per cent is Uranium 238, about 0.7 per cent is Uranium 235. It is this latter isotope which is commonly used in nuclear weapons. Another element in nuclear discussions is plutonium. The fissionable isotope is Plutonium 239 and that is processed from the abundant Uranium 238.

After this all-you-never-wanted-to-know-about-nuclear-physics-so-didn't-dare-ask section it is easier to understand the difference between a conventional explosion and a nuclear explosion.

If one remembers that explosions are about the sudden release of energy, a conventional explosion generates and releases that energy by rearranging the atoms. It is a simple chemical reaction. But a nuclear explosion produces the vast amount of energy by redistributing the protons and neutrons. All that does is form different atomic nuclei.

Everything important that goes on during this reaction takes place among the different nuclei. It is a nuclear reaction. So that is why it is perhaps more correct to talk about a *nuclear* weapon rather than an atomic weapon. The atomic weapon appeared because scientists managed to have some control over the atom itself. But they were really controlling the *nucleus*. It is a *nuclear* interaction, and therefore a *nuclear* bang. It has to release *nuclear* energy and it has to do it in such a way that it becomes self-generating. The essential requirement of the release of this massive amount of destructive and constructive energy is that the self-generating process can produce this quantity of energy in a very short period of time. To do this, scientists use two processes. They either fuse (fusion) or split (fission). The engineering needed to split a fissionable atom is relatively simple by today's standards, but it is nevertheless fascinating when it is considered that the process was being worked on fifty years ago—throughout the world. It involved taking a neutron, finding a fissionable atom, and splitting the nucleus of that atom with the neutron. The most obvious fissionable materials are Uranium 235 and Plutonium 239. To give some idea of the amount of energy that results from this process, sixteen ounces of plutonium could release so much energy that it would take nearly eighteen million pounds of TNT to do the same job.

The other process is fusion. Very simply, two very light nuclei are fused together to form one nucleus of a heavier atom. For example, when what is known as heavy hydrogen, the isotope deuterium, is fused with two deuterium nuclei, the result is the nucleus of helium. And this is where we come on to the thermonuclear bomb; because, in order to carry out this fusion process, very high temperatures are needed, as the adjective *thermo*nuclear suggests. The high temperatures come through the fission process. A fissionable explosion produces the extreme heat, and that fuses the light nuclei which in turn produce the energy. This is, of course, over-simplified but it is basically a correct explanation and certainly sufficient to allow one to understand the process necessary to produce nuclear weapons.

So what does all this energy do? In a fission weapon, about 85 per cent of the energy causes blast and thermal radiation. The different nuclear radiations account for the remaining 15 per cent.

The different effects of nuclear weapons depend to a great extent on where the explosion occurs. This does not mean simply whether it is exploded over Madras, London, New York, Paris, Moscow or the Nevada desert, the sparsely-populated Cumbrian hills or confined islands of Japan. There would be an extreme difference between a bomb exploded high in the air and one on the ground; and the difference might cause some surprise.

For example, a bomb exploded close to the earth's surface will result in more radiation settling on the ground than one exploded higher in the sky. And an explosion high in the sky could cause more damage than one dropped in the middle of a city.

There are five different types of explosions, often defined by their location; an air burst, a ground burst, a high-altitude burst, an underground burst and an underwater burst. (The term 'burst' in this context tends to be used by the military and by civilian organisations engaged in studies of the effects of nuclear explosions.) The five different bursts need not all be examined in detail. But it is certainly necessary to look at ground and air bursts.

The simplest way of differentiating between the two is by describing a ground burst as one that creates a fireball that touches the ground. The bomb may be exploded in the air, but if its fireball touches the earth's surface then it is a ground burst. An air burst is one where the fireball does not touch the earth. A fireball is, as its name suggests, a bright and hot ball of air and the gaseous residue of the bomb or warhead. As a result of the energy released by a nuclear weapon, all the bits and pieces of the weapon (the bomb casing, etc.) become extraordinarily hot – and extraordinary means tens of millions of degrees, temperatures similar to those at the centre of the sun. Not suprisingly, this material is turned into gases. At the very milli-second when all this happens, pressures of millions of pounds per square inch are set up. This intense, almost unimaginable, heat, and these pressures, radiate massive amounts of energy. The result is the ball of fire.

One observation shows that, within a thousandth of a second of the burst, it would be possible to see the fireball fifty miles away at least; and it would be much brighter than the sun high over the most arid desert. The effect on the eyes can be imagined. And, as soon as the fireball assumes its basic form it begins to grow. In much less than that one thousandth of a second, a fireball from a one-megaton weapon would be about 450 feet in diameter. Within ten seconds it would be more than a mile wide. It would probably not get any bigger, but it would be climbing. About a minute after the burst, the fireball would be around four and a half miles above the point of explosion. But, because it would have been expanding, taking in more air to do so, it would not be getting any hotter, in fact it would be cooling.

Not that the average human being could ever notice the change in temperature. In the middle of the fireball, all those bits and pieces from the weapons would be in the form of vapour and, as the fireball cooled, the vapours would condense. Inside that cloud, as tests have shown, would be the millions of particles from the debris of the weapon that caused the bang in the first place. Then, as the fireball rose and widened, it would cool off to some extent and the drag set up through the air would change the shape of what would quickly become a cloud. Inside the by-then fattish mushroom shape, there would be a violent circulation of air and gases. Consequently, the cloud would be sucking up air from below, which is how the spherical fireball changes into the popular concept of a mushroom cloud. In old newsreel shots, the most vivid memory of nuclear explosion is the greyish white mushroom. In fact, at the start of the cloud's formation it is brown, a reddish brown. This colouring is caused by nitrogen oxides and similarly-based chemicals in the radioactive cloud. It does eventually turn white, because it is cooling; the cooling process produces water and it is the water that colours the cloud.

As stated earlier, a surface or ground burst is an explosion either on the ground or one which produces a fireball that touches the ground. For general purposes, an important difference between a surface burst and an air burst is that the former produces a radioactive cloud containing *more* debris.

Those upward drag winds, the ones which produce the 'stem' of the mushroom, suck up debris from the ground. This debris is in the form of dirt, dust, water and tiny particles of anything that is light enough to be sucked up. As the cloud cools, the weapon debris joins with the earth particles. And, very quickly, the outer areas of the mushroom containing these particles are contaminated through the so-called radioactive residues. As the cloud sorts itself out, and stabilises, these drops of water and other contaminated particles come back to earth.

This hazard – contaminated particles falling out of the sky – is what is commonly known as fall-out. And that is why an air burst, an explosion below 100,000 feet but high enough for the fireball not to reach the ground, will not produce the same amount of fall-out as a ground burst. The air burst will not have the same amount of debris to be contaminated.

It is estimated that at least 15 per cent of the energy from a nuclear burst shows up as radiation. This figure, according to some scientists, may be higher, perhaps as high as 20 per cent. In time of war, however, few are likely to get into any scientific discussion on that point. The necessary thing at this stage is to look at these radiations from the fission products in the weapon and see what they would do to people on the ground – the potential victims. Ignoring the radiation from heat (thermal radiation), there are two areax of nuclear radiation. There is initial radiation and there is residual radiation: simply, the radiation that is emitted in the first instance of the burst, and then the radiation that is going to be around for some time.

These nuclear radiations consist of neutrons, gamma rays, beta and alpha particles, although there are few of these final ingredients.

The neutrons and much of the gamma radiation come at the moment of the nuclear burst, the explosion. In other words they are an immediate result of the reaction. The beta particles and the rest of the gamma rays generally come as a result of a decay in the fission products. Because this nuclear process is so quick and the range of some of the particles so short, much of this radiation is of no great interest to us in the present context. For example, although it is very difficult to attempt to define what is and what is not initial radiation, it might be sufficient to say that most of it occurs within about sixty seconds of the explosion. And the alpha and beta particles, although powerful as separate units, would not reach earth from an air burst. And, even in a ground burst, they are not that important. But, during that first minute after a nuclear detonation, the neutrons and gamma rays *are* important. Initial gamma radiation is powerful, it has not lost any of its nuclear punch, so the only protection is a physical shield, perhaps many feet of concrete. There is no medical protection. For anybody in range of gamma rays, it would be necessary to get behind some substantial shield within a second of the explosion. That second is truly a life or death moment.

The difference between a gamma ray and a neutron may best be described as follows: gamma rays are electro-magnetic waves, neutrons are nuclear particles. In imaginative and microscopic terms, you can see neutrons, you cannot see gamma rays. But, however they are defined, both are lethal. To begin with, it is almost impossible to detect either without the aid of scientific instruments. They can both travel huge distances from the explosion, even though in the case of neutrons they only carry about one per cent of the energy produced in the explosion.

Almost all the neutrons are produced inside a millionth of a second of the detonation of the bomb. And it only takes a thousandth of a second for those neutrons to start out from the explosion. (For those with a morbid fascination for the subject, between that millionth of a second and a thousandth of a second, there is mass panic in the reaction. The neutrons, like some manic disturbed anthill, dodge, clash and mix with the reaction nuclei.) Within a second of the explosion they have reached their destination. The effects on people from a neutron would likely be greater than by a gamma ray, in the first instance. It is also more difficult to hide from neutrons. With gamma rays, the object is to put enough dense material about the person. Lead and iron are good examples. But the trick with neutrons is to catch some of them. The first thing to do is to blunt the speed of the neutron. That is where there is a need for dense material. Then the slower rate might be sponged up by elements. There is hydrogen in water, so neutrons would be attracted to the hydrogen, or diverted. A further problem is that, during this nuclear hog-tying operation, the neutron reaction produces gamma rays. So the shielding has to be able to cope with neutrons, gamma rays and extra gamma rays. But this sort of protection, depending on the force, involves at least twenty-four inches of concrete covering – not necessarily easy to find in the average home.

There are those who might say that initial radiation is only effective at a relatively close distance from the bomb, therefore there is little point in believing protection is possible, because the blast effect would destroy any shelter. What is certain is that nobody knows where the bomb would be dropped, so there is absolutely no point in saying that it is not worth building protection in the first place. Also, there is no basic difference from the protection needed for initial and residual radiation. Technically, residual radiation is defined as that which is emitted later than one minute after the detonation.

But, as has been shown, the radiation that will give the survivors of the initial blast the most trouble is evident in the small particles of fall-out – the debris that has been sucked up into the nuclear cloud, has mixed with the weapon debris, the water droplets, and will inevitably fall to earth. And, of course, there is always the chance that the explosion will set up neutronic activity on the surface beneath the original burst point of the bomb.

The residual fall-out might also be seen in two further parts: the delayed and early fall-out. The latter reaches the ground within a short time of the bomb going off. Within twenty-four hours is a reasonable guideline, but it could be thirty minutes from the explosion. It is possible that this is far more dangerous than delayed fall-out, certainly in the short term. Delayed radiation hangs about in the atmosphere and it will decay to some extent. Most of that early fall-out is contaminated by the product of the fission action within the explosion and it too will decay.

To estimate the rate of decay of radiation it is handy to remember two figures: seven and ten. The radiation dose rate will decrease by a factor of ten for every sevenfold increase in time following the detonation of the weapon. So, seven hours after the explosion, the dose rate will be only one tenth of what it was at the beginning. Continuing the arithmetic, at the end of two weeks the dose rate will be down to one thousandth of what it was shortly after the explosion.[1]

In using the term 'will be', there may be some ambiguity. There are a number of factors that cannot be bound by any simple equation. Scientists are always talking about fractionation, which might be described simply as a process or a number of processes which will change the composition of the radioactive debris from the bomb. Fractionation could make the decay equation quite unreliable. Yet, it does act as a rule of thumb guide and it does after all illustrate – even if it does not prove – that radiation will decay. At the same time, it does not reduce the potential threat.

It must be remembered that radiation will possibly arrive from sources other than 'your' bomb. There could be an explosion twenty, fifty, a hundred miles away, but, given the right wind direction, the

1. There are two useful definitions of terms commonly used in discussing the effects of nuclear weapons. Dose: The accumulated nuclear radiation. Rad: The unit of an absorbed dose of radiation. For the technically minded, it is the absorption of 100 ergs of nuclear radiation per gram of body tissue.

radioactive particles from one or all of those explosions could drift into 'your' area.

It is possible that a bomb exploding in one country could produce enough fall-out for people in another country to die. This is obviously truer in, say, Europe than it is in the United States of America, although in the latter case the state boundaries are just as useless as those between perhaps France and Spain. It is even possible, considering that many of the irradiated particles would be so small, for radiation to cross continents and oceans. Of course, the longer they are in the air, the weaker they are when they fall. It must also be remembered that radiation would undoubtedly produce effects that would remain for many years. Indeed, the biological, the genetic, effects may not show themselves for twenty or more years.

One of the difficulties in assessing, or guessing at, the injuries from a nuclear bomb, is the lack of experience. Much of the work in this field, not unnaturally, tends to find its base mark at Hiroshima and Nagasaki. But it would be wrong to point to what happened in Japan as a definitive example of what would, or could, happen in, say, Central Europe, the United States, the United Kingdom or even in Japan today or tomorrow.

To begin with, the types of weapons used were different from those in modern nuclear arsenals. Furthermore, nobody is certain of the yield.[1] At Hiroshima, the yield was about twelve and a half kilotons at a height of 1,670 feet. At Nagasaki, the burst was thirty feet lower, the weapon was about twenty-two kilotons. It is difficult to talk about fall-out, certainly as a comparison, because there were no fall-out injuries due to other forms of radiation. Hiroshima and Nagasaki were almost perfect examples of people being totally unprotected. Looking at the conditions at the time does illustrate the factors that might influence survival chances. Immediately beneath the bomb burst, there were high-density populations, something in the order of 25,000 people to the square mile. This is important because there is a tendency to talk about the average population density. In fact, for Hiroshima it was something like eight and a half thousand people to the square mile; and, for Nagasaki, considerably less – well under six thousand. So beneath the bomb was the highest concentration of people. If you take New York City today, the average density is about 25,000 to the square mile, but in Manhattan it is about 70,000.

1. When scientists talk about yield of a nuclear weapon, the warhead, they refer to the amount of energy released. But there has to be some readily understandable comparison. So the yield is usually shown in the form of the equivalent gonnage of TNT it would take to produce the same explosion. A one-megaton nuclear warhead has the energy equivalent to one million tons of TNT; a one kiloton warhead one thousand tons of TNT.

Another important point was the weather. It was summertime and typically summertime weather. That meant that not only were there more people in the open than there would have been if it were winter and wet and windy, but those people were wearing light clothing. Furthermore, there was not the industrial pollution of recent years. If there had been, for example, a strong haze from factory chimneys, there might have been fewer thermal radiation burns.

It is not the purpose of this book to discuss what might have been, or should have been, at Nagasaki and Hiroshima. But these examples do show how local conditions and the environment could influence injuries, or at least the level of injuries. Japanese housing today tends to be different from that of the 1940s. Constructions might play a major part in protection but not always in the way that one might immediately think.

And there is no reason to believe that casualty rates in Japan, all those years ago, might be taken as a guide to the sort of casualty figures for any given part of the world in any future war. But, for the record, of a combined population of 430,100, 203,000 people were either killed or injured. Hiroshima, the bigger of the two, suffered the heavier casualties as might be expected.

In a nuclear war, people would die from four things. They would die from the utter destructive power of the blast, from nuclear radiation, from thermal radiation and, fourthly, from illnesses that in normal times could easily be treated by drugs or simple surgery.

At this stage it is better to confine explanations to the first three.

Another reason why it is very difficult to use Hiroshima and Nagasaki as examples is that, because the effects of a nuclear detonation vary, the further casualties are away from what is known as ground zero (the point beneath the explosion), it is often difficult to assess the cause of death, even though it is not difficult to identify injuries. Many who died from the blast effect of the weapons were also badly burned. Something like 30 per cent of those who died at Hiroshima took in lethal doses of radiation, but this does not mean they died because of radiation. An examination of the casualty list shows that, during the first day, about 65 per cent of those who died suffered extremely bad burns. Of all the casualties, perhaps half of those who died died of burns. The attention given to radiation and blast tends to obscure the very real threat from burning.

About one third of all the energy released during a nuclear explosion is in the form of thermal radiation, heat and light. There are two types of burns, flash and indirect. Their definitions are obvious; a flash burn comes from the flash of the fireball. An indirect burn is simply injury from fire caused by the nuclear explosion. It is flash burning that is perhaps unusual to us, although death and injury from the latter group may be more widespread. The heat and light from the explosion travels almost at the speed of light, the difference being accounted for by deflection by atmospheric particles. If anybody were to be looking in the direction of the explosion, the chances are they would suffer flash-blindness. But it is not as terrible as it may sound. And the state of the injury would depend on a number of factors, including of course distance from the burst and also the time of day. A moderately-sized weapon, say, one megaton, would or could cause this blindness in people standing twelve or thirteen miles away. But, because it would be, literally, the focus of attention, it could travel well over fifty miles on a clear and very dark night. In addition, there is more chance of permanent eye damage at night than there is during the day simply because, at night, the pupil of the eye is enlarged. But, although flash-blindness would normally be complete, the victim would really go blind only for a few minutes at the most. Its effect is similar to that experienced when somebody inadvertently looks into the sun. Multiply the symptoms and duration, and you have the effect of flash-blindness.

The real danger is that its victim may suffer some other injury as a result. He may be driving a car, he may be driving in a built-up area, or along a fast highway with other cars whose drivers suffer the same injury. The damage taken in the context of a nuclear attack may appear insignificant, but not to the people who might be in the cars. It would also occur at a time when its victim should be taking urgent and perhaps unfamiliar actions to avert further injury for himself or herself and their families. There is also the real possibility of permanent eye injury. The radiation of heat is likely to attack the retinal tissues. If it did, there would be a long-lasting injury, although this would not necessarily mean total blindness. But these are almost insignificant injuries compared with the other effects of thermal radiation.

Much of this radiation from, for example, a ten-megaton warhead might come out of the fireball during the first ten or twelve seconds after an explosion. (This is very much an estimate, but it would seem safe to assume that most of the energy we are talking about would be emitted during the first half of the life of the fireball.) During those brief seconds, a large percentage of the exposed population would be burned. But to what extent? The traditional method of using three categories of burns applies here as elsewhere. First-degree burns are the least harmful. Anybody who has had sunburn has had first-degree burning. Second-degree injuries blister the skin, cause considerable pain and are vulnerable to infection unless treated. Depending on the extent of the burn, they would normally heal within a period of two weeks or so. Second-degree burning does not produce extensive cell damage, therefore new skin often grows with few problems. Third-degree burns can be fatal; or rather somebody might well die as a result of having third-degree burns. The body would char and the cells would be damaged to the extent that they would not be able to produce new skin. Intensive medical care is needed. Depending on how much of the body is burned, it is possible for second- or third-degree burning to induce such shock that death is inevitable. It must also be remembered that the environment, the conditions, would more than likely preclude any normally available medical treatment. A recent report in the United States showed that the entire country had only sufficient facilities to treat a maximum of 2,000 severe burn cases at any one time. In Hiroshima alone, there were 42,000 flash burns. Using that ten-megaton weapon as an example, and imagining it were burst in the air on a clear day, it could produce the following effect in terms of burns.

People would be charred up to eighteen miles away. Charring means third-degree burns. Second-degree burns would affect people caught out in the open twenty-four miles away. And, for first-degree burning, the thermal radiation might reach somebody thirty miles from the explosion.

Taking a city like London and considering the likely effects from even a small weapon, there would be third-degree burning in Bromley, Beckenham, Richmond, Brentford, Hendon, Edmonton, Walthamstow, Ilford – just a few of the towns to show the radius of the effects.

Not everybody would be caught in the same way. Very simple clothing would give some protection. Even clothing of the same material could give different stages of protection. Burns examined in Japan showed that, in some cases, the wearing of a black and white check kimono had resulted in varying burns to the skin beneath. Burns were found beneath the black part of the gown, but not the white sections. It was said at the time that the lighter colour reflected the thermal radiation, while the black fabric let in the heat and caused contact burns. But it should not be taken as gospel that white clothing is going to protect a person against burning. Furthermore, different materials would behave in various ways. It could also be that the heat would be strong enough to ignite certain materials and that people would therefore be burned as an indirect result of the thermal radiation.

People have skins that react quite differently. Just as some people tan more easily than others, so different skin pigmentations would absorb different levels of thermal radiation – although the differences would be likely to occur only for the lesser degrees of burning. Yet it is possible that people with dark skins would suffer more than light-skinned people.

Fire is another major hazard. Firestorms are not confined to nuclear explosions. One of the most infamous must be the firestorm of Hamburg during World War Two. It was started by a heavy incendiary attack and provoked by the high winds. During a nuclear attack, it is expected that great wind currents would be set up and these would be pulled into the centre of the fire area. In other words, the fire would be fanned at its very heart and escape would be made almost impossible. At the same time, these very winds would tend to contain the firestorm in one area.

The greatest destruction in a city would most likely come from the blast of the weapon. The blast would set up two types of pressures.

To begin with, the blast would push out all the air from the immediate area of the explosion. Consequently, there would be terrific pressures around this area. These pressures are static overpressures (pressures in excess of normal atmospheric pressure). It is this overpressure which could crush buildings.

The other type is known as dynamic pressure. It is really a very high wind. It sweeps things aside, knocks them down. These high winds, the dynamic pressures, would probably kill people. The overpressures would destroy their houses, their offices and factories. Put the two pressures together and the effect is truly devastating.

When a blast wave hits a building, it momentarily bounces back – into itself. Consequently, at that point the pressure is increased. The wave bends about the building until it completely engulfs the structure. It is this pressure which can crush the building. And, if there are many openings, the pressure inside will equalise. It may reach the point where it grows to be greater than the outside pressure. It can then explode. It is something that happens during tropical winds. Different structures obviously react to these pressures to varying degrees.

A house in the United Kingdom, for example, may be built quite differently from one in a warmer climate. Timber is going to behave differently from concrete. A barn with open ends will not suffer the same as a barn with closed ends.

Back in the 1950s, tests were made in Nevada on the likely damage from nuclear blast on different houses. Two examples are worth examining. In the first case two houses were built after a style reasonably common in the United States: both wood-framed, with a brick chimney and a basement. They were painted white to see if the colour shade cut down the effect of thermal radiation. Both houses were given window blinds.

The first house was particularly vulnerable. It was subject to a peak overpressure of five pounds per square inch. The house was completely destroyed above ground. There was some damage to one of the basement walls.

The second house was *exposed to less overpressure*. It was in the region of one and three-quarter pounds a square inch, about a third of that applied to the other house. It was, as was expected, badly damaged. But it remained standing. Windows and doors were shattered, although those interior doors that had been left opened were in better condition than the others. Rafters were cracked as were some of the floor joists. But it was easily repairable. Assuming that it was possible to live in the area after an explosion, it would be important to have a building that was simply repaired, because of the few resources that would be available.

In the second test similar houses were used. But this time they were made of brick. They were subjected to the same pressures. The first one suffered the same fate as the wooden building, even though it was brick-built. It ended up as a heap of rubble. Furthermore, the weight of the construction did the basement no good. The first floor partially collapsed into the basement. The second house, further from the explosion, and subject to less overpressure, looked derelict, but once again was easily repaired.

 A recent American report shows some interesting figures for the blast effect of a small bomb, a one-megaton weapon, exploded 8,000 feet above ground. Just under a mile away from the ground zero there would be a peak wind speed of 470 m.p.h. Even reinforced concrete structures would be flattened.

Three miles from ground zero, the peak wind would have been just under 300 m.p.h. Most commercial structures, including factories, would collapse and small houses be destroyed. Even as far out as 5.9 miles, there is a peak wind speed of 95 m.p.h. Steel-framed walls are blown away.

Now, at that bottom figure, the peak overpressure is still about three pounds per square inch. And, says the report, the winds associated with that pressure are sufficient to blow people out of a typical modern office building.

People react differently to blast. Just because a building is damaged, it does not follow that a human being will suffer comparable damage from blast – not directly, anyway. True, the body is subject to the same pressures, but, because the body is small and more flexible, under ideal conditions it stands more chance of survival. There are, in general, expected to be two ways in which people would be killed by blast. They would either die from the high pressure or from the flying debris caused by that high pressure. But, even though the body is small and flexible, it is remarkably vulnerable to the long pressure pulses set up by a nuclear explosion. The body is compressed. Pressure builds up in the lungs. Then the pressure and the general effect of the shock wave is enough to damage other parts such as tissue joints. The result is probably rupturing of the lungs and haemorrhaging. If there is heavy damage, then this is reflected in heart and brain injury, or even suffocation caused by haemorrhaging in the lungs.

It is difficult for the body to avoid these pressures. It is also suspected by Civil Defence experts that the average person would probably take cover as close to a room wall as possible. Apart from the wall collapsing on him, a person would also suffer even further from overpressure than if he were in the middle of the room. Somebody alongside a wall would be subject to peak pressure, because it is at this position that there is maximum reflection.

Distance from the blast is also misleading.

One report suggests that a person would have to be as close as two miles from ground zero before he were killed by the direct blast. But that same report says that if the same person were five or six miles away from ground zero, then, assuming he were standing in the open, he would be carried along by the wind drag forces and could strike an obstacle hard enough for the impact to be lethal.[1]

It is expected that, during a nuclear attack, those affected by blast would die from indirect results. These would include people being hurled against walls with such force that their bodies are actually broken apart, people being blown from buildings, and also those killed by flying debris. By flying debris we are not just talking about glass and slates from roofs. Cars will be lifted into the air, telegraph poles not just blown down but flung through the air like huge lances.

The average motor car would be lifted off its wheels and then hurled through the air according to its distance from the blast and the size of the blast. A ten-megaton ground burst weapon would 'displace', as the scientists say, cars six miles away. A small, one-megaton weapon, again a ground burst, would lift off a car some two and three-quarter miles away. If those same weapons were air bursts instead of ground bursts, then you can increase those 'displacement' figures by as much as 30 per cent.

The size of the blast effect is not so much related to the distance from the centre of the explosion as to the height at which the weapon was detonated. If a bomb is exploded close to the surface, or at the surface, then the overpressures beneath it are greater than if it were exploded high in the sky. But, the overpressures do not reach out so far from the explosion. Consequently, if a bomb is burst at ground level its blast damage might well be less than if it were exploded in the atmosphere.

But, however violent death might be from blast, perhaps the greatest fear would be of the effects of radiation, or rather the likely

1. Based on a document prepared for the British Home Office.

effects. There are short- and long-term effects. Some of the radio-isotopes, or radio-active isotopes, would arrive as a direct result of the explosion, others would be created after the explosion by neutrons, say in the soil. There is also the danger that some irradiated material would come from nuclear power stations destroyed during an air raid. The various radio-isotopes have what are known as half-lives – and often the dangerous strength of the many radio-isotopes is measured in half-lives. Strontium 90 for example has a half-life of nearly twenty-eight years; it will affect lungs and kidneys. Some plutonium radio-isotopes will be around for thousands of years, and uranium for hundreds of millions of years. So, although there is a natural decay process in radiation, the isotopes will not simply disappear in a couple of days. The impression has been given by some Civil Defence planners that the danger from radiation would be during the first few days of an attack. While this is obviously true, the number of long-term injuries from radiation could be equally horrifying.

In the shorter term, radiation would affect most people in the same way. The degree of injury suffered would obviously depend on the amount of radiation absorbed. It would also depend on the time scale for that exposure to radiation. But generally, and during the initial stages, the symptoms would be the same. Even for what defence planners term small doses, say seventy-five rads or so, people would feel sick, then they would vomit. They would suffer diarrhoea and they would not want to eat anything – naturally enough, given the basic symptoms. An increase in that dose would start people coughing up blood, or discharging it through the bowels. Anything over 150 and towards 200 rads would cause a marked increase in the other symptoms. Vomiting would be more violent (assuming there is anything to bring up), haemorrhaging would be almost inevitable, hair would fall out. About a quarter to one third of people suffering in this manner would die.

Now it could be that some of these symptoms would show themselves and then disappear. But the chances are they would return inside fourteen days. At the lower end of the dose rate, they may not amount to much and a person could go about quite normally.

Once the dose rate rose above 200 rads, then the chances of survival would be that much less. Anybody who received more than 200 rads would be, at the very least, dangerously ill. Assuming there were good medical treatment at hand, constant nursing for months on end, blood transfusions and no other infections, up to 50 per cent might survive. For those who did not, it could take anything between one and two months to die.

For double that exposure, the death rate would be that much higher, the time it took to die would be halved. Once the big doses,are examined, really anything much above 650 rads, there could be little hope, especially under the conditions expected during a nuclear war, or its aftermath. And it should not be forgotten that, even at the low levels, the body might be weakened enough to make it susceptible to other infections, and perhaps the effects of less serious diseases would be that much greater on such weakened bodies. One of the problems at the early stages would be the fact that medical attention would be in short supply. There would be a further complication. A person might, because of the general environment after an attack, feel and then suffer some of the early symptoms associated with radiation malaise – and yet be free of it. It would not be at all remarkable for a child, or an old person, to feel ill, perhaps to be sick, to vomit and under such hard feeding conditions to suffer from diarrhoea. It would then be equally natural for him to think he had some form of radiation sickness. The effect of that would be frightening, not only to the sick person, but also to those around. And the fact that sickness is likely to wear off, and not appear for another week or so, could easily be as disturbing as if the individual had the real thing. And, of course, during this intervening period, the person might get radiation malaise. It is an uncertain diagnosis, until made by qualified people. But, for heavy doses, there would be little doubt.

The more obvious signs, certainly after the first eight to ten days, would be bleeding from the mouth and from the intestinal tract. According to a report prepared in the United States by the Department of Defense and the Department of Energy, there would be bleeding in the kidney which of course would be seen in the urine. Because there would be a marked depletion in the number of white cells in the blood, and because the body would be generally in a poor state, an abnormal infection rate would spread through the whole body. There might be a concentration of mouth ulcers, often experienced in normal times when a person is run down. But, because these would be abnormal times, and because of this loss of white cells, those ulcers could easily spread right through the stomach and intestines.

It was noticed in Japan that radiation sickness caused the internal bleeding mentioned above towards the end of the first week. By the third day in some cases there was a marked rise in temperature, in most other cases by the fifth or seventh days. The more serious the illness the more obvious the symptoms. Again in Japan, there was a tendency towards delirium, emaciation and increased fevers. The sufferer took between two and eight weeks to die.

That same report says that those patients who survived for three to four months and did not succumb to tuberculosis, lung diseases or other complications, gradually recovered. There was, among those survivors, evidence of permanent loss of hair. Between three and four years after the attack on Japan, 824 patients were examined. The examination showed that none of the patients had suffered any significant change in blood composition.

It is in the blood where the effects of radiation exposure on the whole of the body take place. And it is not necessary to believe that this effect on the blood will be seen in the patients suffering large doses. Changes are detectable in somebody who has received no more than about 25 rads. Among those white blood cells are neutrophils. Their job is to counter any bacteriological attack. They normally do this by multiplying. But, because there is an overall loss in the numbers of white cells, there are enough to counter the micro-organisms. Even when recovery is apparent, the neutrophils will not be back at full multiplying strength for many weeks, perhaps months.

Assuming a patient survives the initial radiation attack, there is the long-term effect to consider. Recent claim and counter-claim, especially in the United States, indicates that there is still considerable doubt as to these long-term effects. By long-term, we are really talking about years rather than weeks or months, and, in some cases, generations. Because the radiation would attack the germ cells of its victim, it is inevitable that there are great risks of genetic damage. Although the available research is limited, it is accepted that a marked increase in the gene mutation rate might be evident even for small doses, say 50 rads. The mutation rate might even double. The long-term illnesses would include leukaemia, thyroid cancer and general cancers.

Leukaemia might appear between three and six years after exposure to radiation. It was only in the 1950s that the protection of radiologists was taken seriously, and as a result the number of radiologists suffering leukaemia was rapidly reduced. Within three years of the explosions in Hiroshima and Nagasaki, it was noticeable that there was an increase in the normal, or expected, rate of people suffering from the illness – among, that is, the survivors. And it was later discovered that children, who had been less than ten years old at the time of the bomb, were twice as likely to get leukaemia as older survivors.

Other survivors suffered in later years from thyroid cancer. Again, the number of patients was abnormally high enough for scientists to tie the disease directly to the large ionizing radiation the survivors had received. It is thought that leukaemia would appear within twenty years, cancer of the stomach, lung and breast within about twenty to thirty years (and perhaps beyond that period), and thyroid cancer beyond ten years. In the last case, this would show itself mainly in children.

Children might in some cases have a better survival chance. However, there is evidence to suggest the number of stillbirths and abnormalities would increase substantially. Among the survivors from the bombs dropped over Japan were many women in various stages of childbirth. Of those who received a modest radiation dose and who were about three months pregnant, there was a high increase in the number of unhappy births. Births were difficult and there was an increase in the number of stillbirths. Furthermore, of those children who managed to survive delivery, an abnormally high number died within a year. Of those who got through that first twelve months, a number – certainly more than usual – were retarded in some way, including mentally. And all this came from two small bombs and in spite of the medical that followed.

As shown above, the effects of a nuclear explosion may not be confined to the area of detonation. It might well have unacceptable consequences hundreds, perhaps thousands, of miles away. We have touched on the damage from the blast itself, a blast that could reduce a city to rubble and most of those people within it. The blast effect would be felt much further away than the immediate area beneath the explosion. A high bursting bomb would spread out, the shock waves would crumple buildings, sweep cars into the air, crack dams that would then flood whole regions, hurl pylons, poles, people, roofs in all directions. Death from this flying debris alone would possibly be considerable. The effect of the thermal radiation would not only be sufficient to cause its own damage, but the combination of this heat and ruptured systems (for example gas mains) would add to the havoc and death toll. The chaos to normal services, such as emergency relief, medical and law and order, would create wide-spread disorder. Initial radiation would have an almost instant effect. Fall-out, irradiated particles, would not only fall in the general area of the explosion, they might drift for days, certainly might travel hundreds of miles on contrary winds before descending to earth, perhaps on some township, some community, that believed itself immune from an attack that had taken place many miles away.

Dependent on the warning systems and state of readiness of the civilian and military authorities would be the general populations of the so-called war zone and those well outside it. Perhaps, these would include people of no particular allegiance to any one power bloc. The people of Central America, of North Africa, of parts of Asia, could well suffer, some even die, because of the inability of any military command to control the effects of a nuclear explosion. It has always been so. The innocents have always died in somebody else's war. But we are talking about a new kind of war, though not on the whole a novel experience. It is all very well for generals and politicians to duck the questions by saying that the effects would be beyond the experience of anybody; this is not strictly true. Enough is known from the experience in Hiroshima and Nagasaki, from the Pacific tests, from controlled explosions, for government departments to prepare volumes of information on the likely effects of a nuclear exchange.

So the concern at this point must be: is it possible for any to survive? Is it possible to take shelter, either as a community or as individuals? And who is to decide whether or not any or all of this is possible?

EIGHT

Civil Defence

It has been estimated that 40 million people in the United Kingdom will die during an all-out surprise nuclear attack. In similar circumstance 100 million people in the Soviet Union and up to 160 million in the United States would also perish. These are neatly rounded figures, and like most estimates, may vary depending which agency is setting them out and under what political and military circumstances. They also assume attacks and counter-attacks under the worst conditions; yet they should not be dismissed as the rumblings of Pentagon hawks or peace-moving doves. Military analysis may often suffer fools and their miscalculations, but there are sufficient technical denominators and numerators in this field of nuclear weapons effect to put most of the fractions together and produce a credible equation. More than thirty-five years of nuclear weapon-testing have provided the data which, if applied to known population patterns and strategic target areas, will give a reasonable idea of the appalling results of a missile or bomb attack.

During the summer of 1978, shortly after the United Nations special session on Disarmament and NATO's pledge to increase defence spending by a minimum of three per cent in real terms annually, the United States Central Intelligence Agency produced an analysis of the possible effects of an American nuclear attack on the Soviet Union. The analysis was part of an overall CIA study of Soviet Civil Defence and it took into consideration the chances of Moscow being able to operate its Civil Defence programme in time of tension.

The CIA report simulated 'a hypothetical attack against high-value military and economic targets. The Soviet population *as such* was not *deliberately* targeted.'[1] A further condition of the study was that only short-term casulaties would be evaluated, which meant that any hypothetical deaths or fatal illnesses showing up a month after the attack were not included in the analysis. The following is the summary of the CIA estimate:

'Under worst conditions for the USSR, with only a few hours or less to make final preparations, Soviet casualties would be well over 100 million but a large percentage of the leadership elements would probably survive.

1. Author's italics.

'The critical time for preparation appears to be about two or three days, because only by evacuating could the Soviets hope to avert massive losses. With a few days for final preparations, casualties could be reduced by more than 50 per cent; most of this reduction would be due to evacuation, the remainder to shelters.

'Under the most favourable conditions for the USSR, including a week or more to complete urban evacuation and then to protect the evacuated population (sic) Soviet civil defences could reduce casualties to the low tens of millions.'

What the CIA means by 'low tens of millions' is not made clear in the report. However, nine months after the analysis was made, the Defense Department referred to it in some notes on Civil Defence and suggested that those casualties could be '10, 20, maybe 30 million. And the fatalities would be about half that – say 5, 10 or maybe 15 million'. The CIA qualifies its projection as a 'worst case' scenario, but admits that the hypothetical American attack could cause even greater casualties under certain circumstances, some of which seem probable rather than simply possible. It assumes a short, sharp attack. If the offensive were carried out over a protracted period and if a major part of it were to take place during the Soviet evacuation of its major cities, then casualties would be higher. Adverse weather conditions in the Soviet Union could easily slow up the movement of the civilian population, certainly if it had to rely on the existing transport system. Other problems, including the possibility that the Soviet evacuation programme would not work as efficiently as planned, lead many observers to believe the 100 million casualty figure to be a conservative reckoning. At the other end of the projection is the evidence compiled by T. K. Jones of the Boeing Corporation. During 1976, Jones twice gave evidence to Washington inquiries on Civil Defence. The sum of his testimony to the House Committee on Armed Services and to the Proxmire Joint Committee on Defense Production suggested that, if everything went right for the Soviet Union's evacuation and shelter programme, then an American strike would kill no more than ten million people.

Government war-gamers in the United Kingdom and the United States have long played with what-would-happen-if? scenarios. These are no Military Monopoly board games for even with loaded dice there are too many variable to be considered. An attack by American Minuteman Intercontinental Ballistic Missiles would produce different results than would an attack by their submarine-launched missiles and manned bomber squadrons. What would happen, say the war-gamers, if the Minuteman system had been all but wiped out by a Soviet pre-emptive strike? What if some of the SAC bombers could not take off? If some of those that did, failed to reach their targets? It certainly is not a matter of adding up the number of Minuteman IIIs, Titans, B-52s, F1-11s, Poseidon and Trident submarine systems and then saying that means the United States could cause X amount of damage. Other elements are fed into the game, elements such as weather conditions, surprise, weapon failure, strengths of Soviet shelters for missiles, planes, industry and people. There are fairly detailed plans kept of cities such as Leningrad and Moscow showing population densities. The scenario may include the fact that many city-dwellers live in apartment buildings rather than one-family homes, that people in the USSR might live closer to their place of work than their Western counterparts and therefore an attack aimed at an industrial complex might result in higher than expected civilian casualties. For an attack aimed close to the East–West border, consideration may, *may*, be given to the position of Allied troops and civilians at the time of the attack and the likely long-term effects of radiation on those people.

In one American-prepared scenario it was assumed that the Minuteman system had been virtually destroyed by a surprise attack by Soviet missiles. The United States replied with a large part of its strategic bomber fleet carrying one-megaton bombs and 200-kiloton SRAMS (short-range attack missiles) together with submarines firing ballistic missiles containing forty kiloton warheads. The targets were military and economic, which for reasons outlined above meant that civilians were beneath the warheads as they landed or exploded. Three-quarters of Soviet industry was destroyed. Up to 100 million people died. More than three-quarters of the fatalities were due to the immediate results of the attack – blast, heat and instant radiation as opposed to fall-out. When considering the industrial damage, it was even thought that the time of the month would make a difference. Economic intelligence assessments indicate that the major portion of Soviet production takes place during the latter part of the month because of delivery and work schedules. In estimating the casualty figures in cities, it was noted that Soviet towns are 'stronger' than American towns because there are more pre-cast apartment blocks, and therefore Leningrad, for example, is less likely to burn than, say, Boston.

If the submarine-launched attack had been on Leningrad, then the ten forty-kiloton warheads from one boat would have killed more than one million people and injured another one million. If a single megaton bomb had been airburst over the city, there would have been 2,150,000 casualties. About 890,000 of them would have been killed immediately.

At the same time, the war-gamers ran a scenario on Detroit, partly because Detroit and Leningrad have similar populations of something

under four and a half million people. In this war-game there was no
warning and the attack was carried out at night, so that most of the
population was thought to have been in bed. The first one-megaton
bomb exploded on the civic centre and left a crater 200 feet deep and
1,000 feet wide and virtually flattened an area within 1.7 miles radius
of what had been the centre of the town. Population at this time of
night was considered to be extremely low within this business radius,
perhaps no more than 70,000 people. All were dead. If the attack had
taken place during the daytime, then of the guestimated 200,000
business community, all would be killed. Going out a further mile
obviously increased the chances of survival. Most buildings would be
destroyed but, as the circle spread towards three miles, some structures would stand in some form. The night population within this 2.7
mile radius is thought to be about one quarter of a million and fewer
than 20,000 would be injury-free. 130,000 would be dead. It was only
when the scenario projected out somewhere near five miles from the
civic centre that casualties were considered to be on the low side.
There were few if any fatalities due to the immediate effects of the
explosion and only 150,000 or so injuries. But these figures did not
take into consideration deaths and injuries from the fall-out that
would follow from a ground burst weapon. The conclusion from this
one attack was that seventy square miles of Detroit would have been
destroyed and one quarter of a million people killed and double that
number injured.

A further programme on Detroit was run through using the same
time-scale and weather conditions. But this time a 25-megaton bomb
was 'exploded' 17,500 feet above the ground. The effects were felt
beyond Roseville, Madison Heights, Dearborn Heights and Lincoln
Park and to a lesser extent out to Pontiac and beyond. Three million
two hundred thousand casualties was the immediate figure given from
the explosion. Of those, 1,840,000 were dead. It was also noted that
the fewer the survivors, the less chance they have of helping each
other. It is not, therefore, too far-fetched to imagine the chances of
surviving for those who are not killed outright.

Similar studies have been carried out in the United Kingdom
although the British authorities are less willing to produce the results.
But, given the conditions of time, population density, weather and
building constructions, it is easy to get a rough idea of the possible
effects when applied to a British city. The one-megaton ground burst
weapon went out to 7.4 miles and the larger explosion to more than 30
miles. There is nothing new in these studies although the ability of
both sides to fire missiles with varying numbers of independently
programmed warheads on board (the MIRVs) must have caused
both NATO and Warsaw Pact commanders to re-programme many

of their present computer games. One of the more interesting indications of how the United States viewed its chances of surviving a nuclear attack was revealed to a select few in Washington, one afternoon in September 1974.

Earlier that year, James R. Schlesinger, the American Defense Secretary, had presented the DoD's (Department of Defense) annual report. Among other things it contained the apparent assumption that an enemy attack upon US military installations would result in 'relatively few civilian casualties'. But what had he meant by 'relatively few'? It was one of those phrases often overlooked in the usual haggling over contracts, political rights and wrongs and inter-Service rivalries that surround and accompany the DoD Report. This one did not slip by. On 2 July of that year an American Senator, Clifford P. Case, wrote to Schlesinger asking for a briefing on projected casualties, basically asking the Secretary of Defense to explain what he meant by 'relatively few'.

The Defense Department spent some time hedging round the Senator's request. As a result, a very courteous Case wrote once more to Secretary Schlesinger, this time on 25 July. '. . . the actions of your staff to date have not been responsive to my original request . . . I would like this briefing on the total consequences to the US population of attacks against military installations in the United States, to cover the full range of possible attacks, up to and including strikes against all our Minuteman sites, all bomber bases, and all major elements of our command and control system . . .' The result was the sort of briefing rarely heard outside the United States, certainly not in the United Kingdom where there were and remain equally sensitive targets, similar analyses, but also a tendency to slap a Security Classification on anything more revealing than the gender signs on washroom doors.

At 2.30 p.m. on 11 September, Secretary Schlesinger and a clutch of military aides attended room S–116 in the Capitol Building, to appear before the Senate Foreign Relations Sub-committee on Arms Control, International Law and Organisation, of which Senator Case was a member and the then Senator Edmund Muskie was chairman. Reading the ill-informed comment during 1980 following the carefully orchestrated leaks on so-called changes in targeting doctrines and the Carter decision to abandon MAD,[1] Muskie – by then Secretary of State – must have cast his mind back to September 1974 and the sub-committee meeting. It was all about targeting, kill figures, and

---

1. Mutually Assured Destruction, the old theory that defence policy and posture is based on the idea that both sides maintain, deploy and are willing to use such vast nuclear arsenals, that neither side will.

made it quite clear that the so-called flexible response philosophy whereby the United States would have a cross-section of weaponry, instead of relying on one nuclear sledge-hammer, had been a reality for some years.

Senator Muskie opened that meeting by expressing concern about the number of potential casualties. Schlesinger's immediate reply was to preface his remarks with the point that for some years it had been felt at the highest levels that no President should find himself in the impossible position of having to destroy millions of Soviet citizens as a response to a limited nuclear attack by Moscow. This was a reference to President Nixon's 1970 Foreign Policy Report, which in turn was carefully guided by Dr Henry Kissinger. It was a theme continued throughout the Nixon Presidency, and has never changed. In May 1973, President Nixon reaffirmed this policy when he said, 'No President should ever be in a position where his only option in meeting nuclear aggression is all-out nuclear response.' He went on: 'Credible deterrence in the 1970s requires greater flexibility.'

Fixing on this theme, the Defense Secretary then said that the way to make nuclear attacks less likely is to strengthen conventional forces. 'Lowering the level of our general purpose forces is what reduces the nuclear threshold. It drives us to early recourse, either through threat or actual employment of nuclear weapons, be they tactical or strategic.' Secretary Schlesinger was setting the scene for possible use of nuclear weapons. But, knowing the thinking behind the inquiry from Senator Case, Schlesinger was also justifying the large range of nuclear and conventional forces in the American arsenal and budget requirements. Senator Case had told the Secretary of Defense in July: 'Should it turn out that the destruction of our society would be so substantial as to make this cost as unacceptable as all-out attacks specifically targeted against our population centres, then the rationale for the multi-billion dollar family of weapons designed to destroy military targets that has to be funded this year (1974) as well as the basis for the severely stepped-up arms race so many fear could be called into serious question. In the latter event, we might be better advised to continue to rely upon *the former*[1] basis of our strategic policy – that is, mutual assured destruction – and abjure preparations for a kind of nuclear war that we would find ourselves unwilling to fight.' In other words, the Pentagon was being asked to produce the projected casualty figures, but first to justify defence policy and the massive arms bill, which in 1974 was nearly 86 billion dollars at the the then current dollar value – about six per cent of America's Gross National Product. In turn, the Pentagon was saying

1. Author's italics.

that what the committee was about to be told would not be very encouraging and, so as to lessen the chances of people being killed, everything was being done to stop a nuclear exchange ever taking place. But the Muskie sub-committee wanted to know what sort of weapons the Soviet Union might use against American targets.

Schlesinger's guess was that, by 1981 or 1982, the Soviet Union would have roughly 7,000 MIRVed re-entry bodies deployed. He then produced a colour slide to show that the accuracy of these weapons was such that they could strike within 500 or 700 metres of their targets, and these figures would be improved upon. That was all on slide 8. Slide 9 was a detailed list of targets for the Soviet nuclear forces. It showed the Minuteman and Titan II bases as well as 46 Strategic Air Command fields and two nuclear submarine depots. The next illustration was stark. If the Soviet Union launched a full-scale attack, they would be expected to use 1,200 weapons carrying a total of 6,000 megatons. Two-thirds of the targets would be military, the other third civilian. The result would be something under 100 million deaths. No attempt was made to show serious injuries.

In limited attack on the SAC bases, the missile silos and the submarine depots, the mortalities 'could be as high as 5 or 6 million. In an attack on the ICBMs alone, the mortalities would run on the order of a million; and for the SAC bases, the mortalities would be less than that – of the order of 500,000'. One of the missile sites at Whiteman Air Force Base in Missouri was singled out as an example of the death toll extending to the civilian population. Whiteman AFB is close to Kansas City and St Louis. It is considered a good example of how wind direction, and therefore fall-out, could affect one area more than another. Secretary Schlesinger said that, for five of the six Minuteman fields, the total number of casualties would approach half a million and the total number of fatalities would be in the order of 300,000. He went on 'An attack on Whiteman . . . because of its westerly proximity to a major urban-rural population complex, would drive the number of fatalities up to about 800,000. The number of casualties including people who fall ill as a result of radiation sickness coming from fallout, would approach a million and a half'. He then showed the possible death list for three other types of military targets. Attacks on the two missile submarine support bases (one at Bremerton, the other at Charleston) would mean about 100,000 fatalities; the two shipyards at Philadelphia and Hunters Point, 155,000; and at the San Diego, Long Beach and Norfolk Navy Bases, more than 200,000 deaths.

Returning to Whiteman AFB, the Defense Secretary showed that St Louis could suffer 156,000 casualties. Also on the committee was

Senator Symington. He wanted to know the possible casualty figures for Kansas City. Later he was told that, in the worst case, 750,000 people would die. It was, however, emphasised that this was the most terrible possible projection, assuming little warning and shelter.

Warning time is a crucial question for the defence planners and this was emphasised by Secretary Schlesinger in response to a question from Senator Pearson.

Senator Pearson: 'To refresh my memory, what is the time frame between knowledge of a launch against the United States and impact or re-entry?'

Secretary Schlesinger: 'About thirty minutes for ICBMs. Five to ten minutes, depending on the trajectory, for submarine launched ballistic missiles deployed close to the American shore.'

These figures hold good for the 1980s. Much of the September afternoon was taken up with discussing possible fatalities. It was quite obvious that, within the Washington defence community, there existed widely-varying views on the likely outcome of a nuclear strike. Part of the evidence before the committee came from the US Arms Control and Disarmament Agency analysis of possible fall-out effects. This contained considerably higher figures than the Department of Defense analysis, and the conflict between these two offices exists today. Whatever the disagreements, the members of the Muskie Committee were deeply impressed, if not disturbed, by what they had heard. Senator Case, who had started the whole thing with his letter to Secretary Schlesinger, described the session as 'very stimulating'. By 4.45 p.m., two and a quarter hours after they had closed the doors and begun to talk, they called it a day, but not before the Defense Secretary had agreed to furnish them with additional information once he got back to his office. That information was in itself as revealing as the evidence before the sub-committee.

Secretary Schlesinger's office prepared a scenario to show the near-and long-term damage that might be expected as a result of a Soviet attack on purely military targets; they would not make special efforts to minimise the effect of the attack on the civilian population.

Timing for the attack was important. It would occur in March, the worst case for the United States because all the wind directions are at their 'best' for carrying fall-out over long distances. Two Soviet warheads were aimed at each of the 1,054 ICBM silos and one each against the bomber bases and the missile submarine support depots. A total of 2,158 missiles were used by the Soviet strategic forces. The warheads were all air-bursts, therefore the amount of fall-out was negligible, but, as has been shown in an earlier chapter, the violence of the blast was at its optimum. There was also supposed to be sufficient warning time for the civilian population to take cover and 'get out of town'. Quoting from the Defense Department's scenario: 'The estimated near-term collateral effects of this postulated attack were 6.7 million fatalities and 5.1 million non-fatal injuries (largely due to radiation sickness). This is contrasted with the 90 million or more fatalities that would be associated with large-scale direct attack on the US urban-industrial complexes.'

The long-term effects of radiation were summarised as follows:

'7,000 to 30,000 neoplasm deaths per year for several years.

'8,000 leukemia deaths per year for several years.

'5,000 to 10,000 genetic deaths per year during the first generation.

'An average life shortening of about 0.7 years.

'20,000 congenital malformation deaths out of 3 million pregnancies at the time of attack.

'Not estimated are the additional cases of anaemia, cataracts, retarded development in irradiated children and non-fatal malformation from foetal irradiation.'

Some of those 1974 findings appear remarkably sanguine. Certainly there is evidence today suggesting that many of the calculations were underestimated. Indeed, at the time, Fred C. Ikle, who was then the Director of the US Arms Control and Disarmament Agency and who had access to a whole army of government-based computer and strategic predictions, was moved to comment that studies of the effects of nuclear explosions have taught 'the more we know, the more we know how little we know'. Perhaps the Director's point was a little obvious, but it did, indirectly, move Secretary Schlesinger to admit, cautiously perhaps, 'One can never be sure what discoveries may be made in the future that would drastically change the perceptions of nuclear warfare.'

Since September 1974, others have not been so cautious in their warnings of what they believe would happen in the event of a nuclear confrontation. Here it would be simple to quote the doom-and-gloomers one step removed from the brigades of sandwich-board hikers and their predictions that the end of the world is nigh. But some of these warnings have come from people in a position to know what official and quasi-official thinking agrees upon. Some time ago, a former Director of the US Defense Intelligence Agency, Lieutenant General Danny Graham, remarked to the author that he thought that 160 million Americans would die in a surprise attack. He also said that the reason for this was the American failure to understand what the Soviet Union technological advance rate would achieve in a very short space of time. The General blamed the Intelligence community for this misreading of all the signs and was the first to admit that he shared part of that blame. General Graham, who in 1980 joined the defence advisory team of President Reagan, has long believed that one way to cut the chances of his gloomy prediction being proved correct in time of war is to build Western Civil Defence systems. He is not alone in his assumption.

A recent study undertaken in Washington showed that, under the present American Civil Defense system, about 150 million people would die in what was termed 'a Large-Scale Mid-1980s Soviet Attack Versus US Military and Industrial Facilities and Population'. But the scenario and the American reaction were developed in accordance with a five-year plan for the Civil Defense system as organised under the US Federal Emergency Management Agency. If it were possible to have a week or more notice of the attack and during that time remove up to 108 million of the 135 million Americans who normally live in metropolitan areas, more live would be saved. Indeed if all went well with the evacuation programme (of Crisis Relocation as it is called), and fall-out protection had been developed in the outlying areas, then no more than 44 million or so people would die. Remember that this compares with more than 150 million under the present scheme of things.

At the same time it was thought that, if the plans did not go well, and there was not sufficient warning time, then about 132 million would still be dead. Of course all this would cost money, perhaps some 1,600 million dollars at 1979 prices. Furthermore, like so many programmes, there has to be a certain political will to support any scheme. The vagaries of that political support may be seen in the fact that, although President Carter was happy to sign a Presidential Decision (PD 41) in September 1978, little was done to back it. Recent budget increases have done little more than allow the sketchy budget to keep pace with inflation, if that. In fact, on the basis of per capita spending, the United States has a wretched track record in this area in spite of her environmental advantages in setting out a comprehensive Civil Defence programme. And environment is a key element in Civil Defence as many analysts have quickly found when examining the subject. This is especially so in Europe.

A first-class example is that of the United Kingdom. Civil Defence, or Home Defence as it is called in Britain, has long been considered something of a joke. The system of Civil Defence was disbanded during 1968 and, in spite of the 1980 survey carried out by the Conservative government, it does not provide for any real protection for the general population. The weaknesses have been well do-cumented by everybody with even the vaguest interest, partly because the weaknesses are there for all to see. Numerous newspaper, magazine, radio and television surveys have all but ridiculed the system, have increased what is generally called 'public awareness', but have not managed to come up with any solution that would greatly improve the system. The government has had similar troubles. Of course, many have highlighted improvements that may be made to the programme for helping people *after* an attack, but the initial problem of greatly reducing the number who would die in that attack has not been resolved. Nor is it likely to be.

The British government has made no provision to shelter the civilian population. Government ministers, their officials, some local authority personnel, some elected members of local councils, certain police, army and medical officers, will go underground. The remainder of the population will be left to do the best they can with scant and, at the moment, doubtful advance from the authorities. Furthermore, there are no plans to evacuate major towns, cities or obvious target areas. Successive British governments have been quite willing to make do with what is called a Stay Put policy. The two basic reasons for this lack of protection are the cost of providing the shelters and, secondly, the belief that one part of the country would be just as bad as another and that, anyway, the emergency services would not be able to cope with refugees.

Because there is no adequate protection planned for the British population, the vast majority would die in the event of the type of war predicted by many war-gamers. Given this rather alarming picture, it is not unnatural that the public mind has concentrated on the prospect of perishing during an attack. But this is only one part of the grisly equation – although admittedly it is the largest part. Civil Defence is not only about protecting people from an attack, it is also about protecting people from the aftermath, the prospects of which are so horrendous that the former Chief of the Defence Staff, Field-Marshal Lord Carver, has said that he for one would not wish to live through a nuclear attack. Government plans for dealing with this aftermath appear to be no less sketchy than their provisions for the cause. Considering the chances of Britain being right in the conventional and nuclear front line in time of war, this is more than disturbing. Some still doubt whether the United Kingdom would be attacked, either because they believe the British government could 'back away' from any conflict at the last moment, or because they have their quite legitimate political reasons in thinking that some future government would withdraw from NATO. Neither of these hopes is plausible.

But they do help raise the question of why the United Kingdom is such an obvious target. As has already been shown, Britain represents a formidable military base for her own as well as United States forces. Military targets in the United Kingdom include at least four underground major command centres, one third of the ballistic missile early warning system, communications for submarines armed with nuclear missiles programmed to hit targets in the USSR, runways for aircraft designated to handle nuclear weapon-armed jets, interceptors and anti-submarine aircraft. Apart from Britain being a strategic bull's-eye, there is something to be said for the argument that a nuclear strike against Britain might well be used in some conflict as a warning to the United States and the rest of Europe that it was time to call a halt before such a war was transferred to the North American continent.

It has been said there are eighty targets in the United Kingdom. This is, in fact, a figure sometimes used at the Home Defence College at Easingwold in Yorkshire. For them, it is an exercise number, and it should be emphasised that nobody could possibly know which town, city or installation would be attacked during a war. Yet it is a fairly simple pastime to list what might be better described as *potential* targets, some of which are in the middle of high-density areas.

One of these targets is the underground headquarters of one of the three major NATO commands (Supreme Allied Commander Europe at Casteau in Belgium, Supreme Allied Commander Atlantic in Norfolk Virginia and the Commander-in-Chief Channel at Northwood, England.) The Commander-in-Chief Channel, known as CinCChan, is a British admiral who is also the C-in-C of the British Fleet (CinCFleet). His Northwood command post is deep underground and surrounded by the comfortable commuter community of north London. It is a few minutes' drive from another major target, London's Heathrow Airport. Neither is expected to last much more than a few hours. (One CinCChan has stated elsewhere that he would not expect to be in operation beyond eighteen hours.) West of Northwood is the headquarters of the RAF's Strike Command at High Wycombe in Buckinghamshire. Again, it is an underground headquarters and still contains the deep corridor trod by such World War Two leaders as 'Bomber' Harris. In 1981, it remains a prime target. The link between Strike Command, Northwood and the underground complex at Pitreavie Castle near Edinburgh is a strong one in peacetime. The Scottish-based headquarters is the brain that monitors an area which extends to the Soviet territory beyond Norway, the line from Scotland, the Faroes, Iceland to Greenland through which Soviet nuclear submarines, surface ships of the Northern Fleet and Backfire bombers need to pass to get safely into the Atlantic. And, if Pitreavie is on the list, Brawdy in south-west Wales certainly is. Brawdy is part of a huge network of underwater listening posts designed to identify Soviet submarines. It is one of the analysis centres for SOSUS – Sound Surveillance System. Barriers of earphones are able to identify Soviet submarines by their engine, propellor and even hull 'signatures'. A nuclear submarine makes a different noise from a conventional diesel submarine. Even different nuclear submarines make different noises and it is quite easy to identify various classes. At Brawdy, American technicians pick up these sounds and they analyse them. The results are then sent to a higher analysis centre, OSIS or Ocean Surveillance Information System. It is an essential part of the Western need to identify the whereabouts of Soviet submarines, and so it is equally essential for the Soviet Union to knock it out as soon as possible.

Heading north into Scotland, nobody would give much for the chances of the fighter control and radar on Scotland's eastern seaboard at Buchan, nor the Nimrod base at Kinloss. There are similar vulnerable sites throughout the islands. Faslane, not that far from Glasgow, is the base for the Polaris fleet, with nuclear weapon stores not far away; the dockyard at Rosyth on the other side of Scotland is a major repair yard, as is Devonport in England's south-west and the complex of industry, graving docks and housing in surrounding Plymouth. There are the Maritime Headquarters at Plymouth overseeing the Western Approaches, Portsmouth. Further along the coast, are the many airfields in East Anglia, the smaller runways and large commercial airports to be used for alternative bases for bombers, interceptors, tankers and transports. There are the wireless antennae at Rugby, the Government Communications Headquarters at Cheltenham, underground headquarters in Wales, in Somerset, at Horsham in Sussex, at Dundee in Scotland. There are so many potential targets, even if one does not consider the industrial complexes which would include Royal Ordnance Factories at places such as Nottingham and Leeds. Then there is London itself. It is not just a seat of Government, because by then government would have dissolved, scattered throughout the country to the bunkers in what are called, by the defence planners, the sub-regions. But London would be a great psychological target – if that were at all necessary.

But perhaps the first place to go would be far from most towns, inland on the Yorkshire Moors from Scarborough. Fylingdales is the British end of BMEWS, Ballistic Missile Early Warning System. Its radars are constantly scanning the skies for any sign of an attack and have been doing so since the early 1960s. BMEWS is not just switched on during times of international tension. Twenty-four hours a day it watches and waits. If the day should ever come, when a missile attack is launched against the United Kingdom, the RAF personnel at Fylingdales know that one of the first warheads will be aimed at them. They are quite philosophical about this; once they have spotted the lift-off from the USSR missile sites, checked the trajectory and confirmed the attack is on its way, then their job is done. But for the United Kingdom and the Civil Defence system, the war would begin long before that.

The common theme for the UK war-gamers tends to be written in three stages. It begins with the standard 'period of rising tension', goes on to the decision to mobilise troops, and usually ends with a nuclear strike on, say, Birmingham. None of it needs much imagination to put together, and there are those who believe the real thing would produce few quirks or surprises.

If these games were to be played out with great efficiency, which few are, they would involve four elements of the United Kingdom: firstly, the three Services including the Royal Marines (to provide the offensive as well as the defensive troops); secondly the politicians at national (including Cabinet) and local level together with their officials; thirdly, the paid and volunteer emergency services such as the police, medical, fire, the United Kingdom Warning and Monitoring Organisation and the Royal Observer Corps; fourthly, the general public.

There is a remarkable lack of realism in the planning of these exercises. This does not mean there is insufficient blood and gore and live firing. It is quite obvious that exercises have to stick to safety rules. The fault lies in the amount of scope given to the planners, not in the planners themselves. Manoeuvres are obliged to hold to a script otherwise, it is believed, they will not work. There are major headaches in allowing too much flexibility, but at the same time some quite radical rethinking is necessary in future series of Civil Defence manoeuvres. Why should not sirens be sounded to see how the public reacts? And, with plenty of warning, why not run the wartime broadcasting tapes, telling people what to do and expect in the event of an attack? Why could not the public be told to watch for 'suspicious' characters, to check their pantries for fourteen to twenty-one days of food, to see if they could find some emergency shelter? Perhaps such suggestions and elements in exercises would provoke anger. There would be a sense of fear perhaps, and this would not be welcome. But if there is sufficient warning that it need be nothing more than an exercise, this in itself would test the community system which would be essential in an emergency. If these exercises are to run at all, then they should be done properly. The idea that the shop-doors should not be opened until the sale starts at 9 a.m. is perfect for Oxford Street or 5th Avenue, but it does not make too much sense in Civil Defence planning terms.

The general trend for the scenario for an attack on the United Kingdom begins with that period of rising tension mentioned above. It could be imagined that relations between Eastern and Western bloc countries have hit an all-time low, that the Soviet Union and the

United States have taken sides in some Middle East disagreement in spite of earlier announcements that they will not. Britain then announces that she is sending a token force of two frigates to the Gulf in support of the United States naval force in the area. The Middle East conflict settles down to a drawn-out series of border incidents, threatening the whole Gulf security and, yet again, Western oil supplies. During one of these scraps, Omani patrol craft are attacked and retaliate. The following day, an unexpected air attack destroys the Muscat palace of Oman's Sultan Qboos and, in a similar attack in the south, British and American civilians and servicemen are killed in Salalah during an air strike directed from Aden. Accusations fly back and forth, the Soviet Union is accused of being behind the raid on Salalah, and the American President, who has for some time strutted up and down declaring that he alone is willing to protect world interests in the Gulf, is forced to put some of his fire-power where his mouth is. There is a series of 'We shall be forced to act' declarations from Washington and Moscow and there follows a quick naval skirmish between the two sides in the region.

In Europe, Polish workers choose this moment to organise further industrial demonstrations in support of claims they say have not been met following the unrest during 1980 and 1981. Czechoslovak dissidents, who have been carefully watching events in Poland for two years, decide to make their move. The Prague and Warsaw governments say that unless everybody backs down they cannot guarantee that the Kremlin will not be forced to interfere, Washington says that it had better not, the new Moscow leadership sees this as a test of its authority and orders the mobilisation of the Groups of Forces *already* stationed in those two countries. Similar instructions are given to the GSFG commander.

In Western capitals, NATO and national commanders are in constant session with their political masters; Chiefs of Staff in London ask the Cabinet for the necessary authority to call up reserves including the Territorial Army, which would mean the signing of Queen's Order 2. The Cabinet refuses. The General Secretary of the British Trades Union Congress is called to Downing Street. The Prime Minister wants to know how the Unions will react.

Meanwhile the Defence Chiefs argue that, unless they get the go-ahead for mobilisation and reinforcement within the next twelve hours, they are far from convinced that they can carry out the plans to bring Rhine Army to its wartime levels. Downing Street recognises the need, but says that NATO has agreed that any mobilisation will be taken as a sign that the West is going to war, and that could precipitate an attack on the West by the Soviet Union.

Airlines begin cancelling flights, the corridor to West Berlin is closed, a steady stream of refugees begins to move away from the East-West border, adding to the complications of the military trying to clear roads for their own supplies and impending troop movements. Ships heading for European ports are advised to keep clear of the region. Some London commuters fail to check in for work and heavier than usual traffic is reported on all roads leading to the West Country and Wales. The 10,000 or so members of the all-volunteer Royal Observer Corps report for duty and their 870 underground monitoring posts are activated. Both the United States and the Soviet Union have, during the past twelve hours, launched extra satellites. In Downing Street large anti-war demonstrations by trades unions and student bodies are joined by members of the general public. Similar demonstrations are taking place in Bonn, Brussels and The Hague. The Pope broadcasts a message of constraint which is directed to the Polish workers.

At last the order is given to mobilise and Moscow calls this an act of open aggression. Constant probing flights by Soviet aircraft from the Northern Cape region are spotted across the North Sea and heading towards the United Kingdom. Although none of these flights is considered 'hostile', Phantoms from Scottish bases are scrambled to intercept as far out as possible. Similar actions have been taking place for ten or eleven days and, by now, the RAF at Strike Command is reporting that many of the aircraft are in a dangerous state of repair and pilot fatigue is high.

Not too far out into the Atlantic, an ASW (anti-submarine warfare) task group centred on the newly commissioned HMS *Illustrious* is patrolling west of the Iceland–Faroes Gap. The group – the *Illustrious*, guided missile destroyers and anti-submarine frigates – is supported by stores ships, four nuclear submarines, maritime patrol aircraft and an ancient Royal Air Force AEW (Airborne Early Warning) aircraft, a Shackleton. They are on full stand-by following reports that NATO radar is being jammed off Norway, signifying that Soviet Naval Air Force units may be heading into the Atlantic. The task force has also reported three Soviet missile submarines and a conventional boat in the area. Sea King helicopters are searching the area with their dipping sonars, a patrol aircraft has laid a barrier of Jezebel sonar buoys to track the submarines, Phantoms are being sent from Scotland to protect the group, which has launched its Harrier jump jets, and the support ships have stopped refuelling the frigates as the enemy aircraft and submarines close in. And so, the war is on.

By this time it would be evident to the public that Britain really is a massive offshore carrier for the Allies. From the American point of view the main support role for their reinforcement aircraft would be carried out by the United Kingdom. The British Isles would supply recovery bases where American aircraft could be refuelled and maintained after unloading on the Continent.

That US reinforcement would involve perhaps 500 cargo and 300 passenger aircraft. With the minimum of activity now planned by NATO, such an airlift would mean each of those 800 planes making one trip every two and a half days. That means 160 American flights would be coming into the UK every day – assuming everything went according to plan. However, it is assumed that if weather, enemy action and general confusion were taken into consideration, then these rates could readily triple or even quadruple for periods of up to twelve hours or so.

It is against this background that Britain's system for the defence of the civilian population would have to operate. Broadcasts, already prepared, would go out telling people first and foremost to stay where they are. It would be suggested that no one place is any safer than another, although how a Londoner or somebody living close to the centre of Birmingham is expected to believe this is difficult to understand. Somebody in London may not be convinced that he would be better off where he is when, at the same time, he knows that the government has its own plans for going underground in the countryside.

Official policy is that local authorities would not help refugees from another area. But local authority executives know full well they would have to make some provisions. The police know they could not turn people back; physically it would be an impossible task. They are also mindful of the fact that, although the British government sent one and a half million women and children to the the country during September 1939, two million got out on their own accord. When, in the winter of 1944, the population of East Prussia was told to stay where it was, it disobeyed. The movement of people would be a major headache for the authorities, especially as every effort would be made to leave the authority for running the country in civilian rather than military hands. The military would be busy attempting to get reinforcements to continental Europe, maintaining and flying aircraft and making sure every ship that was available could and would put to sea.

There is a large force designated for the defence of the United Kingdom, although it is woefully inadequate for the task; this task does not encompass the thought that there is going to be an invasion. A large part of the force's job would be to protect UK bases and installations from within. There would, for example, be a major attempt to sabotage key points within the United Kingdom. It is expected that, prior to a war, the Soviet Union would be able to

infiltrate sabotage groups into the British Isles. One target often
suggested is the array of offshore oil and gas rigs. A specially trained
element of the Royal Marines, which includes the Special Boats
Section, the SBS, regularly rehearse against such an attack. However,
the simpler action for terrorists or saboteurs would be to hit the points
at which the oil and gas comes ashore. Power stations, including the
nuclear models at Sizewell, Dungeness, Bradwell, Springfields,
Hartlepool, Dounreay, Heysham, Chapelcross, Hunterston, Wind-
scale, Wylfa, Winfrith, Oldbury, Trawsfynydd and Hinkley Point, are
obvious danger points, as are places such as the atomic weapons
establishment at Aldermaston, main railway junctions, ordnance
depots, the Dartford Tunnel, the Severn Bridge, communications
posts, reservoirs, government food dumps, and main airfields.

Yet all this would be largely of academic interest if there were to be
a nuclear strike. By that time, the various underground sub-regional
headquarters would be working with the county and district authorities setting up their operations, often in the basements of county halls,
or in some cases in specially prepared rooms of district council offices.
Far too many of these centres are in disrepair or, in some cases, do not
exist in any form readily convertible to a war-state. Perhaps the most
organised element in the system is UKWMO, the United Kingdom
Warning and Monitoring Organisation. As its name suggests,
UKWMO (often pronounced Uckwermoe) has a job of warning the
public during a nuclear attack. It works on the principle that,
although millions could die during an attack, other lives could be
saved given a few minutes' warning of the attack. Further lives might
be saved if other information such as the pattern of fall-out was
detected earlier enough. It is essentially a volunteer group and has
been seen by some as the most cost-effective system of its kind
anywhere in the world. Whether or not this be so, there is no doubting
its dedication. More than likely, an attack on the United Kingdom
would be signalled from Fylingdales. That information would be
relayed all the way back to Cheyenne Mountain and the North
American Defense Command. It would also go through to, among
other places, Whitehall, to Strike Command at High Wycombe, and
to West Drayton. The UKWMO would be closely involved with the
reaction to that signal. High Wycombe is also the headquarters of the
United Kingdom Regional Air Operations Centre, known as UK
RAOC and referred to as UK Rayock. At UK RAOC there is a
special signal box and, when the nuclear attack warning came
through, a key would be turned in that box to activate alarms
throughout the country. These alarms are called Carrier Control
Points and there are 250 of them scattered throughout major police
stations in the United Kingdom. If an attack were expected, the CCP

(Carrier Control Point) would have been switched up to produce from its small speaker a continuous blip. The key-turning at UK RAOC would interrupt that blipping with a high pitched scream. The officer in the police station simply depresses a switch on the system and this automatically turns on sirens in the area. Throughout the UK there are 7,000 or so of these power sirens, and there are 11,000 further warning points. These are usually hand-cranked sirens, especially in rural areas where they may be in the local pub or even in private homes. In time of war, the public should have been warned what to expect.

Radio and television broadcasts would have given a description of the three warning codes. RED, Attack Warning, is a rising and falling wailing from a siren and means an attack is imminent. BLACK, Fall-out Warning, is meant to be given by the sound of three whistles or three bangs from a maroon. WHITE, All Clear, is intended to come from a siren with a continuous note.

Once the warning attack signal has been given, UKWMO really goes to work. Well before the attack, the Organisation, which includes the 10,000 volunteers of the Royal Observer Corps, would have taken up their stations underground. There are, throughout the United Kingdom, 870 monitoring posts, many of which are within bicycling distance of most small towns and villages, although few know they are there. This fact has little to do with security but is rather a question of safety from vandals in peacetime. From the surface all that is visible is a steel trap door, maybe a couple of box-type constructions a couple of feet in height and looking rather like an odd form of beehive, and a couple of pieces of piping, two or three feet above the surface. The trap door opens on to a shaft measuring about four feet across and twenty feet deep. At the bottom there is a door opening on to a small room about seven feet high, seven feet wide and sixteen feet long. At the far end there is a bunk bed and along one wall a table top with instruments and a communications unit. From the surface, instruments – one of which is called a bomb blast indicator – measure the strength and type of any explosion in the monitoring post's area. An important factor will be the post's ability to tell if the explosion was a surface or air burst weapon, because this may be the first warning that radiation might follow. To get a reading from one of the instruments, one of the three people in the post has to run up the ladder, out into the open, and return with a reading. He or she will go out as soon after the explosion as possible and, because it will take some time for any radiation to reach the post, should be clear in time.

Each Monitoring Post transmits its information to one of twenty-five Group Controls in the United Kingdom. The Group Control will report to one of the four Sector Controls in England or the one Sector

Control in Scotland. The Group Controls monitor the reports from
the posts and attempt to plot the possibility of fall-out in their areas;
and then pass on the information not only to the Sector but to any
other authority in the region. Again the Royal Observer Corps is the
main staffing body for the fifty or so people at Group level who will
include scientific officers. Work from all these centres would be going
out to the 750 warning districts throughout the United Kingdom,
each one of which covers an area of about 100 square miles.

The Sector Control is the biggest unit in UKWMO. It is set up
underground, and is approached through an outer and an inner
reinforced door leading to a decontamination room and then an
airlock. The decontamination room might by-pass the airlock so that
the person entering would go straight through to a dressing room.
Then there would be a corridor. Along the left-hand side there would
be lavatories, a commander's office and the male dormitories. On the
right-hand side, there would be a generator room and an air
circulation chamber. The next door might lead to a galleried room
containing, on the ground floor, teleprinters and communications,
with observers above. At the bottom end of the corridor might be the
kitchens, rest room and briefing section and then the female dormitories. The main room would be the operations centre containing the
state boards for plotting the situation outside. Altogether there may
be seventy or eighty people in the complex under the command of the
Sector Controller, his deputy and the deputy area commander
responsible for logistics, the group commander, the senior duty officer
and others such as the senior scientific adviser and the chief warning
officers. There would also be national liaison officers. At Horsham, for
example, there are two liaison officers whose job it is to keep in touch
with Belgium and France. It could be that fall-out from an explosion
on the Belgian border may be heading for Sussex. In Dundee, the
Sector Control would include a liaison officer from Norway. It is an
important part of the system to defend the public, and an UKWMO
document gives an interesting scenario for its operation.

Time: 0957. Fylingdales, Yorkshire: radar detects an attack on this
country. The United Kingdom Warning and Monitoring Organisation acts immediately.

0958. Enemy attack warning received by 250 Carrier Control
Points in major police stations. Police sound sirens – warning public
to take cover. Every second is vital.

1002. First of the sinister mushroom clouds: nuclear bursts are
recorded in UKWMO Group Controls at the very moment of
explosion by special AWDREY[1] equipment.

1. Atomic Weapon Detection Recognition and Estimates of Yield.

1003. Underground Monitoring Posts also register nuclear explosions. Information is passed to Group Controls in minutes or even seconds.

1008. Position and power of nuclear bursts are calculated at a Group Control from information supplied by Monitoring Posts.

1019. Nuclear bursts are plotted on transparent screens. Likely path of radioactive fall-out is predicted from meteorological forecasts – and the public is alerted.

1023. Carrier Control Points relay fall-out warnings to 18,000 locations all over the country. Maroons detonated from these points warn the public to keep under cover.

1420. By now information on the path and intensity of fall-out is being passed by teleprinter tape network to other Groups and Sectors.

1515. Five Sector Controls exercise overall control and co-ordination.

0600. Life goes on . . . *ten million lives* may have been saved.

As the document says, ten million lives may indeed have been saved. Nobody should poke fun at the work UKWMO is ready to do. But *ten* million lives? In the context for peacetime, however uncertain, it seems a pitiful figure. Furthermore, this all assumes the system will work. Unfortunately, like so many plans for the civil defence of Britain, there are too many unknowns and daunting possibilities. Most plans rely on communications. But will there be any? Electromagnetic Pulses (EMP) from a nuclear explosion are likely to knock out most common communications, to such an extent that even the simplest and sometimes the most vital piece of information will not be passed on. The government expects the public to listen to their radios for the latest instructions. The chances of transistor radios, or any others for that matter, surviving are very slim. Communication may well exist only at the crudest level, word of mouth. And perhaps here lies the key to whatever life exists in Britain, should there ever be a nuclear war. The theme might be, Back to Basics.

The worst scenarios built by war planners not only indicate the horrors of what might be, they also show up the deficiencies in the ability of those who might one day be responsible for the bringing together of whatever society remains and its resources. At some of these war-games, attended by the author, one point common to them all stood out. Most of the players (both military and civilian defence colleges do call the scenarios 'games' and the participants 'players') are people who in wartime would be designated to take part in the running of emergency planning and control services. They would, then be the decision-makers. These same people, as observed by the author, rarely go into the games prepared to exercise a sense of realism, in what would be an almost unreal society. Too many of them give the impression that they are unable to think beyond using a limited version of the resources available in peacetime. The terrible truth is that, in many cases, it is unlikely that any form of peacetime resource in its obvious state would be available.

A few examples may demonstrate this point. If one takes an area the size of one of the Home Counties, the first thing to notice is that the chances of there being any form of telegraphic communication are slim. Without normal, everyday communications, such as telephone, teleprinter, radio or cable service, it would be extremely difficult for anybody who had assumed control in one part of the county to know what was going on in another part; perhaps he would not even know if *anything* was going on. If this possibility is taken to an extreme, he would not know if his small group was all that was left of organised society in the whole country. He probably would not know to whom he should report, if there was anybody to report to, and what powers he might safely assume. He would need to analyse the means of enforcing any powers he did assume. He would not readily know what resources were available, what casualties were like, how much food, fuel and shelter had survived.

He could no longer rely on facilities previously taken for granted. For example, when there is an earthquake, along with the blankets and tents, the Red Cross immediately fly in drugs to combat pain and disease. In a post-nuclear strike, there may only be the drugs immediately to hand. Furthermore, there may not be the means of manufacturing any more. Medical syringes may be available locally but, once they are gone, there would be no industry to make any more. It could take the glass industry and the plastics industry years to be rebuilt. There may be bell-ringing and siren-screaming ambulances. But how long would the fuel last? During one war-game observed by the author, a syndicate spent hours debating whether petrol should be used for emergency transport services, law enforcement or heating for kitchens. It took that long to realise that what little fuel that might be available could not last long enough to make the debate worthwhile, that time should be spent looking for other fuels. When it was decided that forests could provide ready fuel, more time was wasted discussing how to get the fuel to the chain saws and then sawn wood to the kitchens and boilers.

At last, the syndicate, all sophisticated men, realised that the solution was more drastic then they had thought. People would have to gather the timber by hand and axe. No transport would be sent for it. The people who would gather the fuel for the fire to heat the food would bring that fuel to the boiler and be rewarded with the food it had heated. There was another point missed by the group. Even if oil and transport had been available, perhaps it would have been better to use people; better for those trying to pull things together to be able to give out jobs of work. They would soon realise that, by keeping a distressed population occupied, law and order would be that much easier to enforce.

An examination of what might be has shown that a surviving society will go so far back to basics, it will have to re-learn skills often forgotten or never known by the majority of today's society. It is for these reasons, say many who have studied the Soviet Civil Defence system, that the Moscow government has placed so much store on the protection of industrial plant. Much of the responsibility for law and order will be on the police, although there is a great debate as to the role the surviving army might play.

The chances are that the army will be the only section of society actually trained to survive in the crudest of conditions. It is, in general, a fit and young organisation; it is also used to regrouping and setting up, almost by instinct, an efficient command and control system. Anybody who has witnessed this ability in the youngest of modern-day British soldiers will confirm this. Yet the army insists that it will remain at the beck and call of the civilian authorities, and nothing more. It has another advantage: it is the only group with Nuclear, Biological and Chemical Warfare clothing. (Each soldier has three suits.) It may be of course that this advantage may cause some resentment among the civilian population. So, the army will liaise very closely with the police. But the latter will have to work in an environment as alien to them as to any other survivor. Although there is a certain amount of training done in peacetime, it is very limited and it is often not much more than a one-day refresher course every two years or so.

The Police Manual of Home Defence is a comprehensive document, although there seems little reason for it to be Classified. As might be expected, it is full of understatement and just a touch of 'I was proceeding in a southerly direction when I saw . . .' humour. For example: 'On hearing a nuclear explosion, officers at police stations should note the time, and test for fall-out . . . every ten minutes the officer should return to the meter, take a quick reading and retire again . . ..'

'If a prisoner of war is captured by the police, the appropriate Military Headquarters should be told as soon as possible. If this cannot be done for any reason, the nearest military unit should be contacted. Military Headquarters or the unit concerned will then send an escort to collect the prisoner; a receipt should be obtained.'

The guts of the Manual is well prepared for the average constable to get some idea of the enormous task that one day might come his way. There is everything from the effects of a nuclear explosion, to the detention of subversives, to the guarding of Key Points and protected areas, to the correct way to fill in forms and dig latrines.

There are some things that cannot be answered in any manual. In the aftermath of a nuclear war, would the police have to extend their operations in other areas? How would they deal with law-breakers? Where would they put prisoners? How far will they be asked to go to maintain the peace? Who will take the decision to issue them with fire-arms? and when? There are those who believe that that decision would be taken immediately before the nuclear attack. Some police officers say they will be well prepared to use those weapons in the strangest circumstances – for them anyway. Others say they will not. Would they have to shoot looters? Incurable radiation victims? And who would hand down the laws? Surely the laws of the peacetime land would not apply? And who is to decide? When does foraging become looting? How serious a crime is petty theft if it might disturb the harmony of an extra-sensitive community? The people who will have to decide will vary from former government ministers down to former parish clerks. For the chances are that, in such circumstances, the person who has been forced to assume command and control of a community, whether it be a county, a sub-region or, at the other extreme, an isolated village in the Fens, will also have to assume a form of dictatorship as alien to him as the environment. For, although there are communication lines already constructed away from likely target areas between sub-regional and county headquarters, the chances are that small pockets throughout the United Kingdom will be, for a long time, on their own.

As has been shown above, the Government at Westminster would dissolve just before an attack was expected. Senior government ministers would go to their designated regions, which are equivalent to the existing ten Defence Regions, and where he or she would assume the title of Commissioner. Because the minister would not assume any control until some weeks after an attack, the sub-regions would be the highest form of government. Most regions are divided into two sub-regions. Each sub-region would also have a commissioner, and he would run things until such time that the Regional Commissioner and his staff could emerge from the three or four underground shelters. Consequently, the circumstances point to the district and local authorities providing most of the organisation for the possible recovery after an attack. In peacetime, most, if not all, of the real training to ensure fitness for this job is carried out at the Home Defence College at Easingwold and then by the local authorities themselves. It is an accepted fact that, although Easingwold is one of the best training systems in the world, there is a tremendous shortfall in the standard set by local authorities, most of which

HOME DEFENCE BOUNDARIES

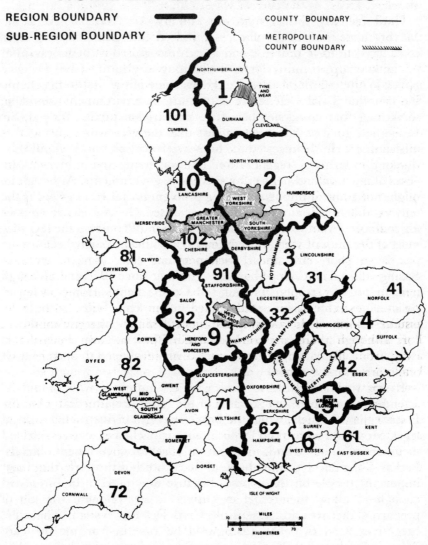

REGION BOUNDARY   ▬▬▬   COUNTY BOUNDARY   ▬▬

SUB-REGION BOUNDARY   ▬▬   METROPOLITAN COUNTY BOUNDARY   ▨▨▨▨

Not shown on this map are Scotland and Northern Ireland. Scotland is divided into North, West and East zones. Ulster is a single region. Most regions are subdivided. Thus, Home Defence region Number 6 includes Hampshire, Berkshire, Bucks, Oxfordshire and the Isle of Wight in one sub-region and Surrey, East Sussex and Kent in the other.

would not be up to the task that might be set them after a nuclear attack.

Until recently Easingwold was run by Air Marshal Sir Leslie Mavor, a retired RAF officer (if indeed Air Marshals are ever considered to have retired), and a man recognised as being essential to thinking up, training for and planning any future Civil Defence policy Whitehall might produce. He was one of the first to ram home the fact that Civil Defence in a post-attack environment would be something that could not be left to prepared manuals. Indeed, Sir Leslie had gone as far as to suggest that the very word 'survival' is misleading. He believes that home defence planners should be thinking in terms of 'regeneration'. He was hampered in his work by years of inaction and neglect by successive governments. Although he might not admit it publicly, one big problem is that Easingwold is the only establishment running these specialised Home Defence courses for civilians. (Another indication of central indifference is the fact that most of the tutorial staff are retired Service officers; partly because the pay is so poor, only those with pensions can afford to work at Easingwold.) The College has been running since 1973 and although it is in no way responsible for the Government's Home Defence[1] policy, inevitably it influences the development. There used to be other establishments doing similar work, but they were closed down. It is now clear to almost everybody in Civil Defence, everybody that is except the Government, that there is a very real need to open at least one more training school.

Easingwold is unable to cope with the numbers who should be attending its courses and so most of the latter are aimed at what Sir Leslie calls the chiefs, while the braves have to be instructed at local level. Most courses are run for local authority chief executives, elected members of councils and, more recently, senior government officials. Perhaps the elected members of local authorities are the most important people on the courses because they need to be interested enough to allow their chief executives to get on with the job of preparing the area for a sensible Civil Defence system. The chief executives need to be at Easingwold because in wartime they are going to be the controllers in many of the underground shelters. The paid officials, such as district and county chief executives, are enthusiastic about the courses which are generally designed to prepare them, both mentally and administratively, for what might one day occur with only a few days' notice. Too few elected members,

---

1. Britain insists on using the term Home Defence instead of Civil Defence, which is stupid because most people understand what is meant by the latter term and not the former. Perhaps this is why the Government prefers the more confusing title.

particularly councillors, have turned up for the courses. There may be very good reasons for this: many, perhaps most, councillors have full-time jobs as well as their civil duties, and getting a week away from work outside their normal holidays may well be difficult. At the same time, it is clear that some local councillors and their authorities are simply not interested. It would be understandable if this attitude were confined to the nether regions of Wales where there could easily exist a sense of security brought on by remoteness. But there are some areas where there seems a foolish lack of interest. They have populations which would be particularly vulnerable in time of war, and it might be considered that the local electorate should be able to demand that their councillors pay more interest to the subject.

One of the courses run at Easingwold is called Hotseat. It is a very apt title because Chief Officers are put in the position of having to make or approve decisions that might well be put forward in Home Defence operations. The course begins, usually on a Tuesday, with background material on Home Defence and the effects of nuclear weapons. This is followed by an outline of current Home Defence policy and a breakdown of government structure in the event of war. In the afternoon of that first day, the students are given a run-down on the job of the police in Home Defence and other services, such as the problems of maintaining food and water supplies in a nuclear environment. By the following morning, they are ready to go into the war-game. The students are normally split into five groups represen-taing different areas in the county of Naptonshire, a mythical county which would appear to be based on somewhere such as Nottingham-shire. Typically, the executives would take on eleven jobs: Controller, his deputy, scientific adviser, emergency accommodation officer, food officer, manpower officer, transport officer, works officer, information officer, the police or military representative, and the health officer.

The scenario might show a large county with a comprehensive industrial base and perhaps an armaments factory (such as the Royal Ordnance Factory at Nottingham), a rural community together with the large suburban population associated with such a county. It is possible that two nuclear bombs have been exploded, one in the Napton area and the other outside it. This latter weapon is important because it demonstrates the possibility that fall-out from another region would reach neighbouring counties. Prepared broadcasts are shown on closed-circuit television, information will come in concern-ing casualties, death rates, looting, transport difficulties, homeless people, refugees from other areas, breakdown in communication systems, contaminated parts of both the city and the rural areas, together with the difficulties of assessing what has survived outside the relative safety of the control centre. There are those who may scoff at exercise Hotseat inasmuch that a group of sane, sensibly-educated people will not be expected to see the four-day programme as anything but a game. Yet it is remarkable how quickly these very professional people do become immersed in the scenario. There is no suggestion that they begin to believe it is real, but the problems are so great, the pace so fast and the natural desire for individuals to shine in front of their fellow students so intense that soon there is an astonishing sense of realism running through the whole course. And, in the bar during the evening break, it is quite common for the groups to spend time discussing the problems almost as if they *were* the wartime controllers and emergency officers.

But, however well Easingwold is able to prepare a few people, the undoubted weakness remains at grass roots level. There are cases where steps have been taken to rectify this, mainly on the initiative of a few people who usually find themselves branded as lunatics or warmongers. One such case where a group has successfully shaken off the lunatic label is in one of Britain's most beautiful villages. In the tiny valley village of Branscombe in East Devon there is the head-quarters of an organisation called CCD, the Campaign for Civil Defence. It is run from the study of a rambling stonebuilt home called, perhaps appropriately, Hole House. Its organising brain is a man who is quite used to fighting battles, both military and bureau-cratic. Tony Hibbert fought through the Second World War and survived actions such as Arnhem. It was not until recent years that he became interested in the organisation of Civil Defence and with others was instrumental in establishing what are known as the Devon Emergency Volunteers. But it is his CCD that may turn out to be the most worthwhile project he has undertaken. Hibbert, along with many other Civil Defence planners, accepts that whatever fine plans central and regional government may produce, if there should ever be a full-scale nuclear war, it would be left to the villagers, wards and tiny communities to do the best they could until some grander form of control and government were in a posiion to emerge from what was left of their shelters.

As Hibbert sees it, essential systems such as telephones would be of no use, transport would be inoperable and regional help would be far away and remain so for some time. He is even sceptical about some of the most elementary systems provided by government. During one exercise in Branscombe, the community was warned that the nuclear warning tests were to be run. Hibbert planned to explode the maroons described in the government booklet, 'Protect and Survive'. The village was told that the tests would be made, at what time they would be made, and what villagers could be expected to hear. After the explosions a survey was carried out. Few people had heard them, yet the valley does not extend to much more than three miles between its longest points. He also discovered that, when he wanted to test the radiation meters, he could not because the batteries were flat. They were not rechargeable and, worse still, were of a type not available in general shops.

The CCD is virtually a one-man operation. The reason for this, says Hibbert, is to avoid the acrimony usually found after a time in such bodies. But his is not entirely a dictatorship. He has on call politicians, military men and scientists who are willing, and have demonstrated their willingness to back him when necessary. One job has been to produce an astonishingly comprehensive document, a Model Emergency Plan. It covers everything any small community, such as a parish, needs to know if it wants to set up its own civil defence system or even to make sure that the one it has is planned along the right lines. There are those who would disagree with what Tony Hibbert is doing, and some of that criticism would be valid, yet the fact that he and others like him are having to take on these tasks does seem to be some indication that, although the 1980 Government Review on Home or Civil Defence emphasised the need for volunteer organisations and local interest, it was little more than lip-service to one part of the system that could, without much financial backing, be made to work. It would, however, take considerable enthusiasm and organisation. One of the problems in gathering together any volunteer group, and preparing it for something which may never happen, is that the group has to be given something to do. Too many local organisations have found that, once the latest media or international scare is over, and with it the initial and inaugural enthusiasm has subsided, then the original team may often fall away. Yet, as Hibbert and others are able to show, there is more than sufficient work to keep a small team going for many years. Although more emphasis should be placed on local organisation, there is no doubt that the existing policy of central government is almost at the point where the Home Office might seriously think about scrapping the whole thing and starting again.

The Division in the Home Office responsible for Civil Defence has much in its favour – especially when it comes to expertise – and it is a reasonable bet that the main problem lies in the elected offices of Whitehall. The complaint heard during the summer of 1980, when Civil Defence was being reviewed, was that the funds were not available for what the Government would have wished to do. Yet there are many in local government who would say that money is not the main problem. It is lack of direction and a failure to channel existing energies. There are some signs that certain authorities are putting more emphasis on emergency planning. There are even those departments who, having been told to cut back on certain areas within the authority, have toyed with the idea of using the government directive on Civil Defence to post would-be redundant officials into emergency planning offices.

It has long been said there are no votes in Defence. This may not be true for much longer. Although there have been some restrictions in Defence Ministry spending, some people are beginning to question the budget. Others might easily point to Civil Defence as a weakness in the overall policy of central government. More has been done than people tend to think. For example, there are more then thirty government papers, known as Home Office Emergency Services circulars, on such subjects as Public Survival under Fall-out Conditions, Ear-marking of Buildings for War Planning, Advice to the Public on Protection against Nuclear Attack, Home Defence Training for Police, National Arrangements for Dealing with Incidents Involving Radioactivity, Community Organisation in War, Water Services in War, and so on. It would be an improvement if more of this information were readily available to the public.

Meanwhile the Government has to get to grips with the basic problems which catch the public imagination: evacuation and shelter. The physical problems of getting people out of towns are enormous. Because Britain is such a small land-mass, many communities tend to run into one another and evacuation is even more difficult. Leaving one suburb for another may not be very satisfactory. Yet people will leave if there is a war and they will tend to head for what they believe to be wider and more open spaces, such as those on the moors and in the Lake District. Their chances of survival in those places are not much greater, especially in winter, as any old newsreel of weather conditions will show. Also, the areas into which refugees may straggle are not likely to be hospitable, whatever faith people may have in the Great British Character. As one South of England councillor remarked publicly and perhaps unwisely during a council debate in 1980, there would be only one reception: 'Shoot 'em!'

For those who actually believe in Civil Defence, a certain amount of comfort might be provided if there could be some means of guaranteeing even limited shelter protection. The Government has been looking at certain buildings, but it would be a better idea if some basic planning instructions were produced that would provide shelter in time of war. A few ideas that might be debated would include the building of a series of underground shelters in every housing estate. The shelters would act as car parks during peacetime and, with a little bit of thought, need not have to cope with more than a dozen families at a time. (The saved garage spaces could mean higher densities or even bigger gardens, who knows?) It would not take much planning imagination to build a basement in more houses or even beneath detached garages. They do not have to be elaborate and, as can be seen in the United States, they have every kind of peacetime use. Nobody is going to survive a direct hit in any nuclear war, but there are developments this or any other British government might consider, to give those outside the immediate blast area a better chance.

For a start, local authorities should be made to comply with the standards already laid down by central government. Some of them do not and Whitehall does nothing about it. Another college along the lines of Easingwold should be established immediately. The costing on this would not be so massive as some might suppose. Easingwold has a principal and a vice-principal. They are supported by twelve tutorial staff, including two seconded officers and administrative staff of about twenty-four and about forty industrial staff. The whole establishment costs a little more than £500,000 a year to run.

More information on Home Defence and what to do in an emergency should be more readily available. The Government should not rely on its booklet 'Protect and Survive', nor on any version of it. Why is it not possible to lay the important information in some publication to which most people constantly refer? Why not put such information in a page or two of the telephone directories? It may be considered alarmist, but then so were Cancer Campaign posters when they first appeared. There is also an argument that if Government had been able to release earlier as much information as it has during the past eighteen months or so, then it would not have found itself subject to such sensational press reporting. There are some very good brains within the Home Office working on this subject; it is a pity they have not in the past been given a little more air by their political masters. Nobody should expect to be shown the army's War Book or the complete details of what Britain plans to do in the event of an emergency, but there is sufficient information of a harmless nature to satisfy most needs.

There are, of course, those who would describe the whole principle of Civil Defence as being an obscene operation. While it does seem the most natural thing in the world to protect people from a possible attack, there is a very good argument against it.

Many would say that, by providing shelters and escape plans, a government is effectively preparing for war. Those same people tend to be those who would argue that Britain should disarm. The argument might continue that, by having an effective Civil Defence system and therefore being in a position to protect the vast bulk of the population, a government feels more assured and even adventurous. In other words, knowing that the population was relatively safe, a government would not think twice about going to war. So, no shelters, no war? Perhaps not. The argument against such thinking tends to point out that an aggressor would not be able to hold a population to ransom and therefore would be less likely to attack. Thus, Civil Defence becomes part of the deterrent. If it is accepted that deterrence must include the ability to show the other side that there are no weaknesses, no gaps, in the defence system, then perhaps Civil Defence may be argued as part of it. In that case, there are few, if any, Western governments up to scratch.

Belgium, for example, does not even have a shelter for its government. One of the country's more controversial generals, Robert Close, appears to feel that Belgium's civil defence system is so poor, almost non-existent, that it would have a terrible effect on the morale of the army. He is said to have stated that it would be impossible to expect the Belgian army to fight if the country behind it was being destroyed. An idea of this antiquated system is given by the national Civil Defence headquarters communications which have outside windows and are considered to be vulnerable to anything beyond the size of a hand-grenade or wire-cutters. Like the United Kingdom, there is no policy to protect the population from fall-out or from chemical attacks, which are likely in wartime in both countries around areas of key installations. The general policy within Western Europe seems to be to order the population to stay where it is. This stay-put policy is unlikely to work and would in particular cause major military problems in continental Europe.

This applies in West Germany more than in any other country. It is inconceivable that the people of West Germany would not leave the border areas in the event of an attack or, more likely, before an attack. The West German government has legal powers to prevent people from leaving their normal homes. It is doubtful whether such a power would work; this is recognised and there are provisions for the people living in certain danger areas to be moved. In the normal course of a projected war, West Germany could expect to face almost every form of attack, air, ground, missile, chemical and nuclear. It is easy to see why the Civil Defence budget stands at about 360 million dollars for 1980, which is better than three times that of the United States. One very sensible attitude in West Germany, which might be adopted elsewhere, is the way in which Civil Defence is presented as the most normal thing. It is effectively a part of the peacetime emergency services even if it does take up the vast majority of the emergency services budget. There are plans to provide Civil Defence advisers to every large community, so that one adviser should be able to cope with about six or seven thousand people. His or her task would be to tell everybody about nuclear protection and how to protect themselves not only from radiation, but chemical and biological warfare. This advice would cover the building of small shelters; and, on a large scale, provisions are being made for construction companies to receive a grant if they intend to put a shelter into some new building. There are similar subsidies for public buildings.

As might be expected, the German warning system is based on sirens and radio and television tapes; the latter have already been made and are ready to go out. The warning system itself is quite comprehensive with more than 1,500 monitoring and warning posts. More than five hundred of them are manned. Rather like the United Kingdom's system, West Germany is divided into wartime warning and monitoring districts staffed by more than 2,000 men and women, the majority of whom are volunteers. (A useful peacetime occupation for these people is the monitoring of pollution standards.[1])

The West German government is only too aware that it would, in time of war, become the most fiercely contested territory in Europe. Apart from the ground actions, there would be desperate air battles and attacks on the numerous West German, British and American air bases and weapon dumps. Yet, in spite of all this and her relatively healthy economy, West Germany has had to admit defeat in one important area of Civil Defence. Her government now approves shelter specifications which are known to be below the standard required for maximum protection. The reason for this is that the specifications that were being approved until recently were too expensive. Time and again, it is the cost element that is quoted as being the reason for a lack of civil emergency systems. The tactical, moral or political arguments are rarely put forward.

In continental Europe, there is a slightly different attitude from that in the United Kingdom and the United States. As these people live in what one day could become a battleground, this is understandable. In the Netherlands, there is legislation that makes it necessary for all new houses of two storeys or more to have in the basement a shelter which includes seals for protection against radioactive fall-out. There is a wider acceptance that dual-purpose buildings such as underground garages could be converted in wartime and more attention is paid to the dangers of chemical weapons. Norway has one of the best systems in the West. The country has four civil defence training colleges, options for those liable for national service to work in Civil Defence, a comprehensive warning and monitoring programme, regular Civil Defence exercises which involve television information programmes, a more or less compulsory shelter policy which provides places for close on 60 per cent of the population, and a

1. See also Assembly of Western European Union Document 838, Rapporteur, Robert Banks MP.

tried evacuation plan. It is an impressive system and, while it is certainly true that the small population of Norway makes it relatively simple for the government to provide protection, there are those countries without adequate systems such as the United Kingdom and Belgium which could learn a great deal, perhaps have, but have failed to do anything about it.

One of the arguments of those who are against Civil Defence appears to be that, if no provision is made to protect the country, then there is less chance of getting into war. There are some merit points to be picked up here, but at the same time it is interesting that the most admired and often quoted Civil Defence system is that operated by the Swiss. The next best is the Swedish programme, also belonging to a neutral country. Neutrality does not lessen the danger of one country to nuclear fall-out or even direct attack. There are all sorts of ways in which a neutral country might find itself involved and in need of protection. During the Second World War, Switzerland was bombarded about a hundred times, and experienced fifty or so minor battles on her borders. The Swiss have been thinking along Civil Defence lines since 1934 when the government recognised that any future conflict beyond its borders would be dominated to some extent by air strikes. It should be remembered that it was not until 1940 that air power was used on any grand scale, but in conflicts elsewhere there were already signs of its military potential.

The Swiss concept of what they call 'armed neutrality' is based on the principle of protecting the population so that most of it will not only survive an attack but will be able to live on afterwards. For the past thirty years all underground cellars in new buildings have had to have a shelter inside them. This does not mean that a cellar is considered to be a shelter. It is worth repeating: the shelter is in the cellar. The shelter would normally be in one corner of the basement and would be built out of reinforced concrete with forty-centimetre ceilings, thirty-centimetre walls and twenty-centimetre floors. The door would be about twenty centimeters thick and made from armoured plate, and a similar door would be used as an escape hatch into a tunnel of reinforced concrete. It is considered that the Swiss provide shelters for about 90 per cent of the population. In addition there are nearly a hundred reinforced operating theatres in underground hospitals together with 290 medical stations and more than 600 first aid posts. By the time the so-called protected medical services are added together, the Swiss government produces 73,000 or so protected hospital beds.

Training for Civil Defence goes on in fifty-five centres throughout Switzerland and manages to cope with the thousands of healthy males between the ages of twenty and sixty. During the next few years, twenty further training centres are to be opened. It is a very impressive operation. It is so impressive that most other countries appear to have adopted the attitude that, because the Swiss system is so far ahead, it is a waste of time trying to catch up. It is certainly not the philosophy adopted by the Soviet Union although it might be said that, in the USSR, Civil Defence is not so thorough as many have suggested. Without going into great detail on the Soviet system,[1] it is worth noticing that the authorities there regard it as an essential part of military planning. It is, after all, the first element in the defence of the homeland – a phrase often heard when discussing Soviet military strategy. The CIA report quoted earlier is quite certain of the miliary connection. Under the heading 'Key Findings', the report says:

'By developing an active and extensive civil defence, in conjunction with their other defensive and offensive strategic programmes, they hope to convince potential enemies that they cannot win a war with the USSR. If war should occur, the Soviets seek through civil defence along with other means to assure survival of the homeland and to leave the USSR in a stronger postwar position than its adversaries.'

That is the CIA's view and, whether or not it be valid, it is one supported by many who have spent a great deal of time analysing the Soviet system. At the same time it must be said there are few who would not be able to guess correctly that the above conclusion might find its way into such a report. Unquestionably, the Soviet Civil Defence System is a massive organisation, although its grossness might easily be thought to be typical of most Soviet bureaucracies rather than a reflection of the importance of the organisation. It is headed by General Altunin, who has a full-time staff of about 100,000. (There are 550,000 or so Swiss doing compulsory Civil Defence service.) It is thought that in time of war there would be sufficient shelters for the whole of the Soviet leadership. This does not mean that only the Party chairman and his colleagues would be protected. The Soviet leadership is spread throughout the different Republics and is generally thought to amount to more than 100,000 senior party officials. There is no certainty that this shelter is safe; most of the units have been identified and so would if necessary be easily targeted by Western military planners.

The general population has a certain amount of protection and by the middle of this decade more than a quarter of the urban population would be sheltered in some form. Although there are thought to be something in the order of 15,000 blast shelters throughout the USSR a great part of the protection plan would rely on early evacuation as indicated earlier in this chapter. Estimates of how much training is

1. For a comprehensive view of Soviet Civil Defence, see Bibliography.

required of the general public vary; but a figure of twenty hours' training a year is thought to be fairly accurate. Official and quasi-official bodies are enlisted into the programme, and so the 100,000 full-time Civil Defence workers may well be reinforced by more than ten million others at some stage or another during the training year. Exercises are held on a fairly regular basis, but, like so many things in the Soviet Union, the multi-cogged bureaucracy in Moscow often fails to turn many wheels in the regions. Factory managers for example, pressed to maintain work targets and bedevilled by local inefficiency, will often ignore and neglect Civil Defence training programmes. A general conclusion on the Soviet system may well be that the machinery is there, the provision of shelter at all levels is well established, there is a recognition of its importance; however, the machinery needs an inordinate amount of oiling and minding.

Yet, if a conclusion is valid, so is a general warning. It may not be assumed that one country's ability – or one power bloc's ability – to protect its population is any indication of its willingness to join in a war, or even start it. Conversely, one side's inability to protect its people should never be assumed to be a sign that it would be reluctant to go to war – or start it.

NINE

Conclusion

Thousands of missiles, thousands of tanks, thousands of jets, millions of men. Some of them good, others very good. Some of them bad. Obsolescent tanks rub tracks with the latest money can buy. Twenty-year-old jets carry ultra-modern missiles beneath their wings. Young men with long-life razors are drilled by older men who have seen it all before and hope to God they will never see it again. Radars stare from hill-tops and moors, while their operators rub their eyes to keep awake. Satellites silently probe for the merest hint of a change in temperature that will tell them a silo lid is sliding back. It is all part of the ill-defined Military Balance. It is what analysts like to call Capabilities.

But there remains one weak link in the analysis. It is possible to present a reasonable assessment of the capabilities of the world military machine as shown in the earlier chapters. Capabilities are there for all to see and, because they are vast, expensive, complicated and cumbersome, they are slow to change. But what any one government intends to do with those capabilities is less predictable.

Capabilities are slow to change, but intentions, normally set in dogma and ambition, can alter within twenty-four hours.

And what of the world outside the direct influence of the two Superpower blocs? It often appears that their intentions and even their long-term capabilities are even less understood. The Western courtship with China is a good example of a relatively new policy being shuffled as if the seal had been broken on some new diplomatic deck. None of the cards are marked, or if they are the players are slow to spot the ink and razor marks.

More than twenty years ago, during conversations with the author, Chinese officials were predicting a war between the Soviet Union and the United States. But who would win? We will, said the Chinese.

During the 1970s the West started to move back to China. Apart from the obvious advantages of re-establishing relations with the vast nation, there were huge commercial prizes to be aimed for. The Chinese military system is only now emerging from the 1940s. Whatever the protestations, it does seem the West is willing to re-arm the Peking government. Britain tried to sell the Harrier jump jet on the grounds that the plane is a defensive weapon, a semantic description and one with which the Vietnamese would hardly agree.

The United States said she would never sell China weapons although it is difficult to see the difference between selling a country military hardware and selling her machinery and technology that eases the production of an indigenous arms industry. If it were at all possible, a joint decision by Western governments not to re-arm China would have its attractions. However, there is no way in which such a joint decision would be agreed in Western capitals. The argument is that if the West does not, then somebody else would. At the moment, that somebody would not be the other great arms exporter, the Soviet Union. But what about Brazil, Israel and, now, Japan? There is every sign that China, the world's biggest nation, will become one of the best armed powers. Peking has already joined the nuclear weapon club, has produced rockets with sufficient range to allow her to enter the inner sanctum of the strategic powers, and has stated and proved her willingness to use military force. And, if the West has second thoughts, there is always Japan.

Japan is now capable of becoming a major arms exporter. She is fast moving towards a constitutional change which will allow the Japanese Self Defence Force to be as well-armed and as wide-ranging as that of any other nation in the Far East. The 1980 defence budget was running at nearly two thousand million dollars, which may not seem very much in NATO terms, but is remarkable for a nation which officially does not have armies, navies or air forces of an aggressive nature. But growing concern over the Soviet build-up in the Far East and encouragement from the United States are giving the Tokyo government any leverage it may feel it needs to build up its forces. Since 1980, Japanese air defence fighters have started to be armed with air-to-air missiles. Before the summer of that year, missiles were kept in storage.

The navy is now carrying charged torpedoes and mines. The United States is supplying her latest F-15 interceptors and the aircraft industry is already capable of building a very good jet of its own. There are those who remain convinced that Japan will never move away from its memories of the Second World War and Article 9 of its constitution, which basically renounces war as a way of settling international disputes. But, with one of the largest middle-class populations of any country – perhaps three-quarters of the Japanese people see themselves as middle-class conservatives – there is every indication that these traditional views are changing. It is not far to the next step in military thinking: the nuclear club.

This is of course the great factor in deciding how little can be predicted by the war-gamers when they prepare their scenarios. Practically every game sees a war beginning between countries other than the two Superpowers. They mostly end with the Moscow and

Washington fingers pressing the nuclear buttons. But what about the other nuclear and near-nuclear nations?

Few doubt that Israel has nuclear weapons. A mistake by the CIA revealed that it at least has long believed that the Tel Aviv government has built such weapons at its plant in the Negev Desert. Certainly the technology exists and Israel has done little to dispel the idea. The standard Israeli reply to accusations is that they will never be the first to introduce nuclear weapons into the region. That does not mean they have not got them. Using typical Israeli logic, it could also mean that as Soviet and American weapon systems have already flown over and patrolled the region with nuclear arms, then Israel would not be the *first* to introduce them to the Middle East. There is also some evidence to suggest that the technology, or part of it, needed to build nuclear weapons, has been passed to South Africa. The United States government is of the opinion that South Africa could become a nuclear power by 1984. That estimate is being revised following a report that the Pretoria government successfully tested a nuclear warhead over the Indian Ocean during 1979.

One problem for the South Africans has been the difficulty in guaranteeing supplies of enriched uranium. This is no longer such a headache although, during the summer of 1980, there were those in Pretoria who were saying that if Ronald Reagan became President, then there would be a change in US policy which would allow enriched uranium more freely into the country. But South Africa is hardly alone in her membership of the nearly nuclear society. Pakistan has been working for some time on what is generally known as the Islamic bomb. India carried out her first 'peaceful' test in 1974, and now some think that Brazil, with West German help, could apply for membership in the not too distant future.

The spread of nuclear arms is perhaps only a generation away from the escalation of the more sophisticated of the conventional armouries. The attempts to restrict the spread have not been particulary successful. The 1963 Partial Test Ban Treaty may be blessed with the signatures of more than two-thirds of the world, but it does not stop nuclear facilities being built. It, or any other treaty, could not hope to prevent the necessary technology spreading to any country that wants it. It is also possible that a nation without the facilities will soon be able to acquire the weapon; that after all is the popular theory behind the Islamic bomb, although it does not stand too much examination – as this stage.

Whoever has a bomb is no more of a threat to *world* peace than he who has to struggle by with conventional weapons. The nuclear bomb-owner may have the ability to be more destructive, but that does not necessarily mean he is more likely to cause a world war than his more conventionally armed neighbour.

It is quite possible that nuclear weapons will be used in some war without the involvement of the Superpowers. The irony is that there are those in both Moscow and Washington who are coming to the belief that, within a few years, they will have less control over the monstrous science they created than they do now with their daunting arsenal of nuclear weapons.

Machiavellian outlines are not normally the distinguishing marks of Western scenario-makers. They tend to stick to the obvious because they are thinking in terms of a setting that would lead to an East-West confrontation. When they do, they still tend to watch for circumstances long described by strategists as the Window of Opportunity. It is a simple hypothesis, which claims that the Soviet Union will attack the West when all the circumstances are right. A typical example might be: a marked Soviet military superiority; Western governments trying to honour too many commitments throughout the world and, therefore, militarily stretched; economic decline; low morale of the people; political and economic rifts within the Atlantic Alliance, making collective decision-making difficult or impossible; and even disaffection among some NATO members.

In other, and perhaps oversimplified, words, the Soviet Union will attack when her power is at its uppermost and Western power is at its lowest. It might not take a brilliant strategist to work that out; any school bully would be able to testify to the logic. Yet it does not take account of the unpredictable, such as war by accident, or one side finding itself on the ropes and deciding to come out fighting rather than take any notice of its seconds, and ducking and weaving until the bell goes for the end of that particular round. It could also be that Western strategists have for too long looked too narrowly at the Soviet capability, and allied it too closely with the different theories about intentions.

In the West there is a tendency to separate nuclear weapons from conventional weapons. Nobody doubts their differing destructive powers, what is assumed is that the Soviet Union sees them as different forms of weaponry. Most Kremlin-watchers are coming round to the understanding that the Soviet Union would never go to war unless it believed it could win. What does seem to have escaped some experts is that the Soviet military mind might not rely on the doctrine that nuclear weapons are to be used if conventional forces fail, and only then. To the Soviet Union the two are indivisible. The nuclear weapon is part of the overall armoury and any planning for a war with the West must include nuclear weapons as a matter of course and not of last resort.

Whether or not this is understood or even important to them, strategists and foreign policy-makers are nervously watching for the signs they so eagerly feed into their possible and probable computers – the think-tanks that attempt to predict the Window of Opportunity. The signs are that some things will change during the next five years or so, World leadership is on the move in the White House and in the Kremlin. China is becoming stronger, the Middle East is looking more unstable, while the major economies and therefore national politics are increasingly under the influence of outside factors such as the price of oil. But there are some things especially in Europe that will not change in the immediate future.

The trend towards coalition governments either by votes cast or consensus will not dig out those countries in trouble. The different cultural and social standards, characters, economies and politics within the European Communities – and therefore in the Atlantic Alliance – will remain fairly constant. The fundamental political system and attitudes in the United States still have much to accept about Europe, and therefore any closer relationship between the United States and her European Allies will be but a temporary bonus for the Alliance. The physical position of countries is not going to change and therefore the traditional fears on both sides of the European borders will continue to haunt the region. While the West may be showing signs of shifting politically to the Right (and therefore could shift back towards the Centre), there is no chance of the Soviet leopard changing its spots. Whatever is thought of the satellite states within the Warsaw Pact, Communism as the form of Eastern European ideology will not alter. This may be stating the obvious, but it should be taken as a reminder that, for all the grandiose schemes and treaties, such as the Helsinki Final Act, treaties banning this or that, or promoting co-operation is one cultural, scientific or economic field or another, the basic character differences, politics, beliefs and systems will remain.

Average Man, blessed as he is with a naïve common sense, might timidly suggest that, while he may not care for the Soviet system, that would seem little reason for a war. He might go further and use the centuries-old argument that he is sure that, if the politicians would step aside for one moment, both he and Vladimir could quite happily get along with each other. He is probably right. However the world has yet to throw up the leaders who are able to put these sentiments into practice. Ideology and simple logic make uncomfortable bedfellows. When ideology is threatened, its guardians tend to lash out. During the next two or three years it is likely that the world will witness major changes as governments and power blocs attempt to strengthen the somewhat rickety fences designed to protect those ideologies.

The West seems determined to re-establish any influence it once had in the Middle East and the Gulf States, and if some of the countries in that area continue to believe that the Islamic Revolution is a threat to their being, then the West may well be encouraged. This will involve military deployments on a more permanent basis than hitherto. As a result, the Soviet Union could find itself having to spend more energy on some of its client states and developing those fringe benefactors of Moscow's military advice. If this all leads to a greater Soviet bloc presence in, say, Libya, South Yemen, and Syria, and a western block presence in Egypt, Saudi Arabia, the United Arab Emirates and, of course, Oman, then there would be little sign of the regional tension being reduced. Such a state of affairs could even lead to other countries trying to play one Superpower off against the other – a dangerous game for everybody.

The Soviet Union must necessarily continue its efforts to decouple European opinion from the United States. Disenchantment with the United States leadership during the past four years, and no clear indications of what to expect during the coming four years, would suggest a very testing time for European and, more particularly, trans-Atlantic unity. Add to this the trend towards the leadership of the West tacitly moving from Washington to the triangular political throne of Bonn, London and Paris, and it seems certain that a great deal of fence-mending needs to be done within the NATO structure. It is the sort of situation the window-watchers love to write up in their strategic notebooks.

Moscow will, meanwhile, struggle with the problems presented by some of her satellites (Poland is an obvious example), and the West will find it more and more difficult to hold its diplomatic tongue. But what if the spotlight continues to shine on the Middle East? What if the Far East once again begins to boil, and one client state or another calls on its super-godfather to honour his pledge of security? For these sorts of reasons, there remains the prospect that, if war should start, it will do so far from the European theatre, because the United States and the West are no longer able to stalk up and down waving their banners of promises while yet another domino falls too neatly into the wrong place.

A war started deliberately in Europe because the Soviet Union believes the time is right is unlikely, because at the beginning of 1981 the time is *not* right. It does not make military sense. In spite of the many weaknesses in the Western military system, the Soviet forces and their allies are simply not strong enough in Europe to make victory certain. But that is no comfort for Europeans, or for others who are uncertain about the future roads the Soviet Union may wish to take to extend its power. Lenin defined Soviet power as 'the road to socialism that was discovered by the masses of the working people, and that is why it is a true road, that is why it is invincible'. He was speaking in March 1919, yet there is no great reason to believe that the present Soviet leadership feels any differently. Politics in Moscow are a little more sophisticated today than they were sixty years ago, but the gut aim is the same.

What is quite different is that the Soviet Union has taken its aims further afield than Lenin could have felt possible. The Soviet Union is now deployed along many roads throughout the world, consequently it is also vulnerable in spite of the daunting vision it presents. It is the kind of vulnerability that causes many to ask what the Soviet Union could hope to gain by invading Western Europe. But that is not the sort of question often asked in the Kremlin. What they do ask themselves, as must the West, is what will happen if the West decides to throw up a roadblock, should the Soviet armies take to the highway once more. That is why the West German Chancellor, Helmut Schmidt, was right to warn of the dangers of a repetition of 1914 and the very real chance of a world, looking for peace, finding itself at war. Chancellor Schmidt knows, as well as any other leader, including those in Washington who pronounce on the theory of a limited exchange, that there could never be such a thing as a limited nuclear war between the Soviet Union and the United States. In fact the only hypothesis that allows any examination is the one which predicts a single nuclear warhead on a European capital as an attempt to hold the rest of the Alliance, including the United States, at ransom.

There has been peace in Europe, if in few other places in the world, for the past thirty-five years. It could be that, as a result of neglecting those few other places, Europe's long-running success is in danger of coming to a terrible end. As a constant reminder, the bottom instrument on the score-board of the Ballistic Missile Early Warning System says simply: Minutes To Impact.

Short Bibliography

CLARKE, Robin, *We All Fall Down*, Penguin Books.

GOURE, Leon, *War Survival in Soviet Strategy*, Centre for Advanced International Studies, University of Miami.

ERIKSON, Prof. John, *The Soviet High Command*, Macmillan.

Outer Space – Battlefield of the Future, Stockholm International Peace Research Institute.

The Soviet War Machine, Salamander Books, particularly the section on the modern Soviet Ground Forces by Christopher Donnelly.

Strategic Survey 1980, International Institute for Strategic Studies.

Foreign Affairs, Council on Foreign Relations Inc., USA.

Index

ABMS (Anti-Ballistic Missiles), 48–9
Aden, 16, 17
Aegis missile cruisers, 84, 95
Aerial reconnaissance aircraft, 99–100
Afghanistan, 117; Soviet invasion, xi, 2, 6, 11–13, 16, 38, 40, 117; and U.S.A., 12–13, 17
Air Launched Cruise Missiles (ALCM), 84
Aircraft carriers, 9, 55, 56 and n.
AK–47 rifle, 50, 53
AKM rifle, 53
Albania, 66; withdraws from Warsaw Pact, 34, 61
Alpha particles, 124
Altunin, General, 173
Anderson, Major Randolph, Jr., 99–100
Andropov, General Yuri, Chairman of KGB, 36, 37
Angola, 12, 16
Anti-aircraft missiles, 84
Anti-satellite development (ASAT), 8
Anti-Submarine Warfare (ASW) (UK), 92
Armiya Sovyetskaya, 43
Arms Control and Disarmament Agency (USA), 146, 147
Atomic numbers, 121
Aviation Work and Space Technology, 8
AWACS (Airborne Warning and Control System), 49
AWDREY (Atomic Weapon Detection Recognition and Estimate of Yield), 158 and n.

B–52 bombers, 78, 79, 84, 107, 141
Backfire (TU-22M) bomber, 9, 15, 59, 84, 150
Baltic Fleet (Soviet), 54; submarines and bases, 58
Barents Sea, 57, 59
Belgium, 93; and NATO, 10, 11, 67, 71; and Cruise missiles, 41, 70; and Brussels Treaty, 66; Civil Defence, 170
Beta particles, 124

Big Bird satellite, 102, 106
Black Sea Fleet, 54, 58
Blackbird aircraft, 99, 100
Blast, 128, 131–4; overpressures, 131–3 dynamic pressure, 131; US tests, 131–2
BMEWS (Ballistic Missile Early Warning System), 151, 181
Boeing jets, 49, 77
Bottom Contour Navigation, 59
Branscombe, East Devon, 166
Brazil, 176; and the nuclear bomb, 177
Brezhnev, Leonid, 33, 40, 41, 43, 59, 88; offices and commands held, 28
Britain and the British, *see* United Kingdom
British Army of the Rhine, 89
Brown, Harold, 41
Brussels, HQ of NATO and North Atlantic Council, 67, 68
Brussels Treaty (1948), 66
Budapest, 42, 50
Bulgaria: and Warsaw Pact, 60, 61; military strength, 63,
Burns, 128–30; flash and indirect, 128, 130

Callaghan, James, 89, 90
Campaign for Civil Defence (CCD), Branscombe, 166–7
Canada, 66, 89; calls for defence pact, 66–7; and NATO, 67, 71; and NORAD, 87
Capabilities, concept of, 175
Carter, President James E., and Carter Administration, xiv, 2, 11, 12, 17, 54, 71, 81, 143, 148
Carver, Field Marshal Lord, 149
Case, Senator Clifford P., 143, 144, 146
Casteau Mons, SHAPE HQ, 67
Casualties from nuclear bombs, 127–38; blast, 128, 131–4, 137; burns, 128; radiation, 128, 133–7; illnesses, 128, 136–7; flash-blindness, 129; firestorms, 131

Centre d'Etudes du Bouchet, 6
CEP (Circular Error Probability), 44–6
Chair Heritage project, 106, 107
Charlie submarines, 57
Chemical Warfare (CW), 5–7, 110–17; in First World War, 110–11, 114, 115; Geneva Protocol, 111; nerve gases, 111–15; US bases, 113; bases in West Germany, 113
Cheyenne Mountain, NORAD HQ, 8, 86–7, 156
China, 38, 179; and the West, 175–6
Chlorosulphate and chlorine gas, 110
Churchill, (Sir) Winston, and the Iron Curtain, 66
CIA (Central Intelligence Agency), 2, 17, 37; study of Soviet Civil Defence, 139–40, 173
Civil Defence, 10, 139–74; estimates of nuclear casualties, 139–48; in UK, 148–69, 171; other Western countries, 170–3; USSR, 173–4
Close, Robert, 170
Commander-in-Chief, Channel (NATO), 150
Communism, 179
Communist Party of the Soviet Union (CPSU), 18; and armed forces, 25–30; Central Committee, 28
Connally, Senator Tom, 67
Copperhead weapon programme, 95
Cruise missiles, 9, 11, 16, 41, 47, 70, 72, 73, 84, 89, 104, 113, 114, 117
Crusader 80 exercises, 89, 103
Cuba, 12, 16; missile crisis, 46, 47, 54, 100
Cyanogen chloride, 112
Cyprus, 17, 71, 88
Czeckoslovakia, 11, 66; events of 1968, 16, 34, 50, 61, 62, 109; Soviet forces in, 39, 42, 52, 61; and Warsaw Pact, 60, 61; military strength, 63

DARPA (Defence Advanced Research Projects Agency), 107
Defence Council (USSR), 28
Defence Regions (UK), 162; map, 163
Defense Intelligence Agency (USA), xi, 147
De Gaulle, President Charles, 67
Delta submarines, 56–8
Denmark: and NATO, 15, 67, 71; refusal to increase defence budget, 92

Department of Defense (DOD) (USA), 143, 146, 147
Detroit, war-game scenario, 141–2
Devon Emergency Volunteers, 166
Directed Energy Weapons (DEW), 107–9
DOSAAF, 20, 25
Dubs, Adolph, 12
Dunking sonar, 56n.
Dutch, the, *see* Netherlands

E–4A and E–4B flying command posts, 77, 83
Easingwold, Home Defence College, 150, 162, 164–6, 169; Hotseat course, 165–6
East Germany: GSFG, 39–40, 42, 52, 61; military strength, 43, 63; and Warsaw Pact, 60, 61
Echo II submarines, 57
Egypt, 180
Eisenhower, General Dwight D., 67
Electromagnetic Pulses (EMP), 159
Electronic counter-measures (ECM), 84, 102–3
Ellis, General Richard H., 78, 104
Enhanced Radiation Weapon (Warhead), *see* Neutron Bomb
Erikson, Professor John, 33
Eurogroup (NATO), 69–70
European Defence Community, 67
Explosions, nuclear and conventional, 119–21

F1–11 jet, 9, 78, 107, 141
F–15 Eagle jet, 4, 82, 83, 176
F–16 jet, 82, 83, 93
F–104 jet, 93
Fall-out, 124, 126, 127
Family of Weapons concept (NATO), 95
Federal Emergency Management Agency (USA), 148
Fencer (SU–24) jet, 9, 59
Fireball, 119, 123, 124, 128, 129
Firestorms, 131
Fission, 122
Flagon interceptors, 49
Flash-blindness, 129
Flying Command posts, 77, 83
Foreign Affairs, 13
Foxbat (MiG 25) interceptors, 49
France, 3, 13, 67, 74; and chemical warfare, 5–6, 110, 111; information system, 65; and Brussels Treaty, 66;

leaves military side of NATO, 67–8;
liaison with NATO, 68, 71; and USA,
71; nuclear warheads, 76
Frunze, Mikhail, and the army's political
bodies, 27
Frunze Military Academy, 27, 36
Fusion, 122
Fylingdales early warning station, 151,
156, 158

Galosh ABM, 48
Gamma rays, 124, 125
Gammon (SA–5) SAM, 49
Geneva Protocol (1925), 111
Germany, and chemical warfare, 110,
111, 114
Giscard d'Estaing, President Valéry, 71
GLAVPUR (Main Political
Administration of the Soviet Army),
28, 37
Goa (SA–3) SAM, 49
Golf submarines, 56
Gorshkov, Admiral Sergei, 35–6, 54, 55
Gosplan (State Planning Ministry,
USSR), 35, 48
Graham, Lieutenant-General Daniel, xi,
147–8
Great Britain, *see* United Kingdom
Grechko, Marshal, 33, 34
Greece, 72; and NATO, 11, 71, 72, 74;
withdraws from military side, 71
Ground Launched Cruise Missiles
(GLCM), 84
GRU (Soviet Chief Directorate of
Military Intelligence), 36, 37
GSFG (Group of Soviet Forces
Germany), 39–43; dispositions, 39–40;
partial withdrawal, 40–3
Gulag Archipelago, The (Solzhenitsyn), 38
Gulags (Labour Camps), 38
Gulf States, 179
Gundersen, General H.F. Zeiner, 70

Haig, General Alexander, 72
Hamburg, firestorm, 131
Harrier jump jet, 175
Hawk missiles, 84
Helicopters, 55, 56n., 60
Helsinki Final Act, 179
Hibbert, Tony, 166–7
Hill-Norton, Admiral of the Fleet Sir
Peter (Lord Hill-Norton), 70
Hiroshima, effects of nuclear bomb, 127,

128, 130, 136
Home Defence (U.K.), *see* Civil Defence
Home Office and Civil Defence, 167–9;
Emergency Services circulars, 168
Hot Line, the, 88
House Committee on Armed Services
(USA), 140
Hungary, 16, 34, 61; Soviet forces in, 39,
42, 52, 61; and Warsaw Pact, 60, 61;
military strength, 63–4
Hydrogen cyanide, 112

ICBM (Intercontinental Ballistic
Missiles), 31, 43–9, 97, 107, 140, 145,
146; and SALT, 44, 46, 47; location,
46; warning units, 84–7
Iceland, and NATO, 67, 71–2
Identification systems, 94
IFF (Identification Friend or Foe)
system, 94
Ikle, Fred C., 147
India, and nuclear weapons, 177
Interceptors, 49
International Institute for Strategic
Studies, 32n., 110
Invincible class aircraft carriers, 56n.
Iran, 2, 4, 12, 17, 38, 73
IRBM (International Range Ballistic
Missiles), 44, 47
Irish Republic, 73
Iron Curtain, the, 66
Islamic bomb, the, 177
Islamic Revolution, 179
Ismay, Lord, 67
Isotopes, radio-or radio-active, 134
Israel, 4, 176; nuclear weapons, 177
Italy, and NATO, 67, 69, 72
Ivan Rogov, marine landing ship, 9, 60
Ivanovski, General, 39

Japan: and Soviet submarines, 58; and
nuclear explosions, 127, 128, 130, 135,
136; military potential, 176; Self
Defence Force, 176
Jasani, Dr. Bhupendra, 99n.
John F. Kennedy, aircraft carrier, 79
Jones, T.K., 140
Jump jets, 55, 56n., 83, 175

Kalashnikov, Mikhail, rifle designer, 53
Kazakhstan, test site, 107
Keegan, Major General George J., 106
Keflavik, base in Iceland, 71–2
Kennedy, President John F., 69

Key Posts (Points) (KPs), 51, 162
KGB (Committee for State Security), 17, 18, 23, 29, 36–8; Chief Directorates and Directorates, 36–7
Khabarovsk, 38, 58
Khmel, General Alexandr, 28
Khrushchev, Nikita, 54
Kiev class aircraft carriers, 55, 56n.
Kirov, nuclear-powered command ship, 55
Kissinger, Dr. Henry, 144
Klauss, Philip J., 8n., 108
Koldunov, Air Marshal, 48, 49
Komsomol (Communist Youth League), 19–20, 25, 26, 29
Kulikov, Marshal Victor, 34
Kutakhov, Air Chief Marshal, 60

Laser beams, 104–9; production, 105; types, 105; US and Soviet development, 105–9; and DEW, 107–9
Lawrence Livermore Laboratory, 107
Legnica, NGF HQ, 42
Lenin, 19, 23, 28, 180–1; on importance of youth, 19 and n.; and the Soviet Navy, 36; Tomb, Moscow, 37
Lenin Military – Political Academy, 27, 28
Leningrad: population density, 141; and Civil Defence, 141
Leningrad, helicopter carrier, 55
Leninskiy Komsomol Academy, 57
Lewin, Admiral Sir Terence, 92
Libya, 180
Lightning jets, 90
Lisbon Treaty, 67
Los Alamos, White House project, 107
Luns, Dr. Joseph, Secretary General of NATO, 68
Luxembourg: and Brussels Treaty, 66; and NATO, 67, 72
Lvov, Warsaw Pact Supreme command HQ, 34

McCormick, Admiral Lynde D., 67
McDonnell Douglas F/A 18 jet, 80
MacGwire, Michael, 55
Macmillan, Harold, 69
MAD (Mutually Assured Destruction) theory, 143 and n.
Mark I Eyeball, 100
Mark 12 identification system, 94
Marshall Plan, 66

Martin Marietta Corporation, 95
Marxist-Leninism on War and Army, 25
Masaryk, Jan, 66
Mavor, Air Marshal Sir Leslie, 164
Middle East, 179, 180
MiG aircraft, 17, 93; MiG 25 (Foxbat), 49; MiG. 23, 63
Military Balance, the, xv, 32, 64, 110, 175
Milovice, Czechoslovakia, Soviet Force HQ, 42
Minuteman missiles, 46, 47, 76–8, 84, 85, 140, 141, 145; description of Minuteman III, 45
MIRV warheads, 44, 45, 142, 145
Moscow: Olympics, 11; Civil Defence, 139; population density, 141
Moskalenko, Marshal, 46
Moskva and Moskva class helicopter carriers, 55
Moss aircraft, 49
Mountbatten of Burma, Admiral of the Fleet Earl, Strasbourg speech (1979), xi–xv
MRBM (Medium Range Ballistic Missiles), 44–5, 47
MRV warheads, 44, 45
Mulley, Fred, 41, 73
Murmansk, 54, 58
Muskie, Edmund, and Muskie Committee, 143–6
Mustard gas, 6, 111–13
Mutual and Balanced Force Reductions (MBFR), Vienna talks, 40–2
MVD (Soviet Ministry of the Interior), 38
MX missile, 16, 43, 84–6, 95, 101; question of its base, 84–5; Test Bed, Lathrop Wells, 101

Nagasaki, effects of nuclear bomb, 127, 128, 136
National Military Command Center, (USA), 88
NATO (North Atlantic Treaty Organisation), 1, 2, 5, 9, 10, 16, 40, 41, 44, 51, 55, 62–75, 82, 83, 88, 89, 92–6, 118, 139, 142, 149, 150, 178–81; and the Neutron Bomb, 5, 117; and chemical warfare, 6, 113–14; signature of Treaty (1949), 65; reasons for it, 65–6; North Atlantic Council, 68, 70; Secretary General, 68; Permanent

Representatives,68; Defence Planning Committee (DPC), 6, 68–70; Nuclear Planning Group (NPG), 41, 69, 72, 73; Eurogroup, 69–70; Military Committee and its Chairman, 70; political element, 70–1; multi-national force, 70–1; position of members, 71–3; trans-Atlantic relationships, 73; strength of forces, 74; expenditure on defence, 74–5; and lack of standardisation, 93–5; identification systems, 94–5; Washington Summit (1978), 94; Family of Weapons concept, 95; lack of cost control, 95; Long Term Defence Programme, 95; comparison with Warsaw Pact, 95–6

Nedelin, Marshal, 46

Nerve gases, 111–15; binary, 5, 6, 114

Netherlands, 93; rejects Cruise missiles bases, 11, 41, 70, 72; and Brussels Treaty, 66; and NATO, 67, 72; Civil Defence, 171

Neutron bomb (Enhanced Radiation Weapons (Warhead)), 5, 6, 41, 116–17

Neutrons, 120, 121, 124, 125, 134

Nike missiles, 84

Nimrod jets, 90, 151

Nixon, President Richard M., 144

NORAD (North American Air Defense Command), 8, 86–8, 156; and false alarms, 86

North Atlantic Treaty Organisation, *see* NATO

Northern Fleet (Soviet), 54, 150; submarines and bases, 58

Northern Ireland, 15

Norway, 83, 92, 93; and NATO, 67, 72; positioning of nuclear weapons, 72; Civil Defence, 172

Nuclear explosions, 119–27; fireball, 119, 123, 124, 128, 129; neutrons, 120, 121, 124, 125, 134; protons, 120, 121; nuclear energy, 121; fusion and fission, 122; types of explosion, 122–3; ground burst, 123–5; air burst, 123–5; fall-out, 124, 126, 127; radiation, 124–30, 133–7; casualties, 127–38; destruction, 131–2, 137

Ogarkov, Marshal Nikolai, Chief of Soviet General Staff, 28, 34–5

Oman, 17, 88, 180

OPEC, 3

OSIS (Ocean Surveillance Information System), 151

Pacific Fleet (Soviet), 54; submarines and bases, 58

Pakistan, and nuclear weapons, 177

Partial Test Ban Treaty (1963), 177

Particle beam system, 104–9; US and Soviet development, 105–9; technology, 106–7; DARPA, 107; and DEW, 107–9

Patriot missiles, 84

Pauly, General John W., 83

PAVE PAWS radar system, 87

Pavlovskii, General I.G., 50

Pearson, Senator, 146

Pershing II missiles, 16, 41, 47, 95

Petrov, General, 39

Phantom jets, 17, 90

Phosgene, 111, 112

Photo-reconnaissance, 100

Pioneers, Soviet, 19, 25, 26

Plutonium, 122; radio-isotopes, 134

Poland, 11, 66; Soviet forces in, 12, 39, 51, 61; and Warsaw Pact, 60, 61; unrest and strikes, 42, 62; Western reaction, 62; military strength, 64

Polaris submarines, 54, 78, 151

Police Manual of Home Defence, 161–2

Politburo, 28, 33, 35, 48

Portugal, and NATO, 67, 72, 75

Poseidon submarine system, 141

Powers, Gary, 99

'Protect and Survive', UK government booklet, 166, 169

Protons, 120, 121

Proxmire Joint Committee on Defence Production, 140

PVO Strany (Soviet National Air Defence Command), 48–50

Pym, Francis, 5

Radar and radar systems, 49, 87, 102–3, 105

Radiation, 124–30, 133–7; neutrons, 124, 125; gamma rays, 124, 125; dose, 126 and n., 134; rad, 126n., 134–5; rate of decay, 126, 134; thermal, 128, 130; casualties, 128, 133–7; radio-isotopes, 134; symptoms, 134–5; long-term effects, 136; genetic damage, 136; illnesses, 136–7

Ramstein, West Germany, USAF HQ, 83
Rapid Development Force (USA), 17
RC–135 aircraft, 99
Reagan, President Ronald, 149, 177
Refugees, 155
Ridgway, General Matthew, 67
Robinson, Clarence A., Jr., 8n., 108
Royal Air Force, 90, 91
Royal Marines, 92, 152; Special Boats Section (SBS), 155–6
Royal Military Academy, Sandhurst, 91
Royal Navy, 78, 92; group deployment, 88–9; manpower problems, 91–2
Royal Observer Corps, 152, 157, 158
Rumania, 11, 66; disagreement with Soviet demands, 15, 61, 62; and Warsaw Pact, 60, 61; withdrawal of Soviet troops, 61; military strength, 64

SALT (Strategic Arms Limitation Treaty), xiv, 34, 35, 44, 46–8, 59; inspection system, 86
SAM (surface to air missile), 4, 48, 94
Sandal rocket, 44, 45, 47
Sarin nerve gas, 112, 113
Satellites, 7–8, 100–10; anti-satellite development (ASAT), 8; early warning, 49; Communications system (USA), 95, 104; photo-reconnaissance, 100; capabilities, 101–2; and ECM, 102–3; information gathering, 103; sensors, 103, 106; bouncing signals, 104; interception, 104; and lasers and particle beams, 104–9
Saudi Arabia, 180
Schlesinger, James E., 143–7
Schmidt, Helmut, 13, 181
Scunner rocket, 47
Sego missile, 47
Senate Foreign Relations sub-committee on Arms Control, 143
Shelter protection, 168–9
Shyster rocket, 44, 47
Sibling rocket, 47
Skylab system, 100
Sokolov, Marshal, 35
Solzhenitsyn, Aleksandr, 13, 14
SOSUS (Sound Surveillance System), 150
South Africa, and nuclear weapons, 177
Soviet aircraft, 49–50
Soviet Army, 50–3; numbers, 50;

disposition, 50; airborne troops, 50; diversionary groups, 50–1; tanks, 51–3, 93; rifles, 50, 53
Soviet military machines, 31–60; assessment of members, 31–2; leaders, 33–7; soldiers as Deputy Defence Ministers, 33; and KGB, 36–8; and GRU, 36, 37; Military Districts, 38–9; forces outside Soviet Union, 39–43, 63; missiles, 9, 43–8; Strategic Rocket Forces, 43, 46–8; *PVO Strany*, 48–50; ground forces, 50–3; Navy, 54–9
Soviet Naval Infantry (marines), 9, 36, 60
Soviet Navy, 35–6, 54–9; submarines, 9, 56–9; cruisers, 9; aircraft carriers, 9, 55, 56 and n.; long-range supply ships, 9; main fleets, 54; manpower, 54; number of vessels, 54; support system, 55–6
Soviet Northern Group of Forces (NGF), 42
Soviet soldier, the, 17–30; ethnic groupings, 18; Pioneers, 19, 25, 26; Komsomol, 19–20, 25, 26, 29; acclimatisation course, 20; DOSAAF, 20, 25; Military Districts, 21; conscription, 21–2; apportionment of recruits, 22–3; KGB, 23, 29; officer candidates, 23; cadet officers, 23–4; living quarters, 24; pay, 24; and Communist Party, 25–30; political bodies and the armed forces, 27–9; GLAVPUR, 28
Soviet Southern Group of Forces (SGF), 42
Soviet Union, 3, 4, 82, 90, 101, 118, 150, 151, 176–81; defence expenditure, 2; and chemical warfare, 6–7, 111–15; anti-satellite development, 8; military strength, 9; attitude to the West, 16–17; regions, 38; nuclear warheads, 76; aircraft shelters, 83; lasers and particle beams, 105–9; and neutron bomb, 117; Civil Defence, 10, 139–41, 161, 173–4; sabotage groups, 155
Spaak, Paul-Henri, 61
Space Defense Operations Center (SPADOC), 87
Space Detection and Tracking System (SPADAT), 87
Space Shuttle system, 8, 109
Special Air Services (SAS) (UK), 50

SR–71 (Blackbird) aircraft, 99, 100
SRAMS (short-range attack missiles),
141
SS–4 (Sandal) missile, 44, 45
SS–11 (Sego) missile, 47
SS–16 (RS–14) missile, 47; and SALT
Treaty, 47–8
SS–17 (RS–16) missile, 47, 48
SS–18 (RS–20) missile, 47
SS–19 (RS–18) missile, 47
SS–20 missile, 9, 15, 44, 47
SS–21 missile, 9
SSBNS (Submarines Ballistic Nuclear),
57–9
SS–N–18 (RSM–50) submarines, 57
Stockholm International Peace Research
Institute, 3n., 99n.
Strategic Air Command (SAC) (USA),
78–9, 86, 99, 104, 145; Omaha HQ,
88; bases, 145
Strategic Rocket Forces (USSR), 43,
46–8
Strontium, 90, 134
Submarines, 9, 56–9; SSBNS, 57–9;
officers, 57; VLF receivers, 58;
organisation, 58; Bottom Contour
Navigation, 59
Sukhoi, Pavel, 59
Supply ships, long range, 9
Supreme Allied Commander Atlantic,
150
Supreme Allied Commander Europe
(SACEUR), 67, 150
Supreme Headquarters Allied Powers
Europe (SHAPE), 15, 67, 117
Supreme Soviet, 28
Sweden, and Civil Defence, 172
Switzerland, and Civil Defence, 172–3
Symington, Senator, 146
Syria, 180

T–54 tank, 52
T–55 tank, 52
T–62 tank, 52, 53
T–64 tank, 53
T–72 tank, 42–3, 53, 63
Tabun nerve gas, 111
Talon Gold project, 108
Tanks, 9, 15–16, 51–3, 93
Tear gas grenade, 110
Thatcher, Margaret, and
Thatcher Administration, 1, 5, 72;
support for White House, 12

Theatre Nuclear Force (TNF)
Modernisation, 41, 69
Third World, weapon exports to, 3
Titan missiles, 76, 77, 85, 141, 145
Tornado jet, 9; interceptor version, 90
Toubko, General V.F., 48
Trident missiles, 9, 16, 84, 141
Turkey, 63, 71, 72; and NATO, 11, 38,
72, 75, 93; complex problems, 93
Typhoon submarines, 56

U–2 aircraft, 16, 99
UKADR (United Kingdom Air Defence
Region), 90
UK RAOC (United Kingdom Regional
Air Operations Centre), 156
UKWMO (United Kingdom Warning
and Monitoring Organisation), 152,
156–9
United Arab Emirate, 180
United Kingdom: defence budgets, 2;
and Chemical Warfare, 5, 111–15; and
Trident missile, 9; and Afghanistan,
13; civilians as defence heads, 33;
information system, 65; and Brussels
Treaty, 66; and NATO, 67, 69, 72–4,
88–9; nuclear warheads, 76; Civil
Defence (Home Defence), 10, 142,
148–69, 171; major targets, 149–52;
war games, 152–4; sabotage targets,
155–6; UKWMO, 152, 156–9; Carrier
Control Points, 156, 158; warning
codes, 157; Monitoring Posts, 157–9;
Group Controls, 157–9; Sector
Controls, 157–9; Police Manual,
161–2; Defence Regions, 162–3; Home
Defence College, 162, 164–6, 169;
Home Office and Civil Defence,
167–9; shelter protection, 168–9;
see also Western defence strength
United Nations, 65, 139
United States, 3, 4, 66, 118, 176–81;
defence budgets, 2; and neutron bomb,
5, 6, 116; and Chemical Warfare, 5–6,
111–15; future weapon programme,
10; level of manpower, 10; Civil
Defence, 10, 148, 170; lack of support
from West, 11, 17; leadership
problems, 12; and Iron, 12; and
Afghanistan, 12–13, 17; civilians as
defence heads, 33; number of
warheads, 44; missile-carrying
submarines, 54–5; information system,

United States—*contd*
    65; call for defence pact, 66–7;
    Vandenberg Resolution, 67; and
    NATO, 67, 69, 70, 73, 86; and France,
    71; soaring cost of projects, 95; lasers
    and particle beams, 105–9; forces in
    UK, 149; *see also* Western defence
    strength
United States Air Force Intelligence,
    Foreign Technology Division, 106
United States Navy, 6th Fleet, 72
Uranium, 120–2, 177; radio-isotopes,
    134
Urey, Dr. Harold, xv
USSR, *see* Soviet Union
Ustinov, Marshal Dimitri, Soviet
    Defence Minister, 28, 33–5

V–2, German rocket, 47
Vandenberg, Senator Arthur, and the
    Vandenberg Resolution, 67
Vegger, General Christian, 92
Venice summit meeting (1980), 13, 71
Vienna, MBFR talks, 40–2
Vietnam, 12, 14, 16, 80, 175
Vladivostok, 54, 58
VX nerve gas, 112, 113

Warsaw Pact, 5, 7, 11, 15, 16, 33, 54,
    60–4, 75, 117, 118, 142; defence
    expenditure, 15, 74; supreme
    command, 34; Liaison Department,
    37; agreements, 61, 62; troop sizes of
    members, 63–4; standardisation of
    equipment, 93; comparison with
    NATO, 95–6
West Germany, 13, 177; and larger
    warships, 9–10; and NATO, 15, 61,
    67, 69, 71; stocks of US chemical
    weapons, 113, 114; Civil Defence,
    170–1

Western defence strength, 76–96; United
    States, 76–88; nuclear warheads, 76;
    silos at bases, 76–7, 85; location of
    bases, 76–7; flying command posts, 77,
    83; missile crews, 77–8; Strategic Air
    Command (SAC), 78–9, 86, 88;
    recruitment problems, 79–80; drug
    problem, 80; question of the draft, 81;
    Draft Registration, 81; air force
    resources, 81–2; need for new aircraft,
    82–3; Military Air Command (MAC),
    82; communications problems, 83–4;
    anti-aircraft missiles, 84; MX missiles,
    84–6; NORAD, 86–8; United
    Kingdom, 88–92; wide involvement,
    88–9; Royal Navy group deployment,
    88–9; defence expenditure, 89, 91; as
    NATO rear base, 89; weaknesses in air
    defence, 89–90; UKADR, 90; new
    aircraft, 90; manpower problems,
    90–2; officer recruitment and training,
    91; ships, 92; Anti-Submarine Warfare
    (ASW), 92; Denmark, 92–3; Turkey's
    problems, 93; lack of standardisation,
    93–5; identification systems, 94–5; lack
    of cost control, 95; comparison with
    Warsaw Pact, 95–6
Western Union Defence Organisation,
    66
White House project, 106, 107
Window of Opportunity concept, 178,
    179
WINTEX exercise (1979), 115

Xm–1 tank, 95

Yankee submarines, 56, 57
Yemen, 16, 180
Ypres, poison gas at, 110, 111, 114, 115

Zampolit (Zampol), 28